"One mark of a great and rare book is that it demonstrates the central importance of a question nobody else was even asking. This, in a nutshell, is what *The God Who Trusts* does. I had never before wondered if trust and faith might be attributes *of God*. When I finished this work, I wondered how I had not thought about that before. In this well-written and hugely insightful book, Curtis Holtzen makes a compelling case that trust is not only an attribute of God, it's an attribute that has significant implications for our understanding of, and relationship with, God. I dare all thoughtful, open-minded Christians to read this book!"

Greg Boyd, senior pastor, Woodland Hills Church, president, Reknew Ministries, author of *God at War*

"Curtis Holtzen is one of the most courageous and perceptive critics of classical theism. This book is Holtzen at his absolute best. If love always hopes, if it always trusts, he asks, What does it mean for a God who *is* love? It means that God also hopes, also trusts, and also has faith. Holtzen offers a profound, unsettling theology for unsettling times. It's a theology that asks us to cling to a God who embraces the mess, lives in the mess, and confronts the mess *with us.*"

Roberto Sirvent, author of *Embracing Vulnerablity: Human and Divine*

"A God who trusts? Why does this simple phrase sound so radically novel and yet biblically consonant? Curtis Holtzen argues that our believing that God has faith helps us understand a host of ideas central to the Christian faith. To develop his argument, Holtzen addressed key doctrines, thinkers, and intuitions. This book offers a new, powerful, and, I think, true contribution to contemporary theology!"

Thomas Jay Oord, author of *God Can't*, and *The Uncontrolling Love of God*

"Curtis Holtzen argues that the faith of God in humans is an aspect, an outcome, and an extension of God's great love for us. While most theists affirm that God's deep abiding love for humans is a constant of God's character, Holtzen also shows that God's faith in humans is dependent upon the understanding that the future, by definition, is open to God. This is more controversial but clearly substantiated by the author, relying on the Bible, reason, and experience. While faithfulness is a divine trait on which theists agree, God's faith in humans depends on God's hope that they will prove to be worthy of faith. This is a risk. Humans who choose to place faith in God rely on evidence from the past and personal experience that God is trustworthy. Does God have the evidence and experience to place faith in humans that goes beyond hope, that goes beyond God's recognition that they have the ability to be cooperative covenant partners? Jesus proved God's faith in him to be well founded, as did others before him. Nonetheless, this is a risky venture. God is a God who risks. This innovative contribution to theology thus affirms not only the hope and faith of God but also the courage of God."

Karen Strand Winslow, professor of biblical studies at Azusa Pacific Seminary

"In this beautifully written book, Dr. Holtzen argues that the apparently shocking statement that God has faith, hope, and trust is both biblical and reasonable. It is a fine contribution to an important modern school of evangelical theology."

Keith Ward, regius professor of divinity emeritus, Oxford University

"According to *The God Who Trusts*, God's care for creation involves not only sensitivity and risk but a deep longing that it will become everything God hopes for it. With its expansive description of divine faith, Holtzen's portrayal of God enhances and complements those of other open theists, such as *The Most Moved Mover* (Clark Pinnock) and *The God Who Risks* (John Sanders). His project also exemplifies theological reflection at its best. He offers an interesting and original thesis, engages the views of others with informed sensitivity, thoughtfully considers pertinent biblical passages, and provides well-developed arguments for his positions—all in clear and accessible language. Students and experienced scholars alike will benefit from this work, and many readers will find it inspiring."

Richard Rice, professor of religion at Loma Linda University, author of *Suffering and the Search for Meaning*

"Wm. Curtis Holtzen has crafted not just an important book but also a necessary one for anyone desiring to understand the essential attributes of God. This vital work fills an expansive gap in the field of relational theology and is required reading for those with similar theological inquiries. Holtzen's sharp mind is on full display with his cogent arguments, making a most interesting and pleasurable read."

Matthew Nelson Hill, author of *Evolution and Holiness: Sociobiology, Altruism, and the Quest for Wesleyan Perfection*

The God Who Trusts

A RELATIONAL THEOLOGY OF
DIVINE FAITH, HOPE, AND LOVE

WM. CURTIS HOLTZEN

Foreword by John Sanders

Academic
An imprint of InterVarsity Press
Downers Grove, Illinois

InterVarsity Press
P.O. Box 1400, Downers Grove, IL 60515-1426
ivpress.com
email@ivpress.com

InterVarsity Press® is the book-publishing division of InterVarsity Christian Fellowship/USA®,
a movement of students and faculty active on campus at hundreds of universities, colleges, and schools
of nursing in the United States of America, and a member movement of the International Fellowship
of Evangelical Students. For information about local and regional activities, visit intervarsity.org.

Cover design and image composite: Cindy Kiple
Interior design: Daniel van Loon
Image: illustration of 2 hands © CSA Images / Getty Images

ISBN 978-0-8308-5255-0 (print)
ISBN 978-0-8308-6667-0 (digital)

Printed in the United States of America ∞

InterVarsity Press is committed to ecological stewardship and to the conservation of natural resources
in all our operations. This book was printed using sustainably sourced paper.

Library of Congress Cataloging-in-Publication Data

Names: Holtzen, William Curtis, author.
Title: The God who trusts : a relational theology of divine faith, hope,
    and love / Wm. Curtis Holtzen.
Description: Westmont : InterVarsity Press, 2019. | Includes
    bibliographical references and index.
Identifiers: LCCN 2019032398 (print) | LCCN 2019032399 (ebook) | ISBN
    9780830852550 (paperback) | ISBN 9780830866670 (ebook)
Subjects: LCSH: God (Christianity)—Attributes. | Theological virtues.
Classification: LCC BT130 .H585 2019 (print) | LCC BT130 (ebook) | DDC
    231.7—dc23
LC record available at https://lccn.loc.gov/2019032398
LC ebook record available at https://lccn.loc.gov/2019032399

P 25 24 23 22 21 20 19 18 17 16 15 14 13 12 11 10 9 8 7 6 5 4 3 2 1

Y 38 37 36 35 34 33 32 31 30 29 28 27 26 25 24 23 22 21 20 19

In memory of my fellow theological wanderer,

tattoo guru, and most of all, friend.

HAL LEIGH SHRADER 1967–2015

CONTENTS

FOREWORD

JOHN SANDERS

THE APOSTLE PAUL SAID, "And now faith, hope, and love abide, these three; and the greatest of these is love" (1 Cor 13:13). Christians have long characterized faith, hope, and love as the three "theological" virtues. These virtues are hallmarks of the genuine Christian life. Of these love occupies the place of preeminence. God calls Christians to love one another, their neighbor, and their enemy. God shows us how to do this by loving and forgiving us. God exemplifies how to love. Jesus, as God incarnate, is the paragon of love who walked the path to show us how to love God and creatures. Christians are encouraged to emulate the love of God—to practice the *imitatio Dei* and *imitatio Christi* when it comes to love. This is as it should be. Yet, what about faith and hope? Christian communities emphasize the need to practice faith and hope and to see God as the object of our faith and source of our hope. Yet, Christians do not say much about the faith and hope *of God*. Seldom are Christians encouraged to imitate the faith and hope of God. Sadly, some Christians do not believe God can be our example of faith and hope.

God's love for us provides a good reason to think that God is our exemplar for faith and hope. Christians have long highlighted the fact that not only does God love others but that "God is love" (1 Jn 4:8). Love is the very being of God—what it means to be divine. God's creative and redemptive love is central to the gospel. If God is love, what do we mean by love? A favorite description of love, often recited at weddings, occurs in the same passage where Paul mentions the three theological virtues. "Love is patient; love is kind; love is not envious or boastful or arrogant or rude. It does not insist on its own way; it is not irritable or resentful; it does not rejoice in wrongdoing, but rejoices in the truth. It bears all things, believes all things, hopes all things, endures all things" (1 Cor 13:4-7). If God is love and this is what love is like, then God is like this. God is patient, kind, and not arrogant. God bears our failings by putting up with us at times. If love believes in others and hopes for a better future, then so does God. God has faith, hope, and love. God is not only the object of our faith, hope, and love but God is our exemplar to imitate the three theological virtues. The way God relates to us shows us how to practice faith, hope, and love.

The God Who Trusts delightfully explores the ways in which God expresses faith, hope, and love. It shows why it makes sense to apply all three theological virtues to God instead of just one. Holtzen carefully unpacks what it means to trust, to believe in someone, and to hope. These concepts always involve relationships with others so Holtzen develops a relational theology that uses the domain of human relationships as a rich source to understand what God is like and how God relates to us. He discusses biblical writers who speak of God entrusting us with a task and God having patience with us. Seldom do Christians stop to think about just what is involved when exercising patience or trusting someone. Holtzen does a thorough job of explaining the theological and philosophical entailments of concepts such as trust and patience. One of these ideas emphasized in the book is that God cares about what we do. It matters to God whether we participate in God's work in the world. God is not indifferent toward us. Sometimes God is disappointed in us while at other times God is overjoyed at what we do. In short, we make a difference to God. One of my favorite lines in the book is "God loves to trust." Holtzen provides several biblical examples where God trusts people and shows why this means that God has faith in us both individually and corporately. When things do not go the way God wants them to, God works with us to improve the situation. This means that God hopes the future will be better than the present. Without this hope, God's faith would be pointless. God's faith is a model for us to follow (the *imitatio Dei*).

A poignant example of God's trust being broken and restored is found in Exodus 32–34. Yahweh, the God of Israel, liberated Israel from the oppression of the Egyptians and then called Israel to be "a kingdom of priests" (19:6 NIV). God entrusted Israel with a vocation to be God's ministers to the world. God formed a covenant with the people regarding this calling. God then instructed Moses to construct a tabernacle (a portable temple) so that Yahweh could dwell in the very midst of the people. However, while Moses was receiving these instructions, the people broke the covenant when Aaron made the golden calf. God then floats a new plan to Moses: God will start over again with Moses' offspring because this generation is not trustworthy. Moses rejects this plan and calls on God to change the divine mind. Amazingly, God does turn away from that route and declares that this generation will receive the Promised Land. Yet, God will not go with the people or dwell in their midst. Instead, Yahweh will send a messenger to guide the people. In response, Moses says that Israel's vocation to the world is jeopardized without the divine presence. He asks God to renew divine trust in the people by accompanying them on the journey. Yahweh then declares that the divine Presence will go with the people (33:14). After this, they build the tabernacle and the divine Presence (glory) dwells in the midst of Israel. Together, God and Moses decide to continue the mission of reaching the world through the people. Though they broke God's trust in them, God decided to continue to have faith in them. God restores the covenant and once again entrusts to Israel the vocation of being a kingdom of priests. This story shows that even though the people sinned greatly, God continued to believe in them. Similarly, God believes in Christians and the church, entrusting us with a vocation to the world.

This book fills a genuine need in Christian theology by mapping out the ways in which God exercises trust, faith, and hope. Holtzen carefully notes the terrain in terms of the important issues and consults the significant guides on each topic. He consults a wide range of people who have written on faith and hope. The sources do not always agree on the way to go and Holtzen proves himself an able guide as he seeks out what is best in his interlocutors. He is sure-footed as he traverses the field. He is fair-minded with these sources, gleaning insights from them while also raising questions. He acknowledges positive features in the views of those with whom he sometimes disagrees. The book makes a solid case for God having faith and hope. Yet, the author is humble and aware that every position has questions. The book explores the theological and philosophical implications of God having faith and trust. In addition, it wonderfully illustrates what it means to trust, have faith, and hope from numerous biblical texts as well as examples from daily life, including many films.

This is a terrific work on what it means for God to have faith, hope, and love. It fills a significant gap in the literature, and it enables Christian communities to better understand what God is like and helps them more fully imitate the God who trusts.

ACKNOWLEDGMENTS

THIS BOOK IS THE RESULT OF A QUESTION I first asked myself several decades ago, "Does my life make a difference to God?" At the time this was not a theological or philosophical question. Like many people, especially when younger, I was questioning my value and purpose. I believed God loved me, but I was confused as to whether my efforts ever helped or hindered God's work in this world. The question began to get its theological legs with two seemingly unrelated events: Christian college and post-punk rock.

As an undergrad I was exposed to ideas and engaged in conversations about free will and God's sovereignty. Classes and conversations with key professors (notably Steve Richardson and Gene Sonnenberg—thank you!) uprooted my embedded theology that God determines, or at least knows, every facet of my entire life. Around this time a Welsh post-punk band called the Alarm, with their crazy hair and stealth Christian lyrics, had become a favorite of mine. One of their more obscure songs called "Time to Believe" was about a man asking God, I presume, to lay healing hands on his soul to help him believe. But it was another line that one day, after dozens of listenings, which caught my attention. The singer Mike Peters says that he is "hurting for someone to hold. Someone to believe. Someone to release. Someone to believe in me." In that moment the realization washed over me that my faith was not simply about my believing in God, but God also believing in me. It was an idea I was not sure how to explore, and my attempts to explain it to others were met with either gentle correction or a quick change of subject.

The idea was rather inchoate until I began to read the works of open theists, especially John Sanders's *The God Who Risks*. Reading this book, I realized that nearly every place where Sanders says, "God risks" I could read that as God trusts, believes, hopes. I began to grasp that my thoughts were not as out there as many had suggested, and that there were biblical, theological, and philosophical reasons to think God has trust in me— that my life makes a difference to God. None of us are but a cog in the machine, for each of us is wonderfully made to be co-conspirator with the divine in this brilliant project of creation, redemption, salvation.

Speaking of co-conspirators and making a difference, this book would not have been possible without those who were generous with their time, talents, skills, and scholarship. I owe a debt to the following people, first of all for their friendship but also for their careful reading and valuable comments on how to improve this book.

Joe Grana, your encouragement and support, especially when disguised as a playful insult, are second to none.

Roberto Sirvent, your talent to read long sections and provide detailed comments all within a few hours is astonishing.

Daniel Speak, your ability and willingness to explain difficult philosophical concepts is greatly appreciated. I'm sorry I made you do it all by text.

Tom Oord, your support and inclusion of me in books, conferences, and committees has been exceedingly valuable to the development of this work and my scholarship in general.

Matthew Hill, thanks for sending all those *Simpsons* clips. Thanks even more for repeatedly reminding me that this is an important subject.

Josh Shrader-Perry, you were a fantastic research assistant. I owe you another cinnamon scone!

My former officemates of suite 216: for me to thank each of you properly would require another hundred pages, so let me just thank you for your friendship, collegiality, and erudition. Kelly Dagley, Kip Lines, KC Richardson, Carl Toney, Phil Towne, and Blair Wilgus you all taught me to take scholarship seriously but life casually.

John Sanders, thanks for nudging me to publish on this. You laid a solid foundation for me to build upon.

Greg Boyd, thanks for agreeing to be an anonymous reader, discussing the project on your podcast, and for pushing me to get my wording right; I hope I did.

Keith Ward, thank you for inviting me to present an early form of this work at Heythrop and for your generosity and hospitality.

Special thanks to Kent Anderson, whose generous gift to Pacific Christian College of Ministry and Biblical Studies allowed me to take a half sabbatical to research and present on this subject.

Hope International University, thanks for all your support over the last twenty years.

And to my editor David McNutt, I am grateful for your patient guidance; you certainly made this a better book.

Writing a book can be a lonely process at times, and I am thankful for the following persons who offered wise words, a sympathetic ear, and general enthusiasm about this project: Peace Amadi, Shannon Bates, Adrian Coxhead, Josh Carman, Steve Edgington, Butch Ellis, Fay Ellwood, Robin Hartman, Natalie Hewitt, Wendy Johnson, Daniel Karistai, Elliott Lawless, Katy Lines, Erik Maiershofer, Tamsen Murray, Duncan Reyburn, Brian Overbaugh, Paul Rogers, Bryan Sands, Mollie Shrader-Perry, Erasmus van Niekerk, Denise Wallace, Jim Woest, James Yuile.

Special thanks to Erasmus van Niekerk who served as my promoter for an earlier version of this work as my DTh in Systematic Theology at the University of South Africa. Thanks also to all of the students who never made teaching feel like a job (you know who you are), Theology Patio/Sojourners Church, and the baristas at Starbucks Pacific Grove.

I want to thank my family for their love and support: my mother, Jackie Holtzen; sister, Jennie Diaz; daughter, Roman; and son-in-law, Judd Barber.

Most of all, thank you to my wife, Wende, for saving me from much embarrassment by proofreading every page of this work before I sent it off to others for their assessment.

1

CONSIDERING A GOD WHO TRUSTS

Your faith in God means much, even more than words
can say; but God's faith in you means more than does
your faith in God. And why do I say that? Because,
when your faith fails, and it is always failing, God's
faith, working by love, faileth never, but continues
to call: "O, My Child, how can I give thee up?"

FREDERICK F. SHANNON, *GOD'S FAITH IN MAN*

WHAT DOES IT MEAN to say that God is perfect? Or that God is a being of maximal greatness? These are questions theologians enjoy pondering. To suggest that God is a perfect being is to say, at the very least, that God possesses qualities that are better for God to have than to lack. That is, if God were missing these qualities God could certainly be great, but not the greatest possible being. Each theologian may affirm slightly different qualities, but all, I believe, would assert that any list would be incomplete if it did not include that God is maximally powerful, knowledgeable, and good. Further complicating matters, even when theologians agree on these great-making qualities, they disagree on just what each means or entails. I would like to suggest that just as holiness, love, and relationality are great-making qualities, so too is faith. Not merely that God is faithful, but that God has faith. God trusts, hopes, believes.

This book argues that if God is authentically relational and humans significantly free, then God is a being of faith. More precisely, if God is genuinely loving, relational, and morally good, while humans are free to accept or reject God's invitation to be partners in the creation of a beautiful world and divine kingdom, then faith, both human and divine, is necessary. Faith not only makes partnership possible but it perfects love itself, for love without faith is distant, one-sided, giving, but not necessarily receiving. It is because God has faith in us that God has not given up on this world. God believes that we are redeemable, trusts us as covenant partners, and hopes that all will accept the invitation of salvation. The love of God entails that God desires and works for the good of all persons, and what greater good is there than maturity in Christ? What greater good is there than that we become virtuous and trustworthy servants? God's love for us means that God desires to make us mature, that is, trustworthy beings. Just as God is faithful—worthy of our faith—God seeks to bring us all to Christlikeness: worthy of God's faith.

Theologians have begun to speak more and more of God being vulnerable and taking risks. William Placher asks us to suppose that God is not a deity who triumphs through raw power but that "more than anything else, freely loves, and in that love is willing to be vulnerable and willing to risk suffering."[1] Notably, John Sanders in *The God Who Risks*, seeks to offer a coherent "model of divine risk-taking . . . conceptualizing divine providence as taking certain kinds of risks."[2] Sanders argues that not only is God vulnerable, but God is even "more vulnerable than we are because God cannot count on our faithfulness in the way we may count on his steadfast love."[3] However, Sanders and Placher, like many others who affirm God's risk-taking and vulnerability, stop short of saying that God is a being of faith.[4] Over the past few decades open and relational theologians have made

---

[1] William C. Placher, *Narratives of a Vulnerable God: Christ, Theology, and Scripture* (Louisville, KY: Westminster John Knox, 1994), 10.

[2] John Sanders, *The God Who Risks: A Theology of Providence*, rev. ed. (Downers Grove, IL: InterVarsity Press, 2007), 33.

[3] Sanders, *The God Who Risks*, 180.

[4] Based on presentations I have heard and personal conversations with Sanders I believe he affirms that God not only risks but trusts as well.

the case that God faces a significantly open future, invites free beings to love and be loved, and to partner with God in the creation of a good and beautiful world.[5] However, to my knowledge, none of these theologians have said that if this is true then God necessarily has faith in these free beings.

This book seeks to correct this oversight and connect the dots that so many theologians have left unconnected. I hope to demonstrate that if certain beliefs about God are true, then it is necessary we affirm that God is a being, even the greatest possible being, of faith. In the remainder of this chapter I will make my initial case for God's faith, arguing that if certain antecedents are true, then the conclusion of divine faith reasonably follows. From there I will briefly address a few prima facie objections to this argument. Finally, I will preview the remainder of the book.

CONDITIONS OF DIVINE FAITH

Why is it that humans need faith? Because we are utterly dependent upon God to reach out and invite us into the divine's presence and purposes. We do not have the power to save or heal ourselves. We do not have the knowledge to navigate the pitfalls and difficulties life brings. If we had the knowledge and power necessary to succeed at life all on our own, we would need no faith. But that is not our situation. God has created us for loving partnerships. God has created us to grow and mature in the virtues. In short, faith is necessary because we need God and others to meet the challenges of this life, to achieve our God-ordained purposes, and to become the persons we were created to be.

---

[5]For a sampling of such books, see Clark Pinnock et al., *The Openness of God: A Biblical Challenge to the Traditional Understanding of God* (Downers Grove, IL: InterVarsity Press, 1994); David Basinger, *The Case for Freewill Theism: A Philosophical Assessment* (Downers Grove, IL: InterVarsity Press, 1996); Gregory A. Boyd, *God of the Possible: A Biblical Introduction to the Open View of God* (Grand Rapids: Baker Books, 2000); William Hasker, *God, Time, and Knowledge* (Ithaca, NY: Cornell University Press, 1989); Richard Rice, *God's Foreknowledge and Man's Free Will* (Minneapolis: Bethany House, 1985); Clark Pinnock, *Most Moved Mover: A Theology of God's Openness* (Grand Rapids: Baker Academic, 2001); Thomas Jay Oord, *The Nature of Love: A Theology* (St. Louis, MO: Chalice, 2010).

Why does God need faith? Why should we even contemplate the claim that God has faith? Analogous to our own situation, it seems God is reliant on others in order to achieve the goals God has established for this world. God desires to enter into loving relationships with others. God desires that we grow in maturity and become virtuous persons. God desires that we willingly partner with the divine, and others, to bring about goods that would otherwise not be possible without such unions.

Let's unpack the reasons for even considering a claim such as God is a being of faith. There are several theological issues that serve as conditions that make this study necessary. However, I will limit this discussion to just four: (1) purpose for creation, (2) human free will, (3) open future, and (4) divine passibility. Each one of these conditions has its own set of presuppositions, and a full exploration for each would require its own lengthy study.[6] The point here is to show that all of these theological suppositions require consideration that God is an agent of faith and that if any one of these suppositions is true then the others are also likely true. And if each supposition is true, then I see no reason not to explore the real possibility of divine faith. This opening chapter, then, is not making a case for God's faith per se but is making a case for this study.

Purpose for creation. Scripture does not reveal God's purposes for creating this world. We can appeal to our senses to show us the nature of creation, to the Scriptures to reveal who the creator is, and to the sciences for reasonable theories regarding how God creates, but we are left to our own imagination to conceive of reasons why God created. The mind of God may ultimately be a mystery on this point, but this does not mean we cannot offer rational theological suppositions. In attempting to

---

[6]It is understood that other conditions might also be necessary, including divine temporality and limitations on power. However, I believe that these "additional" conditions can be subsumed within the conditions stated. For example, the notion that God experiences time sequentially is a logical condition if the other conditions obtain. Likewise, limited power is a necessary condition of divine-human partnership. To suggest that God gives a purpose to creation and shares a task with humans and yet is not limited in power, either voluntarily or necessarily, is problematic. It would mean that God's partnership is merely a façade. So, while I am suggesting that these four conditions are necessary for divine faith, I am not saying these are the only conditions since these have their own logical conditions.

conceive of God's reason(s) for creating it is commonly understood that all acts of creation are born out of God's nature. To discuss why God created is to discuss who God is.

The Reformed theologians from Calvin to today have typically conceived of the creation as the "theater of God's glory"—all that happens in creation is for God's pleasure in glorifying God's self.[7] Twentieth-century Reformed theologian Louis Berkhof affirms this when suggesting that creation's final end is "not anything outside of God, but in God himself," meaning that God's purpose for creation is God's self-satisfaction.[8] Berkhof proposes that human happiness or fulfillment cannot be the intended end for "the theory does not fit the facts." If this were God's intent for creation it would mean that God has taken a risk, but Berkhof declares, "we cannot imagine that a wise and omnipotent God would choose an end destined to fail wholly or in part."[9] For many theologians of this persuasion, the purpose of creation is closed, predetermined, and unilaterally accomplished. God creates for God's own glory without deviation or possible failings. This is true for animate as well as inanimate creation, for each follows the will of God in its own way.[10]

Thinkers such as Emil Brunner, Jürgen Moltmann, and Clark Pinnock propose what I believe is a more suitable approach to God's purposes in and for the creation.[11] For them, creation is the expression of divine love, not absolute sovereign will. Brunner writes, "God creates the world because He wills to communicate himself, because he wishes to have something 'over against' Himself. Hence the revelation of this love of His is at the same time the revelation of the purpose of His Creation, and this

---

[7]Roger Olson, *The Mosaic of Christian Belief: Twenty Centuries of Unity and Diversity* (Downers Grove, IL: IVP Academic, 2002), 173.

[8]Louis Berkhof, *Systematic Theology* (Grand Rapids: Eerdmans, 1962), 136.

[9]Berkhof, *Systematic Theology*, 137. Berkhof does see a place for human happiness, not as an end in itself but as a means of attuning hearts to worship God and express love and adoration to the creator.

[10]Millard J. Erickson, *Introducing Christian Doctrine*, ed. L. Arnold Hustad (Grand Rapids: Baker, 1992), 123.

[11]It should be noted that both Brunner and Moltmann did their work within the Reformed tradition even if their views stray from more orthodox doctrines.

purpose of creation is the reason why He posits a creation."[12] Brunner
does not dismiss God's self-glorification as a purpose for the creation but
argues that glory is love freely received so it can be rendered back to God.
God creates out of love for the purpose of love. Moltmann, likewise,
maintains that love is the motive and end all in one. "If God creates the
world out of freedom, then he creates it out of love. Creation is not a
demonstration of his boundless power; it is the communication of his
love, which neither knows premises nor conditions: *creation ex amore
Dei.*"[13] Divine freedom or sovereignty for Moltmann is inseparable from
divine love. Creation is not an act of power alone or love alone. Rather,
God creates in a most powerful love.

Pinnock employs the image of God as artist who creates out of delight
for the creative process and loves what is made. More importantly, creation is born out of God's loving and relational nature. "Creation arises,"
according to Pinnock, "from loving relationships in the divine nature.
God creates out of his own abundant interpersonal love—it is the expression of his generosity."[14] Creation is an overflowing of the triune love
found within the Godhead—community is the motivation and the intended telos for creation.[15] It is in community where love is given, love is
received, and love is returned. Without community there can be exercises of power but no real love.

I am persuaded that God has authored creation out of God's own
loving nature for the purpose of loving relationships. This means that
God has created the world to form community and fellowship in ways
that reflect and generate unfathomable love. Brunner, Moltmann, and
Pinnock highlight the impetus for God's creative acts, but it must also be
clear that the world is not created simply out of God's love. It was and is
being created to give love back, to generate love in community. To claim

---

[12]Emil Brunner, *The Christian Doctrine of Creation and Redemption*, vol. 2 of *Dogmatics* (Philadelphia: Westminster, 1952), 13.

[13]Jürgen Moltmann, *God in Creation: A New Theology of Creation and the Spirit of God* (Minneapolis: Fortress, 1993), 75-76.

[14]Clark H. Pinnock, *Flame of Love: A Theology of the Holy Spirit* (Downers Grove, IL: InterVarsity
Press, 1996), 55.

[15]Pinnock, *Flame of Love*, 55.

that God created for the purposes of love says more than that God acted on the motive of love—it means God awaits love in return. God created out of love with the intent that creation would love God in return as well as love itself. Love is the reason and the telos of creation. Too often talk of creation as being the product of God's overflowing love can suggest that the creation is simply a result of divine emanation: that the creation has a cause but no purpose. The purpose for creation, as I see it, is to bring about goods that otherwise would not be possible. Some goods that God desires are only possible with a free creation.

Keith Ward argues that God's purposes for creation might include increasing the sum total of value—values that may only be possible in a world of finite, yet free, beings.[16] "The basic reason for creation is that it brings about forms of goodness and value which otherwise would not exist . . . it makes it possible for God to be a God of love, possessing the properties of creativity, appreciative knowledge and sharing communion, which are the highest perfections of personal being."[17] God may know every potential good that could possibly obtain in the lifespan of the creation, but knowing a good as potential pales in comparison with knowing it as actual. When I was a soon-to-be father I had real joy imagining and anticipating holding my daughter for the first time, but when I was able to actually hold her, that experience brought far more value, far more joy, than I experienced in the potentiality of holding her. Likewise, for God, knowing potential goods, even if they are known in the fullest sense possible, is quite different than knowing them as actual goods. And it seems that at least some of the goods God desires are those God cannot actualize alone. In short, actualized values will increase the amount of good even if God knows and enjoys all the potential values.

---

[16]Keith Ward, *Divine Action: Examining God's Role in an Open and Emergent Universe* (West Conshohocken, PA: Templeton Foundation Press, 2007), 22-24. See also Ward's *Rational Theology and the Creativity of God* (New York: Pilgrim Press, 1982), 76-88; *Religion and Creation* (Oxford: Oxford University Press, 1996), 181-82, 223, 256-65; *God, Chance and Necessity* (Oxford: Oneworld, 1996), 50-60, 186, 191, 204; *God, Faith and The New Millennium: Christian Belief in an Age of Science* (Oxford: Oneworld, 1998), 16-17, 29.

[17]Ward, *Rational Theology*, 85.

God as a good and perfect being of love seeks to increase the good and love present in reality. God as immeasurable love and perfect goodness is not constrained by this nature but liberated by it. It would be a sign of limitation if God were not able to increase goodness or able to proliferate love. This is what it means to say God is unlimited love. Only a being of perfect goodness and unbounded love could increase the amount of love and goodness in reality, and God does this by the creation of other persons. Only by there being other agents who appreciate and value beauty, who share in love, can there be an increase in the amount of good in reality. When persons love one another and value and appreciate beauty, good propagates. It is certainly good and valuable that an infinite God appreciates God's own goodness and beauty, but a notable addition to the total good takes place when others appreciate God's beauty as well. In this sense it is not narcissism or some shallow need for affirmation that leads God to call on us to worship, but the divine's desire that good and value be increased by the creation of those who can see, respect, desire, and appreciate true beauty. And there is no greater or more perfect love, beauty, or goodness than God.

It seems then that some goods can only be obtained by the creation of other subjects, beings who have some amount of autonomy. It is not simply that more value-appreciating beings exist, but that goods come only from the existence of other centers of consciousness.[18] The joy that comes from seeing a child make the right choice is a good only possible with a creation like this one. Virtues such as creativity, discipline, kindness, service, and wisdom are goods only possible in a world like ours comprised of personal agents like us. There is a moral development tied into the purpose of creation. God did not create solely out of a desire to be creative or merely as an overflowing expression of God's loving nature. God has brought this world into being with the intent that creation produces values and goods that otherwise could not be actualized by God alone.

---

[18]Ward, *Divine Action*, 24.

Arguably, the greatest of great goods that is only possible with the creation of other persons is cooperation and mutuality realized by loving relationships. Loving relationships between the divine and human, between God and those "over against" God's self, is one such value. Other relational values that foster love are character virtues such as compassion, courage, patience, mercy, forgiveness, hope, and trust. These are virtues that make mutual love possible. God cannot bring about many of these great-making virtues without a creation, even if God exists within a divine community. These goods require beings other than God. This loving partnership that was created to produce goods and virtues requires not just human faith but divine as well.

Human freedom. If it is the case that God has created this world in order to produce goods and values not obtainable without a creation—goods such as partnership and mutual love—then this creation needs to be a world where such goods are possible. The goods and values discussed in the previous section are only possible if this world contains genuinely free beings who can partner with God and respond to divine invitations of love. God, it seems, has created this world for genuine relationship, but relationship is only possible between free agents.

If God is to relate to creation in any meaningful way, it is necessary that humans be significantly free to respond to the will and love of God.[19] Without human freedom there is nothing for God to *relate* with or *respond* to. Without free choice, warm comforting acts of love would merely be cold robotic reflexes.[20] If relationships require that the persons involved be free, then faith, a fortiori, requires the faithful to have genuine freedom.

---

[19]By this I mean to have freedom with respect to options that are right or wrong, good or bad, but also that we fall short of complete freedom.

[20]C. S. Lewis understood that God's good ends are only possible with free persons who can know and enjoy real happiness. "Why, then, did God give them free will? Because free will, though it makes evil possible, is also the only thing that makes possible any love or goodness or joy worth having. A world of automata—of creatures that worked like machines—would hardly be worth creating." C. S. Lewis, *Mere Christianity* (New York: Macmillan, 1952), 52. Likewise Jacob Neusner states, "An act of loving kindness is one that cannot be coerced but is all the more appreciated by God; it is an act of generosity of spirit and shows an attitude of love for the other." Jacob Neusner, *Theological Dictionary of Rabbinic Judaism: Principal Theological Categories* (Lanham, MD: University Press of America, 2005), 117.

If there is no human freedom then all human actions are necessitated and determined either by God or by a mechanistic universe God has set up and ordained. If there is no human freedom God certainly has no use for faith or trust. Faith would be useless since there would be no risk of humans doing other than what God willed. But there would also be no relationship. Relationship requires free agents. So, if relationships of love and virtues are what God desires, then God must create beings capable of such qualities.

Philosophically, free will is a difficult concept. Philosophers and theologians have wrestled over how best to understand and explain this slippery notion.[21] Christians by and large affirm some form of human free will though there are noteworthy disagreements over what constitutes human freedom. By my lights, libertarian freedom makes most sense of human freedom, especially in light of divine directives, sin, love, and morality. To understand what libertarianism is, first let me explain what it is not.

Many philosophers and theologians can be categorized as determinists. Causal determinism is the claim that every event, including human choices, has already been causally determined to take place.[22] Everything that happens, then, is a result of earlier events that cause or determine all future events. Theological determinists regard God as the antecedent cause of every consequent.[23] John Feinberg, writes, "God's will covers all things and . . . the basis for God's sovereign choices is not what God foresees will happen nor anything else external to his will. Rather, God's good pleasure and good purposes determine what he

[21]See Gary Watson, ed., *Free Will* (Oxford: Oxford University Press, 1982); Robert Kane, ed., *The Oxford Handbook of Free Will* (Oxford: Oxford University Press, 2011); Kevin Tempe and Daniel Speak, eds., *Free Will and Theism: Connections, Contingencies, and Concerns* (Oxford: Oxford University Press, 2016).

[22]Thomas Pink, *Free Will: A Very Short Introduction* (Oxford: Oxford University Press, 2004), 13.

[23]For a defense of theological determinism and compatibilism, see Paul Helm, "Classical Calvinist Doctrine of God," in *Perspectives on the Doctrine of God: Four Views*, ed. Bruce A. Ware (Nashville: B&H Academic, 2008), 5-52; Bruce A. Ware, "A Modified Calvinist Doctrine of God," in *Perspectives on the Doctrine of God: Four Views*, ed. Bruce A. Ware (Nashville: B&H Academic, 2008), 76-120; Paul Kjoss Helseth, "God Causes All Things," in *Four Views on Divine Providence*, ed. Dennis W. Jowers (Grand Rapids: Zondervan, 2011), 25-52.

decrees. . . . God has chosen at once the whole interconnected sequence of events and actions that have and will occur in our world."[24]

Most theological determinists emphasize that in the human-divine "relationship" God is the determining power but also that humans are free to act upon their desires. Such theologians, called "soft determinists" or "compatibilists," maintain that determinism and human freedom are logically compatible. Feinberg, for example adds to his statement above: "God includes whatever means are necessary to accomplish his ends in a way that avoids constraining the agent to do what is decreed. Human actions are thus causally determined but free."[25] God then, by virtue of being infinitely powerful and sovereign, determines and thus ensures that "humans will voluntarily make the decisions he would have them make (and thus do what he would have them do.)"[26] For the theological compatibilist, "Agents are free to do as they want and are morally responsible for the choices they make. But all their choices nevertheless fall within the sovereign plan of God, which governs all things."[27] We are free, according to compatibilists, when circumstances allow us to do what we desire, but we are not free, however, to choose our desires. As Steven Roy writes, "God actively, decisively and noncoercively shapes human desires, and then the individual freely chooses to act according to those desires."[28] According to theological determinists, God causes everything that takes place for God's own purposes; nothing, including our free actions, happens outside the will of God. The limits of freedom are linked to one's desires for one is free if one can do what is desired, but no one is free to choose his or her desires.

---

[24]John S. Feinberg, "God Ordains All Things," in *Predestination and Free Will: Four Views of Divine Sovereignty and Human Freedom*, ed. David Basinger and Randall Basinger (Downers Grove, IL: InterVarsity Press, 1986), 29.

[25]Feinberg, "God Ordains All Things," 29.

[26]Basinger, *The Case for Freewill Theism*, 27.

[27]James K. Beilby and Paul R. Eddy, *Divine Foreknowledge: Four Views*, ed. James K. Beilby and Paul R. Eddy (Downers Grove, IL: InterVarsity Press, 2001), 11. This view should be distinguished from fatalism that holds that all things happen out of necessity and that even God has no choice in the matter.

[28]Steven C. Roy, *How Much Does God Foreknow? A Comprehensive Biblical* Study (Downers Grove, IL: IVP Academic, 2006), 15. I must freely admit I do not understand how God "decisively" and yet "noncoercively" shapes our desires so that they are performed freely.

If either theological determinism or compatibilism is true, then there is no need for divine faith. According to each view God is able to ensure the divine will is always met and desires always satisfied—including voluntary human choices. God's abilities are in no way limited by human choice, according to theological determinists and compatibilists, and so God takes no risks. God is wholly independent.

Libertarians maintain that we have free will but add that if any form of determinism is true we are not free. So, libertarians affirm that we in fact have free will but deny that free will and determinism are compatible—thus, libertarians are incompatibilists.[29] Libertarians maintain that deterministic causes are incompatible with free will, and so if God (or anything other than the agent herself) in fact determines any human choice, it is not performed freely.

Freedom is generally expressed by libertarians as *the ability to choose and do (or have done) otherwise.* For example, when faced with the choice to eat a donut or not, one is only truly free if he is able to either choose and eat the donut or choose and not eat the donut. If he is caused (by anything other than his own agency) to eat a donut, then it was not eaten freely, for he could not have done otherwise. Furthermore, libertarians believe that moral responsibility is only possible if an agent is able to act freely—take, for example, eating a donut and knowing it belonged to another person. While theological determinists and compatibilists claim that God is the ultimate cause of our agent eating the donut (even though the agent is still morally responsible), the libertarian claims that the agent himself is the cause and so the agent alone is responsible since he could have done other.

If God, ultimately, is the cause of our actions and, furthermore, we can do no other than what God ordains then God of course needs no faith. But if we are free to do other than what we actually do and God desires that we make particular choices—choices that make a difference to God's

---

[29]Not all incompatibilists are libertarians. So-called hard determinists agree with libertarians that *if* determinism is true then there is no free will, but unlike libertarians they deny that free will is true.

plans for this world—then God must have faith that we will do what is right. That is, God will need to trust us to do what God wants, and furthermore, God as an agent of love will rightly hope that we choose and do what is good and right.

Open future. Libertarianism helps to make sense of the many biblical references to God's anger and grief over sin, as well as the institution of laws, obligations, and covenants. For libertarians, none of these makes sense without genuine free will. God gets angry and grieves in response to freely made choices. If human acts were not genuinely free, it is difficult to make sense of these divine responses. Assuming humans do act freely, a new question arises: Are we really free to do otherwise if God has absolute and infallible knowledge of future free contingent choices? Asked another way, does freedom of the will necessitate that the future be open to real contingency? Open and relational theologians affirm that libertarian freedom is only possible if the future is open to real contingency. Assuming an open future, we will need to rethink God's relationship to time as well as what God knows and in what ways God knows it. But this also means we need to think anew about God's hoping and trusting.

This leads to the third supposition, that the future is genuinely open. On this supposition, the truth of various propositions about the future are presently indeterminate—leaving open a number of possible outcomes. These propositions are not open merely epistemologically but ontologically. That is, the future is comprised, in part, of genuine possibilities.[30] Though the past and present are ontologically settled and, therefore, known by God to be so, there are no current facts about our future free choices and, so, nothing for God's knowledge to be *about*. However, all of the future free actions that you *might* perform—all of your possible actions—are available for God's knowledge. This means we are free to choose because the future is genuinely open to alternatives.

God then is not unaware or ignorant, for God knows *all there is to know because God knows all that is*. Thus, God knows all truth. More carefully,

---

[30]Gregory A. Boyd, "God Limits His Control," in *Four Views on Divine Providence*, ed. Dennis W. Jowers (Grand Rapids: Zondervan, 2011), 194-95.

"God knows with certainty those aspects of the future that are already fixed and certain, and God knows as indefinite those aspects of the future that are, as of now, open and indefinite."[31] Open theists affirm that God knows all truth, but God knows the truth of all actualities *as* actualities and the truth of all possibilities *as* possibilities.[32] Open and relational theists, then, fully endorse the doctrine of divine omniscience, that God knows all truth.[33] The dispute among open theists is whether future free conditional statements have a truth value and, if so, what kind.[34]

Christians, however, from Jacob Arminius to C. S. Lewis have advocated for what some call "simple foreknowledge."[35] This theory seeks to save both human freedom and absolute exhaustive divine foreknowledge by asserting that God knows all future free choices without robbing "the future of contingency or freedom."[36] Roger Olson, for example, argues that divine foreknowledge means that God predestines the salvation of individuals without interfering with genuine free will because "conditional election [is] based on God's foreknowledge of faith."[37] "God foreknows the entire course of the future as well as its end."[38] It is not enough simply to say that God knows all future free choices without causing

---

[31]Michael Peterson, William Hasker, Bruce Reichenbach, and David Basinger, *Reason and Religious Belief: An Introduction to the Philosophy of Religion*, 5th ed. (Oxford: Oxford University Press, 2013), 171.

[32]This view is sometimes referred to as "dynamic omniscience" since the content of God's knowledge changes as future possibilities become present and then past actualities. See John Sanders, "Divine Providence and the Openness of God," in *Perspectives on the Doctrine of God: Four Views*, ed. Bruce Ware (Nashville: B&H Academic, 2008), 199.

[33]Omniscience is generally defined as having "knowledge of all truths." The definition typically includes the statements that one is omniscient if one believes all and only true propositions. For more information, see Edward Wierenga, "Omniscience," in *The Oxford Handbook of Philosophical Theology*, ed. Thomas P. Flint and Michael C. Rea (Oxford: Oxford University Press, 2009), 129-44. I will say more about omniscience in chap. 4 concerning God's beliefs.

[34]Open theists disagree whether future free conditional propositions have a truth value. I address this in chap. 4.

[35]For more information concerning the incompatibility of relational theism and simple divine foreknowledge, see Sanders, *The God Who Risks*, 205-17.

[36]Roger Olson, "The Classical Free Will Theist Model of God," in *Perspectives on the Doctrine of God: Four Views*, ed. Bruce A. Ware (Nashville: B&H Academic, 2008), 156.

[37]Roger Olson, *Arminian Theology: Myth and Realities* (Downers Grove, IL: IVP Academic, 2006), 97. I am unsure if Olson himself fully affirms this approach since he simply begins the quote above with, "All real Arminians believe in predestination. Of course, they mean . . ."

[38]Olson, "The Classical Free Will Theist Model of God," 156.

them, however, "freedom requires more than the absence of coercion. It also requires the presence of genuine alternatives."[39] If the future exists in such a manner that God can infallibly know every future free choice, then there is no need for divine faith. If God foreknows with certainty how every future free choice plays out, then divine trust that individuals will make right choices is unnecessary and the hope that certain free agents will love instead of hate evaporates.

The fact that our knowledge is limited makes human faith necessary. If there were absolute and infallible human knowledge of God's being and acts, both past and future, we would have no need for faith. Knowledge would be able to serve as our detailed and fail-safe road map. However, we do not have such knowledge. Likewise, divine faith is necessitated by the fact that God has created a world in which creaturely free choice is possible because there are genuine indeterminacies. If God cannot know the future as fixed or settled but still desires particular outcomes dependent upon human choices, then God must hope and trust in humanity. Just as humans then have faith and hope regarding God's future actions, God too has faith regarding human free choices.

If God has exhaustive definite knowledge of all future free human choices, in the same way that God has such knowledge of past and present choices, then any discussion of God's faith is irrelevant, because faith is occasioned, in part, by the unknown. Faith is a positive posture when one faces an open future and chooses to hope and trust. Faith not only depends on but is necessitated by an unknown future. If God knows the outcome of every future free choice, then God never risks, trusts, or hopes for anything or in anyone. Obviously, the simple foreknowledge approach will not support a God of faith. But if the situation is that we are free and that God faces an open future, then it is reasonable to continue this discussion of God's faith.

In this section I have endeavored to articulate tersely God's omniscience in light of an open future. God knows all truths. God knows

---

[39]Rice, *God's Foreknowledge and Man's Free Will*, 20.

some truths as actual ("I was born in California") and some truths as possible ("I will die in California"). God's knowledge of all truth also entails that God knows some statements are false ("I was born before my grandfather"). But in conventional language this can be stated as *God does not know false statements* and thus God does not know that "I was born before my grandfather" because that statement is false. Out of convention and readability I will from time to time speak about God not knowing, but this should be read in light of what is said in this section. Thus, if I say, "God does not know what tie I will buy ten years from now," that means "God knows every tie I might buy ten years from now, but God does not know what tie I will actually buy."

Divine possibility. I will consider one final supposition. Does God genuinely care if the creation reaches its intended ends? Does it make a difference to divine happiness if humans respond positively or not to God's invitation to share in this divine project and to enter into relationships of mutual love? It seems to me it does, but let's consider how it might not. It may be that creation has a divinely appointed but undetermined telos. It may also be that humans are genuinely free to achieve or reject God's desired ends for the creation. Furthermore, it may even be true that God cannot know if we will be successful (however that might be understood) or whether this divine plan will see its end. But in all this, God would still not need faith if God did not have anything invested in this project. If the success of creational plans makes no difference to God, then divine faith and trust is unnecessary. Without risk, there is no need for trust. Without hope, faith is pointless.

What reasons might there be for God being unaffected by creation? I can see two possibilities. First, it may be that this creation is merely a bit of divine research. While existentially difficult to admit, this world may simply be a grand divine empirical experiment. It might be that all God anticipates getting from this experiment is the knowledge of whether or not we meet divine expectations. The creation may be one giant mouse maze, and when it is all over, win or lose, God will know whether we get to the cheese or not. If that is the case, God needs not faith, only curiosity.

While this is a possible conclusion, it is most definitely not a plausible one from a Christian perspective. The idea that God is curious but uncaring sounds more like the plot of a Philip K. Dick novel than the offering of a Christian theology. A more considerable problem to divine faith, however, is divine impassibility, the view that God's emotional life is unaffected by human affairs.

Impassibility, in its modern form, is "immutability with regard to one's feelings, and the incapacity of being acted upon and having one's emotional experience changed by an external force."[40] Said another way, impassibility "declares that nothing can disturb God's heart or rob him of his joy."[41] The doctrine is born out of classical conceptions of divine immutability, which basically state that God is not subject to change in any manner.[42] Certainly, if God is unable to change in any way, then impassibility is a logical consequence. But impassibility does not require immutability, for God could be a temporal being who experiences real change that comes with causing the universe to exist in the manner it does and acquires new truths as contingencies become actualities, but God nonetheless remains emotionally unmoved by those changes. Logically, those who affirm divine immutability would certainly reject divine faith.

It could be then that God experiences the changes that come with being creator, fashioning creatures who are genuinely free, and facing an open future, and yet remains emotionally unaffected. This approach to impassibility would highlight God's inability to have emotional experiences changed by an outside force. By this, God's eternal blessedness would be unaffected by our faithfulness or unfaithfulness.[43] But could a

---

[40]Roberto Sirvent, *Embracing Vulnerability: Human and Divine* (Eugene, OR: Pickwick, 2014), 38.

[41]Ron Highfield, *Great Is the Lord: Theology for the Praise of God* (Grand Rapids: Eerdmans, 2008), 375.

[42]Though many have made exceptions concerning the incarnation. See Thomas G. Weinandy, *Does God Suffer?* (Notre Dame, IN: University of Notre Dame Press, 2000), 172-213.

[43]Richard Creel (*Divine Impassibility: An Essay in Philosophical Theology* [Cambridge: Cambridge University Press, 1986]) seems to take just such an approach. Creel argues that God has created the world so that "there might also be others to enjoy the great good of existence under his sovereignty" (207). He affirms libertarian freedom, arguing that human relationships with the world and God are "up to us" and that "the fundamental purpose of God's granting subjective freedom to creatures is to enable them to make a radical choice for or against his kingdom"

person exercise faith in another without being emotionally vulnerable or passible? As I seek to demonstrate, faith—trust, hope, and love—is not possible without vulnerability. To enter into a relationship of faith is to become exposed and risk whatever it is you have entrusted to the other. I see no reason to think that God can have faith without being passible. But why should I think God is passible? Let me offer a very brief and woefully inadequate response to this question—hopefully though, one that satisfies the reader enough to continue with this inquiry.

What reasons are there for embracing the passibility and suffering of God?[44] First, the Bible attests to a God who is not only passionate but also passible. God suffers *because of* the choices and actions of humans. For example, Judges 2:18 says God raised up judges and delivered the people from their enemies because "the LORD would be moved to pity by their groaning because of those who persecuted and oppressed them." Psalm 78:40 says, "How often they rebelled against him in the wilderness and grieved him in the desert!"[45] Some defenders of impassibility argue that passages that speak of God suffering or having a change of mind speak anthropomorphically or anthropopathically in order to accommodate human understanding. Millard Erikson, for example, regarding passages like Genesis 6:6 (which depicts God as sorry for making humankind) says these are anthropomorphisms since "the plan of God in terms of its specifics is unchangeable. God does not change his mind

---

(206). Creel also affirms that such radical freedom means that there is no "way to compatibilize human freedom and divine omniprescience [foreknowledge]." Furthermore, if "God has no such knowledge . . . the future free actions of creatures are something that in principle cannot be known" (206). And yet Creel concludes that God remains impassible in feeling (emotion) since "it is intelligible that a being is blissful by nature, and therefore God, a perfect being, should be thought of as such. God is dependent on no other individual for the actuality or perfection of his existence or happiness" (206). While Creel offers an interesting argument, I find his conclusion problematic. He says that God "honors the decisions of those" who do not choose God's kingdom and, furthermore, that "God would rather that no one suffer innocently," and yet he maintains that God's blissfulness is never altered even though many do not choose the kingdom and do suffer innocently.

[44]When I speak of God suffering because of the action of others I am assuming two things about suffering. First, that it is an undesirable state of mind. Second, it is inflicted by an external power. God suffers because humans (external power) sin in various ways, yet God desires we not sin. Suffering is likely much more but minimally suffering entails this.

[45]See also Gen 6:6; Ex 2:23-25; 3:7-8; Is 63:9b; Jer 3:7; 32:35; Hos 11:8-9.

or alter his decisions regarding specific determinations. . . . We must keep in mind here that constancy is one of the attributes of God's greatness."[46] Essentially, any biblical narrative that speaks of God emoting or having a change of mind or heart is simply not literally true in what it claims or suggests about God. This means that Scripture obfuscates certain basic truths concerning God and we are left with unreserved equivocation, but no one wants this conclusion. Modern impassibilists argue that God does experience the emotions attributed to God in the Bible. However, God freely choses these emotions, they are not caused by human deed but are self-caused. God then, having "impassible emotions," is passionate but not passive.[47] But here again we are plunged into ambiguity since the biblical narratives do not merely suggest that God has emotions but that human choice is the cause of, at least in some cases and in some respects, these emotions.

Second, since humanity is made in the image and likeness of God (Gen 1:26-28), it stands to reason that our emotional life is imaged after and like that of God's. I am not suggesting that humans are a perfect analogue for the divine. But it may be that emotions are not human traits metaphorically attached to God, but divine traits imperfectly possessed by humans. That is, emotions and passibility may be better understood as speaking theopathically rather than anthropomorphically.[48] John Peckham contends that it may be "more accurate to say that the canon

---

[46]Erickson, *Introducing Christian Doctrine*, 113. See also John Calvin, *Institutes of the Christian Religion*, ed. John McNeil, trans. Ford Lewis Battles, 2 vols., Library of Christian Classics (Philadelphia: Westminster, 1960), 1.13.1; 1.17.12; 3.21.4. Paul Helm, "The Impossibility of Divine Passibility," in *The Power and Weakness of God*, ed. Nigel M. de S. Cameron (Edinburgh: Rutherford House, 1990), 119-40. Weinandy, *Does God Suffer?*

[47]John C. Peckham, *The Love of God: A Canonical Model* (Downers Grove, IL: IVP Academic, 2015), 171. Several theologians have affirmed this idea directly or indirectly. Karl Barth states this view clearly: "But the personal God has a heart. He can feel, and be affected. He is not impassible. He cannot be moved from outside by an extraneous power. But this does not mean that he is not capable of moving Himself. No, God *is* moved and stirred, yet not like ourselves in powerlessness, but in his own free power, in His innermost being." *Church Dogmatics*, ed. Geoffrey W. Bromiley and T. F. Torrance (Edinburgh: T&T Clark, 1957), vol. 2, part 1, 370.

[48]Jürgen Moltmann, building upon the works of Abraham Heschel, argues extensively that suffering is not alien to God but is essential to God as a being of love. Furthermore, "God and suffering belong together." Jürgen Moltmann, *Trinity and the Kingdom of God*, trans. Margaret Kohl (Minneapolis: Fortress, 1981), 49. For his full argument, see pages 21-52.

considers humans to be theomorphic and theopathic than to say that language of God that Scripture also uses of humans is anthropopathic."[49]

Third, as a being perfect in love and goodness, God must be passive and emotionally vulnerable. I, like many others, understand love to necessitate vulnerability. Jürgen Moltmann famously stated that "the one who cannot suffer cannot love either."[50] Paul Fiddes argues that love involves suffering, and "suffering must mean change and being changed. To love is to be in a relationship where what the loved one does alters one's own experience . . . the lover's existence is shaped by the other's needs."[51] Not only does impassibility lead us to question divine love, it raises questions about divine morality. Roberto Sirvent sees vulnerability as a moral virtue and concludes that if God is a moral agent then God is passible. "Imitatio Dei . . . asks us to reject divine impassibility on moral grounds. To put it bluntly, an impassible God is not worth imitating."[52] Furthermore, as I have been suggesting, if God is impassible, "then we are left with a God who undertakes no emotional risk with his creation" and thus a God who has no place for faith.[53]

If it is true that our choices make a difference to God, that divine happiness is in some part dependent upon our faithfulness, then God needs faith. If God is passible and God's blessedness depends, in part, on a relationship with humans, then faith is a necessary divine virtue, for without mutual faith there is no hope of divine happiness.

Conclusion. I concede that any one, or even all four, of my suppositions (purpose for creation, human freedom, open future, divine passibility) could be false. This world may have ends wholly independent of human action and may have been created purely out of God's sovereign freedom. Perhaps we are not free in any sense that necessitates an open future. Perhaps the future is closed and so God does indeed have exhaustive

[49]John C. Peckham, *Canonical Theology: The Biblical Canon, Sola Scriptura, and Theological Method* (Grand Rapids: Eerdmans, 2016), 244.
[50]Jürgen Moltmann, *The Crucified God: The Cross of Christ as the Foundation and Criticism of Christian Theology*, trans. R. A. Wilson and John Bowden (Minneapolis: Fortress, 1993), 222.
[51]Paul Fiddes, *The Creative Suffering of God* (Oxford: Oxford University Press, 1988), 50-51.
[52]Sirvent, *Embracing Vulnerability*, 177.
[53]Sirvent, *Embracing Vulnerability*, 177.

foreknowledge. Perhaps God is beyond the impact of anything outside the divine will. I concede that if any one of my assumptions is false, then my thesis might be in serious trouble. However, if any one of these conditions is true, then we need to consider the others earnestly. Further, I think that my assumptions can, under ideal conditions, be supported by forceful argument that I am simply not in a position to provide here.

But if this world was created to bring about forms of goodness and value that otherwise would not exist, then this world invites us to consider not only that God is a God of love but also a God of faith. If the reader believes that each of these conditions is true and accurate, then it is appropriate (and maybe even necessary) for us to speak about trust and hope, along with love, as divine virtues. If all that I have laid out is as I have supposed, then it is perfectly reasonable to consider a theology of divine faith and trust.

PRIMA FACIE OBJECTIONS

Before beginning the formal argument for God's faith, it may be helpful to briefly address a few possible objections.

Humans are completely untrustworthy. Many Christians affirm that humans are totally depraved, and I agree, but not totally. We should understand *totally* in reference to the scope, not depth, of depravity. There is no one who is without sin (Rom 3:23). There is no aspect of our world unaffected by sin. Sin pollutes every part of our lives—social, psychological, political. Christ died for all, the totality of humanity, because of the totality of sin (Rom 5:18-19). If that is what is meant by total depravity, then I agree. I disagree, however, that the totality of our being is absolutely perverted by sin.[54]

Biblical calls for obedience and a general belief in responsibility constitute reason to consider whether humans can be trusted and be

---

[54]Even Calvinists argue that the "total" in *total depravity* does not mean that "humans are as bad as we can possibly be." It means that "we are all guilty and corrupt to such an extent that there is no hope of pulling ourselves together, brushing ourselves off, and striving (with the help of grace) to overcome God's judgment and our own rebellion." See Michael Horton, *For Calvinism* (Grand Rapids: Zondervan, 2011), 41.

trustworthy. Should husbands and wives have faith in one another? Is it good and right that children trust their parents? Can we call someone a friend if we can never count on him or her to be trustworthy? It seems to me we should trust those whom we have close and intimate relationships with. I will say more about this, but it seems we have a prima facie moral obligation to trust our spouses, friends, and in the right circumstances our children. Furthermore, can a society function if there is a fundamental distrust and suspicion of all persons and systems? If it is good, right, and even necessary to trust and hope in one another, then it seems wrong to suggest that every human is utterly and totally depraved. There may be many a person who demonstrates total depravity, but anyone who strictly and consistently lives out a fundamental distrust and suspicion of all persons and systems would be either an antisocial relentless conspiracist or simply unhinged.

It is clear: we are sinful creatures. Sin has alienated us from God, nature, one another, and ourselves (Gen 2–3). Sin is estrangement, a rupture in all kinds of relationships and a denial of relatedness. Sin is far more than a violation of a moral code; it is "the disruption in our relationship with God."[55] We cannot save ourselves and I do not hold that God trusts us to do so. But, as I will argue, God's trust does not begin only after we have shown ourselves trustworthy. No, God trusts us first. Perhaps the first act of divine faith in each of our lives is God entrusting us with grace.

Sin is not what makes faith in another a mistake; it is what makes it necessary. If there were no possibility that we would ever act selfishly, then there would be little need for faith—divine or human. Faith supposes one may not be faithful, but there is trust and hope in spite of the risk. As Terence Fretheim rightly affirms, commenting on Genesis 2:5 and 2:15, that because we have failed does not eliminate either responsibility or trust: "Even in the wake of human sin, God still entrusts the human with power and responsibility . . . still entrusting the human

---

[55]Daniel L. Migliore, *Faith Seeking Understanding: An Introduction to Christian Theology*, 2nd ed. (Grand Rapids: Eerdmans, 2004), 151.

creature with important creational responsibilities even though they have failed."[56]

Divine faith is not explicitly biblical. Perhaps scholars, pastors, and priests considered but rejected a theology of God's faith because it is not an explicit biblical teaching. Nowhere in Scripture is there a description of God's faith like those of God's wrath, anger, love, or even patience. While it is true that the Bible never explicitly mentions God's faith, this should not keep theologians and pastors from considering the idea. The history of theology is filled with creeds, doctrines, teachings, and exposés that are not explicitly found in the pages of the Bible. Such ideas include, but are not limited to, omnipotence, omniscience, *creatio ex nihilo*, and the Trinity. The Bible never makes explicit mention of these deeply held doctrines. I am not saying there is no way to make a biblical case for these doctrines, it is just that they are unlike explicit biblical teachings such as the love of God, humanity of Jesus, or salvific work of Christ. My own theological heritage has long maintained the maxim, "where the Bible speaks, we speak, and where the Bible is silent, we are silent."[57] This does not mean that we cannot speak or theologize about such matters, but only that they will not be a test of fellowship. As noted above, Christians have much to say about doctrines not explicitly found in the Scriptures. Nonetheless, I believe the Bible does have something to say about the faith of God, even if not explicitly, and in the following chapters I will try to demonstrate that the Bible is not wholly silent on such matters. Even if the Bible does not speak as obviously about divine faith as it does other doctrines, a case can be made that the Bible at least allows for such interpretations.

No Christian tradition of divine faith. Some may also hold that because there has been no prior tradition of addressing God's faith such an idea should be rejected. However, as most theologians know, Christian

---

[56]Terence E. Fretheim, *God and World in the Old Testament: A Relational Theology of Creation* (Nashville: Abingdon, 2005), 54.

[57]Historian Leroy Garrett argues that while this affirmation had the potential for harmony, it also brought with it controversy. See Garrett, *The Stone-Campbell Movement: The Story of the American Restoration Movement*, rev. ed. (Joplin, MO: College Press, 2002), chap. 13.

doctrines are developed and codified over time, often over long periods. It is also true that now and then doctrines fall out of favor with the majority of Christians. Examples include the long-held ransom theory of atonement and postmillennialism. It seems that there is room for conceptual innovation. The last century, to the joy of some and lament of others, has produced many conceptual innovations in the doctrine of God. New discoveries and paradigm shifts in the sciences as well as in philosophy have led to reexaminations of creation as well as God's being. These new understandings are not always meant to supplant the tradition but to supervene upon it. Sometimes they are corrective, but often these new theologies explore and unpack the logical, though un-noticed, implications of our tradition. One of this book's primary direc-tives is to make explicit what has only been implicit in the open and relational approach to God. A theology of divine faith may not fit within everyone's theological tradition, but it is clearly linked to and is a logical outworking of the great Christian tradition. This study is a new leaf on a newer branch but is nonetheless a part of the great family tree.[58]

All language concerning God as dynamic is anthropomorphic and metaphoric. In his *Institutes of the Christian Religion*, John Calvin fa-mously argued regarding any scriptural depiction of God having a change of mind: "Because our weakness cannot reach his height, any description which we receive of him must be lowered to our capacity in order to be intelligible. And the mode of lowering is to represent him not as he really is, but as we conceive of him."[59] Earlier in the text Calvin suggested that anthropomorphisms are akin to God "lisping" to us like a nurse speaking to a newborn.[60] The conclusion some reach is that any depiction of God having either humanlike body parts or emotions

---

[58]A theology of divine faith is not without a tradition. Theology of divine faith is a logical out-working of relational theologies. Just as relational theologies are logical developments of Armin-ian and freewill traditions, my theology of divine faith is an expression of open and relational theism. A theology of divine faith, while seemingly new, is nonetheless directly linked to the great tradition.

[59]Calvin, *Institutes*, 1.17.13; see also 1.17.12 and 3.21.4.

[60]Calvin, *Institutes*, 1.13.1.

should equally be treated as anthropomorphic accommodations to human weakness. If this is so, then any biblical passage that lends itself to speaking of God's trust, belief, or hope are not to be understood literally but as crude metaphors that need to be literalized.

I agree that "all speech about God is anthropomorphic" because human language itself is anthropomorphic.[61] However, it might be helpful to make a distinction between poetic imagery of God, anthropomorphisms, and anthropopathisms. Poetic imagery for God makes use of common objects in order to help us better understand a divine character trait. God is imagined as a rock (Deut 32:31) and fire (Heb 12:29). Divine anthropomorphisms speak of God having physical human characteristics or "forms" such as eyes (Heb 4:13), feet (Mt 5:35), or in general human movement like walking in the cool of the garden (Gen 3:8) or repenting (Gen 6:6-7). More precise and more appropriate to this work are anthropopathic utterances, which apply to God (or any other non-human things) human emotions or pathos. While I believe it is appropriate to understand anthropomorphic statements as metaphoric, some anthropopathisms are more literal than others—though none are perfectly analogous to human emotions.

It is important to distinguish the purpose and use of anthropomorphic and anthropopathic Scriptures. First, if we treat all utterances about God as accommodations that never represent God as God actually is, then what can be said of God's love, plans, will, wisdom, or goodness? Can it even be said that God is a *living* God or that God has *being*? Second, it seems that Scripture is meant to communicate something true about God. An anthropomorphism such as "And before him no creature is hidden, but all are naked and laid bare to the eyes of the one to whom we must render an account" (Heb 4:13) is meant to communicate that God knows our thoughts and intentions—we cannot hide from God. While the passage makes use of anthropomorphic and metaphoric imagery, it nonetheless communicates something true about

---

[61]Justo L. González, *Essential Theological Terms* (Louisville, KY: Westminster John Knox, 2005), 9.

God—not literal, but true.[62] But what of anthropopathisms? When we are told that God is patient (2 Pet 3:9), what does this communicate about God if it is simply an anthropomorphism? What about divine changes of mind? As Greg Boyd argues, "If God in fact never changes his mind, saying he does so doesn't communicate anything truthful: it is simply inaccurate."[63] Hermeneutically, we need to ask what anthropomorphizing a passage brings to the table. Does it bring clarity and understanding to an otherwise difficult text? Or does it obfuscate and lead us to conclude that the text does not mean anything near what it says?

Finally, it may be better that we speak not of anthropopathism but of theopathism. Depictions of God's emotions may not be mere reflections of the ways God is like humans but ways in which we are like God, and these depictions give us examples of how we should feel and emote. Scripture reveals God's thoughts, feelings, and responses in part to teach us how we, in certain times and ways, should think, feel, and respond. We are made in God's image (Gen 1:26-27) and are meant to be imitators of God (Eph 5:1). John Sanders, following the lead of Abraham Heschel, says, "Instead of saying that God is like us we should say we are like God since we are created in the divine image. . . . God's concern for justice and love is not anthropomorphism, rather our concern for justice and love is a theomorphism."[64]

Certainly all theology is tinged with anthropomorphisms, metaphors, and analogies. Anything we say about God is incomplete since all language is human language. But this does not mean we cannot speak about God in ways more literal than other ways. I contend that while depictions of God's trust and hope are asymmetrical to human trust and hope they are not mere anthropomorphisms.

---

[62]Notice this passage not only uses anthropomorphic imagery of God's eyes but also uses a spatial metaphor of "before him," suggesting that God has a front and a back, a before and a behind. For more on theology and metaphor, see John Sanders, *Theology in the Flesh: How Embodiment and Culture Shape the Way We Think About Truth, Morality, and God* (Minneapolis: Fortress, 2016).

[63]Gregory A. Boyd, "The Open-Theism View," in *Divine Knowledge: Four Views*, ed. James K. Beilby and Paul R. Eddy (Downers Grove, IL: InterVarsity Press, 2001), 39.

[64]Sanders, *The God Who Risks*, 29.

Throughout this work I employ several metaphors—notably God as lover, parent, and friend—in an attempt to explain and articulate God's faith. Some may bristle at such use, arguing that this is nothing less than "creating God in our own image." Such a critique is taken seriously. Sallie McFague reminds us that "metaphorical statements . . . always contain the whisper, 'it is *and it is not.*'"[65] Thus, the danger in using metaphors is forgetting that they are images and depictions of what God is but also what God is not. Furthermore, while metaphors are "anthropomorphic, they are legitimate to use, for God has created us in the divine image and comes to us in our history."[66] So while I am not seeking to create God in my own image, I am seeking to understand God through the images given us in Scriptures as well as through my own humanity.

Not all statements about God are metaphorical. To say "God loves you" is a literal statement, though it will need to be fleshed out, often with the use of metaphor.[67] Likewise, I suggest that "God trusts you" is also a literal statement, but again one that needs to be fleshed out. I suggest God's faith can be compared to the trust between spouses, parents who believe in their children, and friends who entrust one another with joys and hardships. But these comparisons will also come with contrasts since our human relationships are imperfect examples of a perfect being.

According to McFague, "good metaphors shock, they bring unlikes together, they upset conventions, they involve tension, and they are implicitly revolutionary."[68] One of the most shocking biblical metaphors is found in Hosea where God's relationship with Israel is depicted in metaphors of sexual intercourse, love, passion, anger, disillusionment, and other anthropopathic imagery.[69] It is unknown whether this work will

---

[65]Sallie McFague, *Metaphorical Theology: Models of God in Religious Language* (Philadelphia: Fortress, 1982), 13. This whisper is a warning against what McFague refers to as the idolatry and irrelevance of religious language.

[66]Sanders, *The God Who Risks*, 37.

[67]Sanders, *Theology in the Flesh*, 63-64.

[68]McFague, *Metaphorical Theology*, 17.

[69]For an outstanding treatment of Hosea as anthropopathy of God, see Abraham J. Heschel, *The Prophets*, 2 vols. (Peabody, MA: Prince Press, 1962), 1:39-60.

upset and shock conventions—that is up to the reader. It is my belief, however, that this discussion of divine faith will spark new conversations about the relationship between God and humanity.

CHAPTERS PREVIEW

Chapter two is an exploration of faith itself. I argue that faith cannot be reduced to a single notion but is a dynamic integration of belief, trust, hope, and loving devotion. I further suggest that faith is a kind of relationship and when that relationship is most intimate and healthy it will include all four of the aspects noted above.

Chapter three begins my argument that God is a being of faith by maintaining that any person who genuinely loves another must have faith in the other or, minimally, desire to have faith. I explore God's love through the metaphors of lover, parent, and friend, pairing these with the Greek terms eros, agape, and philos, demonstrating that each of these kinds of love requires mutual faith.

Chapter four explores how we might understand God's *belief that* and *belief in*. The first part of the chapter unpacks how various open theists articulate God's omniscience in relation to an open future. What does God believe in regard to future free conditional statements? The second half of the chapter explores how God can be said to believe in us as well as have doubts about our faithfulness.

Chapter five unpacks the character of trust as "reliance plus." I will show that trust is a willingness to risk something of value to the care of another person and that God is such a being of trust. God's trust is also explored in relationship to divine omnipotence and also covenant. The chapter concludes with an exploration of several biblical texts that support the idea of divine trust.

Chapter six unpacks the character of hope and makes the case that God genuinely hopes. Because the future is open and humans are free, God cannot control our choices, but God has hope that we will respond to God's invitation. The second half of the chapter makes a biblical case for divine hope utilizing both the Old and New Testaments.

Chapter seven moves on from making the case for divine trust and explores the relationship of mutual faith between God the Father and Jesus of Nazareth. By understanding the incarnation through a kenotic Christology, we see that Jesus related to the Father through faith, and at times it was faith mixed with doubt. The chapter also considers God's faith in the efficacy of the cross, suggesting that if salvation is a restoration of a broken relationship, then God must trust the cross will move us to respond to God's grace.

Chapter eight, concluding the text, makes a brief argument for *imitatio Dei*, inviting the reader to consider that if God is our moral example then perhaps God too is our faith example. God's faith is not a response to our faith but a model for all to imitate.

2

THE MOSAIC OF FAITH

Sadly, God is not our ultimate concern, as Paul Tillich
would have it. Rather, we are God's ultimate concern.

Jerome Gellman, "The God of the Jews and the Jewish God"

"Faith" undoubtedly is one of the most widely used words in Christian theology. Countless books, articles, sermons, and devotions have sought to proclaim, define, clarify, and classify faith.[1] Faith can be understood as a creed or set of beliefs when used synonymously for Christianity itself when we speak of *the* Faith. For example, "There they strengthened the souls of the disciples and encouraged them to continue in the faith" (Acts 14:22).[2] Faith is a noun when we are called to have faith ("Have faith in God," Mk 11:22), increase in faith ("The apostles said to the Lord, 'Increase our faith!'" Lk 17:5), or one is of little or no faith ("You of little faith, why are you talking about having no bread?" Mt 16:8). The Greek also has a verb form of the word "faith" (*pisteuō*), but since English does not, it is generally translated as believe or trust: the same root word is a verb when faith entails actions such as believing or trusting ("Whoever

---

This quote is Gellman's summary of Abraham Heschel's theology. See Abraham J. Heschel, *God's Search for Man: A Philosophy of Judaism* (Northvale, NJ: Jason Aronson, 1987).

[1]William Lad Sessions, regarding faith studies, wonderfully uses John 21:25 out of context to suggest, "If it were all to be recorded in detail, I suppose the whole world could not hold the books that would be written." William Sessions, *The Concept of Faith: A Philosophical Investigation* (Ithaca, NY: Cornell University Press, 1994), 1.

[2]See also Gal 1:23: "The one who formerly was persecuting us is now proclaiming the faith he once tried to destroy"; and Jude 3: "I find it necessary to write and appeal to you to contend for the faith that was once for all entrusted to the saints."

believes in the Son has eternal life," Jn 3:36). Faith is spoken of in terms
of character such as faithfulness or fidelity ("Whoever is faithful in a
very little is faithful also in much," Lk 16:10). Of the theological virtues—
faith, hope, and love—faith, in its various Greek forms, outnumbers
hope and love together by over two hundred references in the New Testament.[3] While sheer numbers do not equate with importance, it is
nonetheless striking to see that faith is such a pervasive word and
concept in the New Testament.

Given that faith can be depicted in terms of belief, trust, doctrine,
feeling, attitude, and devotion, it is difficult to reduce faith down to a
single notion or concept. And yet many have tried, perhaps even suc-
ceeded. I, however, seriously question whether faith can be boiled
down to a single conception.[4] Faith, by my estimates, is dynamic,
complex, and irreducible. This does not mean I disagree with every
definition offered; it means I agree with many of them, but not to the
exclusion or negation of all others. It is good and helpful to develop
such definitions and conceptions—and not merely because I will make
use of them in this book. Continuing explorations and careful articu-
lations of faith help us weed out misunderstandings and sloppy formulations even if there has yet to be a perfectly univocal one-size-fits-
all conceptualization.

In what follows I will offer what I believe to be the key features of faith.
I will not necessarily speak of these as different kinds of faith but as differing aspects or elements of faith.[5] Specifically, I look at faith through
the lenses of belief, trust, hope, and love. This is not to suggest that faith
is exhausted by these features. Nor am I suggesting that all four of these
must be present to rightly label an attitude or disposition as faith. I have,

---

[3]Faith, in its various forms, is used over 550 times, while hope and love are used just under
350 times.

[4]Richard Rice also eschews using "definition" in his book and instead uses terms like "descrip-
tions," "dimensions," and, of course, "contours." For more information, see Richard Rice, *Reason
and the Contours of Faith* (Riverside, CA: La Sierra University Press, 1991).

[5]Throughout this work I will use various terms in discussing faith such as *element, aspect, feature,*
and *facet.* I am not trying to say anything unique when using one term instead of another but
am simply trying to reduce reader fatigue by not using one term exclusively. You're welcome.

nonetheless, chosen these for a few careful reasons. First, many other features of faith such as risk or devotion can be discussed under one of these other aspects of faith such as trust or love. Second, belief, trust, hope, and love tend to be the most widely discussed facets of faith by both scholars and laity. Third, biblical authors seem to associate faith with each of these various elements at one time or another. Once the concept of faith has been unpacked, I will use the remainder of the book to show how God is the subject of faith.

FAITH AND BELIEF

Perform even a casual search of books about faith and you will find title after title pairing faith, in some fashion or another, with reason—reason being one way to gather true beliefs and faith being another. While few would suggest that faith is exclusively about right believing, there are those who hold that faith's essential feature is propositional belief.[6] Arguably, the most important champion of this approach is Thomas Aquinas, and in my experience his influence is widely felt.[7]

According to Aquinas, faith is belief (*credo*), which holds a position between knowledge (*scientia*) and opinion (*opinio*) since all three are concerned with propositions.[8] With knowledge the truth of a proposition is certain but compelled by natural reason. The mind cannot help but believe. Regarding opinion, one holds the proposition willfully, yet tentatively. The believer recognizes she could be in error. Aquinas argues that faith, like knowledge is firm and certain. But faith, like opinion, does not compel us to believe. If a belief "be accompanied by doubt or fear of

---

[6]John Calvin, for example, wrote that "unless there is knowledge present, it is not God we worship but a spectre or ghost." See John Calvin, *The Gospel According to St John: 1–10*, ed. David W. Torrance and Thomas F. Torrance, trans. T. H. L. Parker (Grand Rapids: Eerdmans, 1995), 98.

Modern philosopher Richard Swinburne states, "All kinds of faith . . . involve attitudes towards, behaviour in the light of, *propositions*. They are not necessarily always so phrased, but my claim is that talk about believing in God or trusting God can without loss of meaning be analyzed in one of these ways." Richard Swinburne, *Faith and Reason* (Oxford: Clarendon, 1981), 124.

[7]Aquinas's thoughts on faith are found in the second part of the *Summa Theologica*. All quotations are from *The Catholic Encyclopedia* (New York: Robert Appleton), available on the New Advent website: www.newadvent.org/cathen/03791a.htm.

[8]Aquinas, *Summa Theologica*, 2-2.1.2.

the opposite side, there will be opinion, while, if there be certainty and no fear of the other side, there will be faith."[9] Faith then, for Aquinas, is a firm and certain propositional belief affirmed willfully, and this is why faith is meritorious, a virtue.[10]

It is with this Thomistic approach in mind I would like to explore the nature of belief as it relates to faith. So, what does it mean to believe some proposition is true? Richard Swinburne defines belief in terms of probability against an alternative.[11] For example, to believe there is a God is to believe that the proposition "there is a God" is more probable than the proposition "there is not a God."[12] The closer the probability is to 1, the greater the certainty felt, and the closer to .5, the less certainty felt. Just how much more probable a proposition should be compared to its alternative is debatable.[13]

Daniel Howard-Snyder says that belief is "something mental, specifically a mental state, not a mental occurrence like an act of mental assent or a process of deliberation. More specifically still, it is a dispositional state that manifests itself under certain conditions."[14] Howard-Snyder further states that believing p will include several dispositions such as feeling that p is the case, affirming p when asked whether p is so, using p to support other premises, and being surprised to learn not p.[15]

---

[9]Aquinas, *Summa Theologica*, 2-2.1.4.

[10]It is this voluntary character of faith that helps Aquinas make sense of the believing demons of James 2:19: "You believe that God is one; you do well. Even the demons believe—and shudder." "The demons are, in a way, compelled to believe, by the evidence of signs, and so their will deserves no praise for their belief" (Aquinas, *Summa Theologica*, 2-2.5.2). The demons have no meritorious faith for they lack the ability to not believe.

[11]Swinburne, *Faith and Reason*, 4.

[12]Swinburne does note that the alternatives can be plural, in which case one need only believe the proposition is more probable than any of the others. For example, after Thanksgiving dinner the proposition that "I will have pumpkin pie" is not only more probable than "I will not have pumpkin pie," it is more probable than "I will have cheesecake" or "I will have pecan pie." Though the next day it is more probable that "I will have a slice of all three" than "I will not have any slices." See Swinburne, *Faith and Reason*, 5-6.

[13]Swinburne, *Faith and Reason*, 5.

[14]Daniel Howard-Snyder, "Propositional Faith: What It Is and What It Is Not," *American Philosophical Quarterly* 50, no. 4 (2013): 359.

[15]Howard-Snyder's list of dispositions is taken from William Alston's "Belief, Acceptance, and Religious Faith," in *Faith, Freedom, and Rationality*, ed. Jeff Jordan and Daniel Howard-Snyder (Lanham, MD: Rowman & Littlefield, 1996), 4.

Questions concerning evidence, rationality, and just what makes a proposition worth believing are too massive, but also unnecessary, for this study.[16] Questions concerning the truth value of a propositional belief, however, are pertinent and will also be discussed in chapter four. For now, it will suffice to say that it is generally held that we only believe propositions we hold to be true. I believe that "I parked my car under a tree last Monday" is a true proposition about the past. I believe "I am eating jelly beans as I write this" is a true statement about the present. These simple statements are true if they correspond to reality. "I am eating jelly beans as I write this" is only true if I am in reality eating jelly beans as I write.[17] The truth value concerning future free conditional propositions is a very different matter. For example, is the proposition "I will buy my wife a necklace for our fortieth anniversary" (which is nearly a decade away) currently true or false? Philosophers are divided on this question. I take up this discussion in chapter four since this is important to understanding what God might believe about the future.

Propositional belief is a good and helpful aspect of religious faith. But to reduce faith to propositional belief or propose this is faith's essential feature is quite problematic. To suggest "faith that p entails belief that p"[18] has encountered criticism that, in my opinion, has rendered this view highly dubious. Howard-Snyder, for example, argues that "one can believe something and not be *for* its truth, but one cannot have faith that something is so and not be for its truth."[19] This is an important point, it is quite easy for me to think of all sorts of statements that I believe are true but would not say I have faith that they are true. I believe it is true that America will be plagued by racism for decades to come, but I would not say I have faith that this is true. Likewise, one will feel disappointed

---

[16]For those interested in such issues, two good starting places are Alvin Plantinga, *Knowledge and Christian Belief* (Grand Rapids: Eerdmans, 2015); and Steve Wilkens, ed., *Faith and Reason: Three Views* (Downers Grove, IL: IVP Academic, 2014).

[17]If you must know, they are a combination of cinnamon, black licorice, and buttered popcorn.

[18]This can also be articulated as "faith in p entails belief that p."

[19]Howard-Snyder, "Propositional Faith," 545.

to learn that something he had faith in was true turns out to be false, but this is not the case for many beliefs.[20]

I think this distinction that we necessarily care about the truth of faith propositions while belief propositions need not always involve our appeal or desire is a helpful way to approach James's believing demons. Demonic belief entails believing certain statements about God are true but there is no desire that they are true. There may even be hope that the belief is false. Faith, on the other hand, desires the truth of the proposition. Thomas Nagel gives us an excellent example of faith—faith that atheism is so. "I want atheism to be true. . . . It isn't just that I don't believe in God and, naturally, hope that I'm right in my belief. It's that I hope there is no God! I don't want there to be a God; I don't want the universe to be like that."[21] Nagel plainly states that he not only believes that atheism is so but deeply cares about it being so. He hopes that atheism is so. Nagel would be disappointed to learn that theism (or his misunderstanding of theism) is true. Therefore, Nagel has faith that atheism is so. While Nagel is admittedly an odd example, I think it shows that faith and belief are different animals.

Belief and faith are also differentiated in that "being in doubt about something *need not be* at odds with having faith that it is so."[22] One can have faith that *p* while being in doubt about *p*, but one cannot believe that *p* and doubt that *p*. If belief that *p* entails attitudes such as feeling that *p* is so and being surprised to learn not *p*, then it is hard to see how simultaneous belief and doubt about *p* can be reconciled. It would seem rather odd to simultaneously believe and doubt the Cubs won the World Series. How would I answer if asked if I think the Cubs won? Would I be surprised to learn they lost? I can say that I have faith they won even though I have my doubts. By faith here I mean I believe it is possible they won, and I am in favor of them winning. But the doubt means I would not be surprised to learn they lost.

---

[20]Howard-Snyder, "Propositional Faith," 545.
[21]Thomas Nagel, *The Last Word* (New York: Oxford University Press, 1997), 130.
[22]Howard-Snyder, "Propositional Faith," 546.

While it is possible to have doubts about something and still have faith that something is so, one cannot deny, disbelieve, or have unbelief and faith. I can have real doubts about whether a prescribed medication will cure my particular ailment, after the first two have failed, but still have faith that the medication will help. I should be clear: I can perform a particular act and yet deny, disbelieve, or have unbelief. I could take the medication, disbelieving it will help, but still take it in order to prove my doctor wrong. But in this situation, I cannot have faith that the medication will work while also disbelieving the medication will work.[23] For an act to be one of faith means that we do not deny, disbelieve, or have unbelief, but we are not required to believe, affirm, or be certain.

What about Aquinas's claim that faith as belief is meritorious because it is voluntary? Many philosophers hold that we have ample reason to reject doxastic volunteerism—the notion that people have direct voluntary control over their beliefs—for several reasons. First, if we had direct control over our beliefs, we could will to believe something while at the same time judge that belief to be false. That is, I could will myself to believe that God exists while at the same time judge that "God exists" is a false statement. But this seems like I am believing and disbelieving, affirming and denying the same proposition at the same time, and that does not work. Furthermore, as Swinburne observes, believing something is what happens to a person and not something a person does.[24] I believe that I am wearing my glasses, not by an act of the will but because I cannot help but believe this. It just seems that I am wearing my glasses and cannot directly change that belief voluntarily. Louis Pojman says it well, "Believing seems more like seeing than looking, falling than jumping, catching a cold than catching a ball, getting drunk than taking a drink, blushing than smiling, getting a headache than giving one to

---

[23]Howard-Snyder notes that while one can be in doubt about a proposition and thus not believe that it is so, there is still some cognitive stance that one will act on. He calls this "beliefless assuming." To act on a proposition that one does not believe or disbelieve requires minimally that one *assume that*. See Daniel Howard-Snyder, "Does Faith Entail Belief?" *Faith and Philosophy* 33, no. 2 (2016): 148.

[24]Swinburne, *Faith and Reason*, 25.

someone else."[25] If faith is a virtue, meritorious, as I think it is, then it has to at least in part be up to me. However, direct or immediate propositional beliefs are not under our immediate control.[26]

While it is highly dubious that we have voluntary control over our direct beliefs, it seems that we do have some control over our indirect beliefs. For example, I could tell my wife that I have properly repaired the kitchen sink by replacing the faucet. Given my track record of home repair and my usually causing more problems than solving, she would be justified in doubting, or even plainly disbelieving, my claim. And despite my petitions for her to believe me, she cannot, by an act of the will, directly believe I changed out the faucet properly—even if she genuinely wants to believe I finally did a home repair right. But, assuming I have properly fixed the faucet, she could do certain things to change her belief. She could repeatedly turn on and off the water, pull the spray hose out and replace it, inspect under the sink for leaks, maybe even ask a qualified individual to double check my work. It might take a few days or weeks, but eventually the evidence would lead her to believe it was installed properly, and so she would have indirectly, yet willfully, believed.[27] So even if someone does not believe that God exists, but wills to believe that God exists, she could seek out evidences and arguments and this process could lead to a belief happening to her.

This brief walk through belief as it relates to faith shows that faith does not necessarily entail belief, that belief is not an indispensable element of faith. One can express faith that *p* without believing *p*. God may not believe certain humans, collectively or individually, will love God but God certainly can have faith that this will be true.

---

[25]Louis P. Pojman, "Faith, Hope, and Doubt," in *Philosophy of Religion: An Anthology*, ed. Louis P. Pojman and Michael Rea, 7th ed. (Boston: Cengage Learning, 2014), 562.

[26]It could be added that if belief is understood to be meritorious, then unbelief should be understood as willful and therefore vicious and punishable. Daniel Speak takes issue with this given the Kantian dictum that "ought implies can." If we cannot willfully choose our beliefs, we cannot, ethically, be held accountable for failing to believe. For more on this see Daniel Speak, "Salvation Without Belief," *Religious Studies* 43, no. 2 (2007): 229-36.

[27]People can also will to indirectly believe by rational arguments in addition to empirical evidences as in my example above. For more information see Rico Vitz, "Doxastic Voluntarism," *The Internet Encyclopedia of Philosophy*, www.iep.utm.edu/ (accessed May 22, 2017).

FAITH AND TRUST

As shown above, it is quite common to see faith understood in terms of belief *that*. Others, however, affirm that faith is better understood as belief *in*, that is, as trust. Martin Luther, for example, conceived of faith primarily in terms of trust.[28] He argued that faith is trust, personal commitment or investment in the promises of God that unites the believer with Christ.[29] While Luther's approach was overshadowed by Enlightenment and modernist preoccupations with epistemic justification, there have always been those who have highlighted the trust element of faith.[30] In this section I introduce the concept of trust and its relationship to faith, but I will have more to say about the nature of trust in chapter five.

"Trust is at the centre of a whole web of concepts: reliability, predictability, expectation, cooperation, [and] goodwill," to name but a few.[31] While there is much to be said about trust and its place in the virtue of faith I will limit my comments to three aspects since these are the most pertinent for this study. First, trust is personal—we trust persons, not things. This is especially applicable to our trust in God and God's trust in us. Second, trust is risky. There is no perfectly safe way to trust anyone, even God. Third, trust is volitional. We decide, to a great extent at least, who to trust and what to entrust to them.

Trust is personal. Swinburne says, "To trust a man is to act on the assumption that he will do for you what he knows that you want or need, when the evidence gives some reason for supposing that he may not and

---

[28]I later make a distinction between trust and belief *in*.

[29]For more on Luther's conception of faith, see Alister E. McGrath, *Reformation Thought: An Introduction*, 3rd ed. (Malden, MA: Blackwell, 1999), 111-14.

[30]Even today trust is a neglected aspect of faith. For example, Terrence Penelhum has only one section (two and a half pages) devoted to trust but eight sections devoted to belief in his book *Reason and Religious Faith* (Boulder, CO: Westview, 1995)—an odd situation given that Penelhum states that "Faith entails trust, not merely belief" (72). One encyclopedia on the philosophy of religion has no entry on trust, or even faith, but does include one on belief. See Anthony C. Thiselton, ed., *A Concise Encyclopedia of Philosophy of Religion* (Grand Rapids: Baker Academic, 2002).

[31]Katherine Hawley, *Trust: A Very Short Introduction* (Oxford: Oxford University Press, 2012), 3. Interestingly, Hawley makes no mention of faith, God, or religion in her book. Perhaps her introduction is a bit too short.

where there will be bad consequences if the assumption is false."[32] A few pages later Swinburne speaks of trusting God in the same terms of trusting *a man*: "acting on the assumption that God will do for him what he wants or needs, when evidence gives some reason for supposing that he may not."[33] Swinburne should have simply said, "To trust a person" since his depiction applies to trusting a man, woman, or God.[34] What his trust statement does not include is trust in objects. This is a good omission since an object cannot "do for you what it knows that you want or need." Objects, be they ropes, chairs, phones, or computer programs can have our reliance, but they do not, properly speaking, have our trust. This is because trust, as I and others see it, is a personal relational quality.

"In the primary sense of 'trust'—which is the sense in which one trusts a person to perform an act—one cannot trust a machine, the weather, or a plant. None of these is a person or performs acts."[35] We trust persons; we rely on objects. More specifically, we depend on objects, while we place our trust in persons because of their character and/or entrust them with a task because of their specific skills.[36] We might speak of trusting our car to get us to work or trusting a watch to keep accurate time, but these are metaphors. We only metaphorically trust these objects because we do not feel let down or belied by our car when it gets a flat tire or betrayed by the watch when the battery dies.[37] Even though I can certainly feel frustrated when objects fail to work properly—I've even been known to offer a few choice words directed at them when they do—it

[32]Swinburne, *Faith and Reason*, 111.
[33]Swinburne, *Faith and Reason*, 115.
[34]Swinburne defines a theist as "a [person] who believes that there is a God. By 'God' he understands something like 'a person without a body' (i.e. a spirit) who is eternal, free, able to do anything, knows everything, is perfectly good." Richard Swinburne, *The Coherence of Theism*, rev. ed. (Oxford: Clarendon, 1993), 1.
[35]Ted Guleserian, "Can God Be Trusted?" *Philosophical Studies: An International Journal for Philosophy in the Analytic Tradition* 106, no. 3 (2001): 295.
[36]Katherine Hawley makes this helpful distinction between trusting persons and having "mere mechanical reliance" on objects. See Hawley, *Trust*, 4.
[37]Some may disagree with my claim that we only metaphorically trust objects. That is fine; this is not a make or break claim, and I believe the argument works whether one agrees on this point or not.

seems odd to think the car has failed me. The car has not let me down or cheated me (though a mechanic might have).

Trust is something that can be morally evaluated. We can consider the virtues and vices of good and bad trusting and ask what it means to trust well and be trustworthy. The trust I am interested in is between persons; that kind of trust has deep moral implications. We can have mere mechanical reliance on persons without necessarily trusting them. A pickpocket in a crowded concert may rely on the band to distract his targets, but a shoplifter can trust her accomplice to distract the salesperson.[38] Trust, as I see it, is reliance *plus*. It is relying on a person plus an attitude or openness to a person. It is this openness that makes us susceptible to feelings of either betrayal or gratitude.[39]

Borrowing from ethicists, we can distinguish between thin and thick trust.[40] Trust that is primarily reliance or merely mechanical is "thin trust." This trust has little to no moral implications and is rarely accompanied by feelings of gratitude or betrayal.[41] "Thick trust" has moral implications and can rightly produce feelings of appreciation or disappointment. Trust between couples, parents and children, or close friends is thick trust since it is the kind of trust we work hardest to foster and would bring the deepest feelings of hurt if betrayed.[42] Thick trust is most often reserved for those we know and who know us intimately. Thin trust is given to the nameless other. I trust the stranger walking next to me not

---

[38]Hawley, *Trust*, 4. Once, when driving home after a holiday break, I was following behind and going slightly slower than a car going faster than the speed limit, relying on that driver to get a speeding ticket instead of me. Unfortunately, the police officer pulled us both over. While I was disappointed, I did not feel betrayed by that unknown driver.

[39]For more on the difference between reliance and trust, see Richard Holton, "Deciding to Trust, Coming to Believe," *Australian Journal of Philosophy* 72 (1994): 63-76; specifically 63-68.

[40]Pekka Väyrynen, "Thick Ethical Concepts," in *The Stanford Encyclopedia of Philosophy*, ed. Edward N. Zalta, Winter 2016 ed., https://plato.stanford.edu/archives/win2016/entries/thick-ethical-concepts/. Paul Helm speaks of thick and thin belief in God. Thin belief for Helm is philosophical in nature, belief that God exists, while thick belief adds to that devotion, love, and obedience. For more, see Paul Helm, *Faith with Reason* (New York: Oxford University Press, 2000), chap. 6.

[41]I understand being grateful the airbag deployed and protected a loved one from great harm, but it seems misguided to be grateful to the airbag itself and wish to thank the airbag for saving the driver.

[42]Those who have had loved ones murdered or killed by drunk drivers will certainty feel hurt and anger, but if they did not know the killer, any feelings of betrayal or unfaithfulness might be minimal or absent altogether.

to rob me. I will feel great anger toward the stranger who robs me but something less than personal betrayal.[43] This may be because the greater the love between the persons, the thicker the trust. Ideally at least. The more we love another, the more we desire to trust and be trusted.[44] Thin trust is not bad by any means. It is a very good communal kind of trust that helps society run well. While there is not space to unpack all the implications of thick and thin trust, I think it is important to note that trust is not all or nothing. Trusting persons will not always include thick trust, but it seems to me the more intimate the relationship the more it should involve personal thick trust.[45]

While trust is personal, it need not include love. It is perfectly reasonable for an individual to trust someone whom he or she has found to be trustworthy but not be in a relationship defined as loving. I may trust a coworker, student, or any individual with whom I have entered into a mutual agreement, and each of these relationships could include personal trust and yet fail to meet the typical benchmarks of love.[46] I may not love them, and they not love me, and yet there is a relationship of personal trust between us.[47] At the same time, one can deeply love another individual and yet not trust the person. A woman, for example, may have a spouse with a gambling addiction. She may love her spouse deeply even though circumstances might prove that the spouse should not be trusted, at least in certain respects. While love is possible without trust, it will never be an intimate love without trust. I will say more about this in chapter three.

---

[43]I am not saying a person cannot feel a sense of betrayal, only that such feelings would either be rather unusual or would require special circumstances. For example, a Republican may learn that a fellow, but unknown, Republican voted for the Democrat candidate in the last presidential election and feel personally betrayed. It may be that the person does not have a logical justification for this feeling but may feel it nonetheless.

[44]Or in some cases respect. I will say more about this in chap. 5.

[45]Notice even that thicker trust is spoken of as "trust of" or "trust in," while thinner trust as "trust that." And yes, I am aware that discussions of thin and thick trust bring to mind images of New York and Chicago-style pizza.

[46]For a very nice summary of mutual loving relationships and their characteristics, see Vincent Brümmer, *Atonement, Christology and the Trinity: Making Sense of Christian Doctrine* (Burlington, VT: Ashgate, 2005), 28-31.

[47]I understand that as Christians we are called to love (agape) all persons, especially fellow Christians. Here I am speaking of being in a relationship constituted by love, whether the love is philia, storge, or eros.

Trust and risk. Risk is the essence of trust. While there is risk without trust, there is no trust without risk. Adriaan Peperzak rightly says, "there is always certain risk that cannot be eliminated by any calculation or deduction."[48] Peperzak further argues that no matter how well we might know a person, trust is never 100 percent foolproof since "this would exclude the trustee's freedom and such an exclusion is incompatible with the respect without which no trust can be sincere. . . . Risk therefore is inherent in all trust."[49] The willingness to trust another with what is valuable to us is the attitudinal or openness aspect of trust.[50] Sometimes we trust another contingently, that is, *if the occasion arises* I trust that my friend will help me. Trust moves from attitude to action when I entrust another with what is of value to me. This attitude and disposition is risky because in "choosing to be vulnerable by putting a matter into another's care and thus subjecting it to another's neglect, incompetence, or ill will" there is no way to guarantee the outcome one desires.[51]

Trust comes with the necessary fact that those we trust may not be competent in their skills or mature in character.[52] This is true whether we trust friends, family, or God. I understand it sounds heretical to say that trusting God is inherently risky, but by placing trust in God we risk that God may not do what we want or need God to do. God may not exist. God may be constrained by metaphysics,[53] by God's own loving

---

[48]Adriaan P. Peperzak, *Trust: Who or What Might Support Us?* (New York: Fordham University Press, 2013), 33.

[49]Peperzak, *Trust*, 18-19.

[50]Jeffrey Godfrey speaks of "openness trusting," a term I rather like. While Godfrey intends the idea to say much more than this, "Openness trust is an orientation or disposition . . . healthy intentionality." Jeffrey Godfrey, *Trust of People, Words, and God: A Route for Philosophy of Religion* (Notre Dame, IN: University of Notre Dame Press, 2012), 49-50.

[51]Godfrey, *Trust of People, Words, and God*, 32.

[52]There is also an element of self-trust in that we are trusting our ability to rightly assess the trustworthiness of another.

[53]Process theologians argue that God can only persuade but never control, and so "God is responsible for evil but not indictable for it." John B. Cobb and David Ray Griffin, *Process Theology: An Introductory Exposition* (Philadelphia: Westminster, 1976), 69. Tom Oord as well argues that because God has no physical body, God cannot unilaterally act on the world: "God cannot prevent evil with a localized divine body because God is an omnipresent spirit." Thomas Jay Oord, *The Uncontrolling Love of God: An Open and Relational Account of Providence* (Downers Grove, IL: InterVarsity Press, 2015), 179.

nature,[54] or unable to do what we want or need because God does not have the power to act in this physical world.[55] On the other hand, God may be so absolutely and totally free that God chooses not to do what God knows you want and need.[56]

It is common and acceptable to minimize risk when trusting another. Parents should check references before hiring a nanny to care for a child. This does not eliminate the risk, but it can minimize unnecessary risk. However, the more trust I exercise the less monitoring I will do.[57] Risk management with regard to trusting God may mean I am one of "little faith." But then again, if God is who I have faith God is, then there is no safer place to be. "To entertain whether to trust God is paradoxically to entertain both absolutely no risk and supreme risk, is to be absolutely invulnerable and absolutely vulnerable."[58]

Belief is understood to be strong when the belief is held with a greater sense of certainty due to convincing evidence, arguments, or warrant. Strong trust, on the other hand, is not about certitude (though one may have those thoughts) but a "risk-readiness."[59] The stronger the trust the more "I am disposed to rely with more risk" and "the more habitually this

---

[54]Oord argues that because God is essentially love, God is necessarily uncontrolling: "Divine love limits divine power. God cannot deny God's own nature, which necessarily expresses self-giving, others-empowering love." Oord, *The Uncontrolling Love of God*, 169.

[55]Cobb's, Griffin's, and Oord's theologies suggest that trusting God, at least for a physical need, such that it requires God to act unilaterally or coercively upon the world would be misplaced trust.

[56]Some may have placed their trust in God to save them from hell, but this may be misguided trust if God freely decides who to elect to heaven and who to send to hell.

[57]Lara Buchak has an eye toward risk management when she says "a person has faith that X, expressed by A, if and only if that person performs act A, and performing A constitutes taking a risk on X; and the person prefers to {commit to A before he examines additional evidence} rather than {to postpone his decision about A until he examine additional evidence}." It seems then, for Buchak, I could check references before hiring the nanny, but if I am to actually trust or have faith in the nanny, I would not install "nanny cams" throughout the house. See Lara Buchak, "Can It Be Rational to Have Faith?" in *Philosophy of Religion: An Anthology*, ed. Louis P. Pojman and Michael Rea, 7th ed. (Boston: Cengage Learning, 2014), 531.

[58]Godfrey, *Trust of People, Words, and God*, 55.

[59]I should note that some see risk attached to belief more so than trust. Paul Helm writes, "The riskiness of faith, where it is risky, attaches not to trust per se, but to the degree of belief. The different degrees of trust correspond to the different degrees of belief in the case of those who exercise faith. Some degree of trust is compatible with some degree of doubt, and if one trusts at the same time as one entertains doubts one is knowingly taking a risk." Paul Helm, *Faith with Reason* (New York: Oxford University Press, 2000), 156.

openness characterizes me."[60] Strong trust is being vulnerably open to the care of another and willing to risk much. Strong trust is not always active, and thus I may not know how strong my trust is until it is put to the test.

Trust and volition. Risk, reliance, and resolve are key features of trust; the latter of the three speaks to our willfulness. "It is unusual for someone to speak of relying upon someone else unless he has come to a definite *decision* to rely on him; and clearly, there is no need for such a decision if no risks are believed to be involved."[61] Trust, it seems, at some point, is volitional. Riskiness often brings with it mindfulness. When we risk we often assess whether the risk is worth it and then decide to trust or not trust.[62]

It is quite likely that not every circumstance of trust is immediately willful. Katherine Hawley observes that we can come to realize that we have been trusting one person or distrusting another.[63] Does this mean trust, like propositional belief, is involuntary? I don't think so. While I cannot, by an act of the will alone, simply *believe* that a person is trustworthy I can, nonetheless, act *as if* she is trustworthy. I can, in spite of my beliefs, and maybe even against my better judgments, entrust someone with my care or the safety of something I care about. I can put my well-being in the care of another even when that person is unreliable.[64] Maybe it is better to say that I can freely rely on someone even if I do not yet believe the person to be trustworthy. Thicker trust at times may be a curious blend of deciding to rely on another so that I might eventually come to trust them more habitually than willfully. Our initial

---

[60]Godfrey, *Trust of People, Words, and God*, 196. While thick trust is deeply relational, strong trust is about readiness to act. Thick trust then will always be a strong trust, but strong trust need not be thick.

[61]H. J. N. Horsburgh, "The Ethics of Trust," *The Philosophical Quarterly* 10, no. 41 (1960): 344. Emphasis added.

[62]Benjamin McMyler, however, holds that "trust and belief are equally non-voluntary" (163). But even if trust, unlike belief, is noncognitive, trust is nonetheless an attitude of the type that "ensures that trust cannot be voluntary" (175). See Benjamin McMyler, "Deciding to Trust," in *The Philosophy of Trust*, ed. Paul Faulkner and Thomas Simpson (Oxford: Oxford University Press, 2017), 161-76.

[63]"This can be very distressing: the realization that you distrust your partner or close friend may be a real shock, one that makes you reevaluate your evidence in retrospect. Conversely, discovering that you trust a new friend or colleague can be a pleasant surprise, even if you can't say exactly why you feel this trust." Hawley, *Trust*, 9.

[64]Godfrey, *Trust of People, Words, and God*, 32.

trust in God was most likely a willful act of reliance that has, over time, developed (hopefully) into trust, or more correctly, faith.

If trust and distrust can be evaluated ethically, then they have a volitional character. Can we say to a husband that he should trust his spouse or to a mother she should trust her children? It seems to me we can. Is it unethical for a husband to not trust his wife any time he cannot keep tabs on her? It seems to me it is.[65] And so, if trusting has a moral dimension to it then it also has a volitional aspect since we can only be responsible for what we have some control over.[66] The willful aspect of trust allows us to affirm that, in the right situations, we should trust someone who is trustworthy or that we should not trust someone who is duplicitous. Even when a person is trustworthy we can talk about the ethics of right and wrong trusting since it would be inappropriate, if not outright immoral, to burden a coworker or casual friend with our deep dark secrets simply because she is trustworthy. The trustor trusts, in part, by an act of the will—the trustee, however, may not be so fortunate.

The volitional aspects of trust mean that in the right situations and with the right people trust is obligatory. We have a moral obligation to trust those who are trustworthy when the conditions are right or the situation calls for it. The ethics of trust then include more than being trustworthy; they include giving trust in the right ways. Since *pisteuō* can as easily be translated as "to trust" as it can "to believe" the New Testament therefore contains calls (commands) to trust.[67] Jesus says, "Do not fear, only trust" (Mk 5:36 translation mine) as well as "trust in God, trust also in me" (Jn 14:1 translation mine).[68] In short, if faith is meritorious but belief is involuntary, then it seems that trust needs to be at least minimally volitional.[69]

---

[65]At least prima facie it is. Assuming there are no good reasons to doubt the other's faithfulness, it seems a husband or wife should trust one's spouse.

[66]I am here assuming that Kant's dictum "ought implies can" is basically correct.

[67]Paul R. McReynolds, *Word Study Greek-English New Testament* (Carol Stream, IL: Tyndale House, 1999). McReynolds translates every use of *pisteuō* as "trust" in this text.

[68]Some Hebrew Bible examples include Ps 9:10; 37:5; Prov 3:5; Jer 17:7-8.

[69]Not all hold that we can obey when instructed to trust. Baier, leaning on Hume, suggests that it is not trust that needs explanation since we naturally and reflexively trust as infants but "ceasings to trust, the transfers of trust, the restriction or enlargements in the fields of what is trusted." See Annette Baier, "Trust and Antitrust," *Ethics* 96, no. 2 (1986): 244-47.

Before leaving this discussion of trust and the will I should make a quick comment about the difference between trusting and obeying. God does not simply call us to obey. God calls us to trust. Obedience can be demanded while trust must be invited. The penalties for failing to obey can bring condemnation and retribution, but failure to trust, even though it is willful and moral, cannot be rationally punished, even if immoral. To punish a lack of trust would only result in less trust—which means a damaged relationship. Trust and obedience are not mutually exclusive, for out of trust I may obey. By trusting I may come to recognize God's authority, listen to God's voice where it may be found, and obey God's teachings. Even though both trust and obedience are willful events, trust brings with it certain attitudes unnecessary for obedience. Trust brings with it a kind of positive cognitive stance. When I trust, I plan or hope that the good I have entrusted to another will be cared for. I plan or hope that the situation will bring happy results. This is not necessary for obedience. I can obey while expecting the situation to end poorly. I can obey, following every command, secretly desiring that my perfect obedience will show just how feeble that authority truly is. So, while I can obey and hope the situation goes very badly, the same is not true for trust. Obedience is easier when we trust those who demand, and may even be due our obedience, but trust is not necessary. It is better for soldiers to trust their commanders—but not required. It is good to obey God; it is better to trust God.

Finally, just as one can obey and not trust, one can trust and not obey. Parents need to trust their children but are not required to obey them. It seems quite healthy for spouses to be working toward unreserved trust in one another, but unreserved obedience seems oddly suited for a couple to be working toward. While I believe our relationship to God should include obedience born out of trust, other relationships can rely on trust alone. As I will show, our relationship with God is one of mutual trust, but not mutual obedience.

Faith in God may be much more than trust in God, but it seems to me that for faith to be healthy and growing, trust is a much-needed element. The contrary to faith here is not doubt but distrust, not a failing to believe what is true about God but a failing to trust in the love, will, and wisdom of God.

FAITH AND HOPE

I cannot envision any conception of faith that would be absent of hope. If we believe God exists then we surely also hope our beliefs are true. We hope that God's love, power, and wisdom will one day make right all the evils and atrocities. If we trust God to save us through the work of Christ, then we certainly have hope to one day enjoy the beatific vision (Rev 22:4). Hope, like trust, looks to God to do what is good, loving, just, and ultimately, in the best interests of the hoper. For some, more than belief or trust, hope is the "defining characteristic of those who seek God and experience his Grace."[70] Hope has been defined as "a uniquely human emotion that energizes us to engage in projects we believe will enhance our future well-being, even though they are of no immediate value to us."[71] The reader should, at this point, anticipate that I have doubts about hope being "uniquely human." In this section I briefly explore the nature of hope; however, space requires I set aside questions less important to this study.[72] In chapter six, I will discuss hope further and illustrate how it fittingly applies to God.

To hope is to wait with a sense of positive anticipation. Hope, at its most basic, involves a desire for some state of affairs that is possible, but not inevitable. A person can hope that p if that person desires that p and believes that p is not logically impossible but also that p is not necessary. Before discussing that hope entails what is possible, let's look at the desire aspect.

---

[70]Allen C. Myers, ed., *The Eerdmans Bible Dictionary* (Grand Rapids: Eerdmans, 1987), 500.

[71]Anthony Reading, *Hope and Despair: How Perceptions of the Future Shape Human Behavior* (Baltimore, MD: Johns Hopkins University Press, 2004), 3. Reading goes on to explain that hope is not simply belief about the future but also taking an active role in bringing the hoped-for future into being.

[72]I have in mind here issues regarding whether hope is reasonable, whether one has an excess of hope, whether animals hope, and, in Kantian terms, "for what may I hope?" I will also assume that hope is a good trait even though some ancient accounts of hope had a negative reputation. See Claudia Bloeser and Titus Stahl, "Hope," in *The Stanford Encyclopedia of Philosophy*, ed. Edward N. Zalta, Spring 2017 ed., https://plato.stanford.edu/archives/spr2017/entries/hope/.

I know of no philosopher or theologian who suggests we can hope
for something without desiring that something. Could someone reasonably say that she hopes the Anaheim Ducks win the Stanley Cup but
at the same time offer that she does not care if they win? That she is
indifferent to their winning? This makes no sense. Can I hope to one
day enter into God's glory and at the same moment be indifferent to
entering into that glory? It hardly seems possible. Hope necessarily
entails desiring (or wanting) some condition to obtain.[73] The desire
found in hope, theological hope anyway, cannot be mild or halfhearted.
When thinking about options for dinner if I say to myself, "I kinda feel
like Thai food," this would mean I have a faint desire for pad Thai. I
want it, yes, but this wanting seems something shy of hope. Even if we
think of hoping for Thai food in terms of desire that it minimally meets
what might qualify as hope, I do not think this would quite apply to
theological hope.

Desiring the beatific vision is not hope if the desire is only slightly
more than not caring. If someone were to say that they are on the fence
about God but, if push came to shove, they probably hope there is a God
more than they hope there is not, this does not qualify as genuine hope.
Here I agree with William Sessions when he says to hope is to "greatly
desire" the apparent good.[74] Christian hope is a virtue because it longs
for, seeks, and intensely desires, not only what God has promised but
what God desires as well.

Philosophers like Aquinas,[75] Descartes,[76] and Hume[77] speak of hope
as both a desire and a passion. But if hope is a virtue, "a stable, positive

[73]One bit of qualification, it seems to me that I can desire and at the same time not desire something. For example, I can desire and in the same moment not desire pie. I can have conflicting
desires that are attached to the pie in that I want the pleasure of eating the slice but also desire
not to feel sickeningly full. This reveals a difference between desire and hope. I can desire and not
desire something at the same moment, but I cannot hope for some event and in the same moment
hope against that event. I cannot hope and at the same moment not hope to have a slice of pie.
[74]Sessions, The Concept of Faith, 114.
[75]Summa Theologica, 2-2.17.1.
[76]Rene Descartes, Passions of the Soul, trans. Stephen Voss (Indianapolis: Hackett, 1989), 53, 110-11.
[77]David Hume, A Treatise of Human Nature, ed. David Fate Norton and Mary J. Norton (Oxford:
Oxford University Press, 2007), 283.

inclination of the will that prompts and facilitates good actions, binds humans ever more closely to their last end, and makes their self-realization possible," then it seems hope should be understood as something other than a passion.[78] It seems we can be praised or reprimanded for our hopes and desires but not our passions.[79]

Louis Pojman develops the argument that God minimally accepts hope as faith since belief is involuntary and God can only rightly judge us by what we can do.[80] In making his case, Pojman says, "hoping—unlike believing—is typically under our direct control."[81] Furthermore, "hoping—like wanting—is evaluative in a way that believing is not."[82] We cannot rightly fault someone for believing ocean levels will rise in the next year, but we can fault someone for hoping that such an event occurs. And if we can fault someone for what they hope, we can fault them for what they fail to hope. I *should* hope that ocean levels decrease even if I cannot make myself believe they will. Some Christians experience doubts about Jesus' bodily resurrection. These Christians may deeply desire to believe it happened as the biblical texts purport but may lack belief. For Pojman and others, this lack of belief should not be met with condemnation if the Christian is a hoper even when not a believer. If the message of the resurrection inspires hope and leads one to decide to live according to that hope, then it should be counted to them as faith. The soundness of this argument will have to be decided by the reader.[83] My point is that there is very good reason to hold that hope is willful since it is not purely an emotion but is subject to moral scrutiny.

---

[78]Paul O'Callaghan, *Christ Our Hope: An Introduction to Eschatology* (Washington, DC: Catholic University of America Press, 2011), 5.

[79]For two philosophers who believe that hope is not a passion, see J. P. Day, "Hope," *American Philosophical Quarterly* 6, no. 2 (1969); and Anthony Kenny, *Action, Emotion, and Will* (London: Routledge & Kegan Paul, 1963).

[80]I am unsure whether Pojman categorizes hope as an emotion or passion, but I am sure that he believes hope is volitional.

[81]Pojman, "Faith, Hope, and Doubt," 565.

[82]Pojman, "Faith, Hope, and Doubt," 566.

[83]For more on the subject, see Speak, "Salvation Without Belief"; and Louis P. Pojman, "Faith Without Belief?" *Faith and Philosophy* 3, no 2 (1986): 157-76.

While hope entails desire, desire does not necessarily entail hope. I can only hope for the possible while I can desire the impossible. That is, I can wish for the impossible but hope is specious where there is logical impossibility.[84]

Aquinas argued that hope, which sits between impossibility and necessity, does not exist within the blessed or the dammed. He writes, "When happiness is no longer future, but present, it is incompatible with the virtue of hope."[85] We no longer hope for what we have obtained and know we have obtained, which is the place of the blessed. More interesting however, is his take on the damned. For hell to be truly hellish, Aquinas argues, those in hell must know that they will never leave even though they desire to be released.[86] Dante must have had this in mind when, in his *Divine Comedy*, there is written above the gate to Hell, "All hope abandon, ye who enter here." Both the blessed and the damned know their fates and know those fates will not change.[87]

Hope, as I see it, is the forward facing, anticipatory feature of faith. Trust operates in the present as we, day by day and moment by moment, entrust our lives to God's supremacy and goodness.[88] Hope looks to and acts for a future good.

We may trust with the thinnest sense of hope. I may act so as to show the drug addict that I trust her all in the hope that she will respond positively. The hope may be razor thin, that is, the phenomenon of hope feels very uncertain, but it is there. Hope in this way gives endurance to trust. As long as I have hope that my trust will not be in vain, even if I cannot

---

[84]J. P. Day says this means that "*p* is possible" is contrary to "*p* is true," "*p* is false," "*p* is certain," and "not-*p* is certain." Day discusses this in terms of "*p* is probable," but notes that others speak in terms of "*p* is possible." See Day, "Hope," 95.

[85]*Summa Theologica*, 2-2.18.2.

[86]*Summa Theologica*, 2-2.18.3.

[87]I should make it clear that when I suggest that hope does not apply to the impossible I mean the logically impossible not the physically impossible. For all we have known and experienced, it is physically impossible for the dead to rise to life again. But this is a reasonable hope if there is a God. It is not reasonable to hope that the number four be greater than five. This is a logical impossibility that, by my lights, even God cannot effect.

[88]Robert McAfee Brown seems to wrap both belief and hope into trust when he says, "Trust in what God has already done in the past makes it possible to trust in what he will do in the future." See Brown, *Is Faith Obsolete?* (Philadelphia: Westminster, 1974), 64.

believe this, my trust may remain. Without hope, however, there is no will to trust.

Hope as an element of faith relieves the tension, as Paul Tillich put it, "between the cognitive function of man's personal life, on the one hand, and emotion and will, on the other."[89] Hope keeps faith from being reduced to either belief or trust, and it gives a sense of courage and confidence that each may lack.[90] I not only employ hope in trust-filled actions and attitudes but also in my strained or tentative beliefs. Hope produces courage, giving one the strength to trust and act despite fears or doubts.

FAITH AND LOVE

Devotion can take many forms. It can be robust, mindful, and deeply affective in the form of love for family or friends. It can be enthusiastic and public or quiet and private. Our devotion can feel volitional and involve committing one's self and energies to a person, idea, or institution.[91] Devotion can also have noncognitive, even mystical qualities that at times render devotion hard to put into words. Here I have in mind someone who struggles to believe God exists and may even lack any real hope that God exists yet feels strangely attracted to God—or at least the idea of God. The person may wish to let go but feels oneself to be grasped by the transcendent.[92] Devotion, as I am speaking of it, can be articulated by ideas and concepts such as allegiance, loyalty, and commitment. At its most mature, devotion as a feature of faith is expressed and demonstrated in love for God.

I can believe that all sorts of things are true with regard to my enemies. I can choose to trust those I despise, and I can put my hope in those I hate. However, I can have no animosity toward God if I have faith in God. "Faith involves the kind of connotation that may fairly be called '*love*': a

---

[89]Paul Tillich, *Dynamics of Faith* (New York: Harper & Row, 1957), 7.
[90]Perhaps *courage* would be a better word choice since *confidence* literally means to "have faith," but then again, hope might entail "faith in faith."
[91]An example of this might be Joshua 24:15.
[92]Lament psalms often express such feelings. For example, see Psalms 10 and 13.

firm, deep and lasting desire for personal relationship with the other person."[93] Anthony Kenny writes that faith in God is

> more than mere intellectual commitment to the truth of certain propositions as revealed by God. It involves a resolution to act upon these propositions: a commitment of oneself to the revealed purposes of God, trust in His enabling one to enact them in one's life. It can be described not only as belief in God, but also as love of God: in its fullest manifestation, as the love of God above all things.[94]

Aquinas proposes that belief and hope can exist without love, but they will be unformed and less than virtuous without love.[95] This may be true if we still count "dead faith" as faith nonetheless. As Juan Alfaro says, "Faith reaches its fullness when it is love of God," and if "charity is lacking, faith itself is mortally wounded."[96] In this section I will briefly discuss love (sometimes expressed as commitment, loyalty, or devotion) of God as integral to faith. In chapter three, I will say more about how love necessitates trust and hope and seeks to believe.

It may be too demanding to suggest that love be included in every expression of faith. Can't we be faithful to God and not (yet) love God? Terrence Penelhum says, "Love is commanded from the faithful," implying that faith can be genuine, though inchoate, and still not love.[97] Maybe I should simply speak of faith including some affective attitude. This may be the case for some, that they have trust but not yet love. For some, trust in God may be like an arranged marriage in which they pledge to be faithful, but only hope to one day love. By my lights, this would be a case of *little* faith, but not *no* faith. Of course, lacking trust and losing hope are examples of weak and fractured faith, but can we say someone is of great faith if he believes, trusts,

[93]Sessions, *The Concept of Faith*, 33.

[94]Anthony Kenny, *What Is Faith?* (Oxford: Oxford University Press, 1992), 4.

[95]Aquinas, *Summa Theologica*, 1-2.65.4.

[96]Juan Alfaro, "The Dual Aspect of Faith: Entrusting Oneself to God and Acceptance of the Christian Message," in *Man as Man and Believer*, ed. Edward Schillebeeckx and Boniface Willems, Concilium 21 (New York: Paulist Press, 1967), 58, quoted in Avery Dulles, *The Assurance of Things Hoped For: A Theology of Christian Faith* (New York: Oxford University Press, 1994), 250.

[97]Penelhum, *Reason and Religious Faith*, 71.

and hopes but does not *love* God with all his heart, soul, mind, and strength (Mk 12:30)?

If the object of faith is some good, such as to live the life eternal in paradise, then perhaps loving God is an addition added on to faith. But if God is the object and telos of faith then faith without love is at best contractual but not covenantal. Augustine says, "There is no love without hope, no hope without love, and neither hope nor love without faith."[98] In 1 Corinthians 13 Paul unequivocally joins love and hope with trust. "And if I have prophetic powers, and understand all mysteries and all knowledge [read as "believe all truths about God"], and if I have all faith [read as "trust in God"], so as to remove mountains, but do not have love, I am nothing" (1 Cor 13:2). A few verses later we again see that the features of faith—belief, trust, and hope—must be wedded with love since love "bears all things, believes all things, hopes all things, endures all things" (1 Cor 13:7).

In "Reflections on Faith, Hope, and Love," H. Richard Niebuhr argues that "the theological virtues cannot be reduced to one of the three, as often seems to be suggested." Niebuhr continues:

> But without love and faith hope is empty, or does not exist at all. Each of the virtues has its distinctive character, but none of them can be in action without the others. . . . In the one instance faith is perfected by love, in the other case love is perfected by faith. . . . Hope is not only the expectation of faith and love; it is the exercise of faith and love in the temporal dimension. . . . The more trusting the hope or the more hopeful the trust, the more it is possible now to respond to God and companions with anticipations of love and faith shall be.[99]

These three virtues seem analogous to the vital organs. We can distinguish the brain from heart, from the lungs, but without any one of these no life can be sustained. Trust, belief, hope, and love are weak, small, and frail on their own, but enhanced and bolstered by each other.

---

[98]Augustine, *The Enchiridion on Faith, Hope and Love*, ed. Henry Paolucci and J. J. Shaw (Chicago: Henry Regnery, 1961/1996), ix.

[99]H. Richard Niebuhr, "Reflections on Faith, Hope, and Love," *The Journal of Religious Ethics* 2, no. 1 (1974): 154-55.

Perhaps commitment, instead of love, is a better way of talking about devotion. Too often we cannot shake our affective and passive notions of love. We know we are *in* love when we feel affection and are overcome by certain emotions. When I think of my wife or daughter, I *feel* something. Yet love is not merely emotive or passive but at times willful. The spouse who forgives after sexual unfaithfulness may have no positive feelings about the other. When trust is broken and hope trampled by despair, commitment may remain. Out of love the spouse is committed to the other. In spite of feelings of betrayal, they make plans to repair the relationship. This commitment is love. This commitment is faith. A drug-addicted child has once again stolen from his parents. The parents' feelings of love are choked out by thoughts of anger and helplessness. They cannot trust this child, and multiple rehab stints leave them feeling hopeless. Their resolve to remain committed to do whatever they can to help the child is the resolve to love. Commitment is a bare-bones approach to relationship and thus the bare bones of faith. Commitment to God—even when belief, trust, hope, and feelings of love are sinking under the weight of doubt and despair—can still be called faith.

Job is an example of one who remained in faith, committed to God (or perhaps merely grasped by God), in spite of a loss of belief, trust, and hope. Job repeatedly laments and cries out, "My days are swifter than a weaver's shuttle, and come to their end without hope" (Job 7:6). Job knows there is still hope for the tree when cut down since it can sprout again, but he has lost hope because mortals simply die and humans expire (Job 14:7-10). Hope and trust are gone when Job understands himself as God's foe:

> He breaks me down on every side, and I am gone,
>   he has uprooted my hope like a tree.
> He has kindled his wrath against me,
>   and counts me as his adversary. (Job 19:10-11)[100]

---

[100]It is interesting that Job says that a cut down tree can sprout again but God has uprooted him—certainly not an image of hope.

Here Job expresses that he cannot trust God,

> I am terrified at his presence;
>> when I consider, I am in dread of him.
> God has made my heart faint;
>> the Almighty has terrified me;
> If only I could vanish in darkness,
>> and thick darkness would cover my face! (Job 23:15-17)

But, strange as it sounds, through it all Job is committed to God. Angry with God, frustrated and wronged by God, but still devoted. Job blames God, but never curses God.[101]

Perhaps I have overstated my case. Maybe in the midst of unjust suffering Job bounced between moments punctuated by hope and at other times trust. But it seems to me this narrative calls on us to think about just what keeps Job in the story. What is it that keeps Job in conversation with his interlocutors and seeking an answer from God? One thing of which I am convinced is that it was not Job's unflinching and certain belief. I do not see Job's faith as J. Kellenberger sees it: "Even when Job was made to suffer, and could not understand God's way, he did not doubt His goodness and was certain that the God he believed in had not forsaken him. What we should note here is that if he had doubted, it would have been a failure of his faith. The commitment of Job's faith requires certainty."[102] Yes, Job was committed, but to God, not to the certainty of his own faith!

Paul Tillich famously said that "faith is the state of being ultimately concerned. . . . It is the state of being grasped by the holy through a special medium."[103] For Tillich "ultimate concern" refers both to the act of faith and the object of faith.[104] Much of what Tillich says about ultimate concern is deeply dependent on his understanding of existentialism and

---

[101]Thank you Kelly Dagley for helping me formulate these thoughts.
[102]J. Kellenberger, "Three Models of Faith," *International Journal for Philosophy of Religion* 12, no. 4 (1981): 219.
[103]Tillich, *Dynamics of Faith*, 1 and 58.
[104]Tillich, *Dynamics of Faith*, 10; "*fides qua creditor* (the faith through which one believes) and the *fides quae creditor* (the faith which is believed)."

our struggle for authenticity. I am using this phrase in a much simpler way.[105] Authentic faith is faith that is concerned about what is truly ultimate—our highest concern for the Ultimate. Idolatry is placing one's trust and hope in that which is not ultimate. On the subjective side of this, we all have something that grasps us—something we are most concerned about and that has our devotion. That which has our ultimate concern is what we treat as holy and worthy of our concern. Another way to talk about Job is to suggest that in the heaviness of his suffering and the brittleness of his hope and trust, Job still held God as his ultimate concern.

Perhaps in those weakest and thinnest moments of faith, it is not our faith that keeps us in the game but God's. Perhaps those moments we feel lost and alone but somehow taken by the life and death of Christ, it is actually God's faith vicariously substituting for our own. "God can have faith in us just as we can have faith in God. It's God's faith in us that justifies. This divine faithfulness triggers trust within us. God's faith grasps us in our faith."[106] Perhaps minimally to have faith is to allow one's self to be grasped by the faith of God. But I will say more on this in the following chapters.

FAITH IS RELATIONAL

If what I have said is true and faith, at its best or most mature, includes the features belief, trust, hope, and loving devotion, then faith looks a lot like personal relationships. When I believe true things about another person, trust them with some good, have hope in them for those goods, and am lovingly devoted to them, it seems that I have faith in them. I cannot see faith being anything other than, ideally, a relationship. Faith at its fullest is intellectual and contemplative, emotional and willful, dependent and free. Faith at its best is complete *and* still growing. These are all features of an intimate relationship. I believe true things about my

---

[105]Tillich has much more to say about faith as ultimate concern that does not apply to this discussion. For more on "ultimate concern," see his *Dynamics of Faith*, and Paul Tillich, *Systematic Theology*, 3 vols. (Chicago: University of Chicago Press, 1951–1963), discussed in all three volumes.
[106]Ted Peters, *Sin Boldly!: Justifying Faith for Fragile and Broken Souls* (Minneapolis: Augsburg, 2015), 301.

friend; I trust him with my secrets, and I hope our friendship will continue to develop—all while feeling and acting in love toward him. This can and should be said about our wives and husbands, daughters and sons, parents and siblings. It simply strikes me as odd to say one is to have belief, trust, hope, and love for God, but that faith is something other than a relationship.

James Fowler writes, "Faith is a *verb*; it is an active mode of being and committing, a way of moving into and giving shape to our experiences of life." Fowler adds, "Faith is always *relational*; there is always *another* in faith. 'I trust *in* and am loyal to . . .'"[107] Saying that faith is always relational means that faith is a way of relating, a deep and intimate kind of relating. Faith is not a means to relationship but a descriptor of particular relationships. Intimate relationships require faith. Faith is not the object of desire but the means to it. When we long for more faith, we do not simply desire confidence or greater assurance; we desire God. When we divorce faith from relationship with God in Christ, we risk *pistalotry*, the worship of faith itself. It is this point that Karl Barth so aptly makes when he states, "it was never a desirable tendency to exalt faith into an ontic and central concept, displacing the real object of theology, as though faith were the theme and the true event of salvation."[108]

Faith is personal and thus relational. In this overview of faith, I have emphasized a nonreductionist approach to faith, seeking to avoid the error of understanding it through only one lens or by a single feature. It may seem that I am doing just what I argued against by understanding faith as a kind of relationality. But this is to misunderstand the nature of relationship, for it too cannot be reduced to any single concept or notion. Relationship is dynamic by its very nature.

Relationships can be understood in terms of family, marriage, or friendship, as between coworkers or neighbors. What each of these has

---

[107] James Fowler, *Stages of Faith: The Psychology of Human Development and the Quest for Meaning*, rev. ed. (New York: HarperOne, 1995), 16.

[108] Karl Barth, *Evangelical Theology: An Introduction*, trans. Grover Foley (Grand Rapids: Eerdmans, 1963), 99.

in common is a kind of interconnectedness, a "coming together, a common thread existing or developing between people, with members being tied to one another in some manner that each constrains the other. We speak of being involved, of being socially bound to one another, of being *in* a relationship."[109] Certainly relationships can be prefaced with terms like "personal" or "working" to denote the level of intimacy between the subjects, but what is common is an interconnection, though one among differences. It is in fact differences that require relationships to involve faith.

Faith becomes theological when the relationship is with God. F. Gerrit Immink writes, "Faith is a relationship between subjects, a communal bond between God and humans. A life of faith is not just a matter of taking certain beliefs about God and his salvation to be true; it is also a matter of our trust in God and God's trustworthiness. These notions are given with the structure of faith as a relationship between two subjects."[110] Relationship may be the only category in which elements of belief, trust, hope, and devotion (and perhaps others unexamined here) can all be used and understood in personal terms. Not to make too fine a point of it, "To have faith in God is to be in right relationship with God. It is to love and trust who God is. Likewise, for God to be in relationship with us means that God loves us and trusts us to be a faithful partner in the divine mission for the world."[111]

CONCLUSION

Martin Luther affirms the mosaic of faith when he says, "A quick and living faith is not only the common belief of the articles of our faith, but it is also a true trust and confidence of the mercy of God through our

[109]L. Edna Rogers, "The Meaning of Relationship in Relational Communication," in *The Meaning of "Relationship" in Interpersonal Communication*, ed. Richard L. Conville and Lilian Edna Rogers (Westport, CT: Praeger, 1998), 70.

[110]F. Gerrit Immink, *Faith: A Practical Theological Reconstruction*, Studies in Practical Theology (Grand Rapids: Eerdmans, 2005), 26-27.

[111]Wm. Curtis Holtzen, "Faith in Relations," in *Relational Theology: A Contemporary Introduction*, ed. Brint Montgomery, Thomas J. Oord, and Karen Winslow (Eugene, OR: Wipf and Stock, 2012), 36.

Lord Jesus Christ, and a steadfast hope of good things to be received at God's hands."[112] Faith is an umbrella concept. When I think of faith in Christ I think of a life of devotion seeking to grow in love, trust, hope, and belief. It is a single precious gem with many facets and, at its best, when held up to the light, will reflect love, trust, hope, and belief. Robert Audi says, "Faith alone, particularly propositional faith, does not exhaust religious commitment." But what if faith is best understood as religious commitment? What if we said, "A true religious commitment is both wide and deep. It is a commitment of the heart and not just the head, of a lifetime and not just its Sabbaths. It affects moral and interpersonal conduct, as well as attitudes towards the universe and toward human existence within it," and this religious commitment is best understood by the robust and dynamic term "faith"?[113]

In the chapters to follow I will demonstrate that faith, this dynamic relational concept of love, belief, trust, and hope is not simply a human virtue but a divine one as well. God's relationship with humanity can be understood in many ways (creator, sustainer, savior) and through many metaphors (lover, parent, friend). I am arguing that these ways and metaphors can be seen in a new light when perceived through the lens of divine faith. God's love and relationship with this creation is not merely risky, it is faithful, that is, filled with love, hope, trust, and even belief.

---

[112]"The Freedom of a Christian," §11 in *The Reformation Writings of Martin Luther*, trans. B. L. Woolf, vol. 1 (London, 1952), from his "Sermon on Faith, Part I," quoted in Swinburne, *Faith and Reason*, 110n4.

[113]Robert Audi, "Faith, Belief, and Rationality," *Philosophical Perspectives* 5, *Philosophy of Religion* (1991): 234.

3

GOD LOVES

Love . . . ought to be a stimulus to faith. Because faith
is fiducia no real love is possible without faith.

STEPHEN T. DAVIS

"LOVE IS PATIENT, LOVE IS KIND. It does not envy, it does not boast,
it is not proud. It does not dishonor others, it is not self-seeking, it is not
easily angered, it keeps no record of wrongs. Love does not delight in evil
but rejoices with the truth. It always protects, always trusts, always hopes,
always perseveres" (1 Cor 13:4-7 NIV). "God is love" (1 Jn 4:8). Do these
two passages speak to one another? If we declare God is love but also that
love has the characteristics and qualities listed above, then it seems
1 Corinthians is telling us, indirectly perhaps, something about the
nature of God. This list of qualities and characteristics matches what
Christians experience in God.[1] God is patient and kind (Rom 2:4), God
is not self-seeking (Rom 15:1-6) and God keeps no record of wrongs
(Rom 2:7-8). But what about verse 7? If love always trusts and always
hopes can we say the same about God? Is God's hope and faith limitless?[2]

"The Theological Virtues: 'And the Greatest of these Is Love'" in *Faith, Hope, Love, and Justice:*
The Theological Virtues Today, ed. Anselm K. Min (Lanham, MD: Lexington Books, 2018), 64.
[1]Craig Blomberg suggests that we could replace the word "love" in 1 Cor 13 with "Jesus" since Jesus
Christ was perfect and sinless. See Blomberg, *1 Corinthians*, The NIV Application Commentary
(Grand Rapids: Zondervan, 1994), 262.
[2]The word for "always" is *panta*, which can have both inclusive and exclusive connotations. The
inclusive in this passage is a bit awkward, for it would suggest that love as trust and hope is
without discernment. But there is no virtue in always trusting or in trusting all things. Anthony
Thiselton argues that in this passage *panta* more logically conveys exclusion in that there are no

It is difficult, perhaps impossible, to fully love another and yet not trust them. Love is risky because we entrust our secrets, aspirations, well-being, our very selves to other persons. We delight in them and desire their love as we promise ourselves and hope to be a delight as well. But these are acts of faith since love is a fellowship of free persons. Whether love is felt and then given by the infatuated lover longing for love in return or a convivial love between family and friends—love is an act of faith. Without faith love is anemic. We may act benevolently, doing generous and kind acts, but without faith the love between friends and family is guarded or distant. To love is to be open and exposed, vulnerable but hopeful, to give and to be given back.

Love is more than kind and caring acts but also includes allowing others to love in return. Love is openness to the other, openness to great goods but also great anguish. Fiona Utley says it well:

> We need trust to experience love as openness, as joy, as tenderness and renewal, and as the possibility of emergence into authentic being. Love as openness is also the possibility, indeed inevitability, of loss, heartbreak, and unyielding grief. Love as openness contains the possibility of betrayal and pain. Love as openness also holds the possibility of violence, cruelty, and death. . . . trust is the ground for love.[3]

God is a God of faith because God *is* love. Faith is a logical and natural extension of love. To love is to trust and hope that love is accepted and returned. In short, to be in a fellowship of love is to hope and trust that the beloved will be faithful, trustworthy, and true. If God is passible, subject to passions and suffering, vulnerable and desirous, then God not only risks but also hopes and trusts that love will not return empty. If God desires our partnership, then God desires our maturity, but maturity

---

limits to trust or hope. "There is nothing love cannot face; there is no limit to its faith, its hope, its endurance." Anthony Thiselton, *The First Epistle to the Corinthians*, The New International Greek Testament Commentary (Grand Rapids: Eerdmans, 2000), 1056. This certainly works well if "love" is replaced with "God." "There is nothing God cannot face; there is no limit to God's faith, God's hope, God's endurance."

[3]Fiona Utley, "Trust and the Experience of Love," in *Thinking About Love: Essays in Contemporary Continental Philosophy*, ed. Dianne Enns and Antonio Calcagno (University Park: Pennsylvania State University Press, 2015), 175.

comes when we are given opportunity to show ourselves trustworthy—worthy of God's trust. God surely laments our faithlessness, but too many theologians stop here. We should also recognize that God also enjoys and celebrates our fidelity.

In this chapter I demonstrate that God's risky and vulnerable love means that God necessarily exercises faith in us—that we will return God's love with our own, albeit inglorious, love. God trusts that divine love will be made manifest in our love for one another. Furthermore, if we hold that the metaphors of God as parent, lover, and friend tell us something true about God, then we should understand that God wants to trust us because being in intimate relationship means each lover desires to be trusted and also to trust. As Christians, we desire to trust God fully, but we should be mindful that God desires to trust us as well. To be complete in Christ is to be trusting and trustworthy.

GOD IS LOVE

"'God is love,' is the most transforming, soul-subduing proposition ever propounded to a fallen world. . . . There is not in the universe a more positive, a more substantive, a more real existence than love; for *God is love*."[4] Scripture is clear in its claim that God is love. While there is disagreement on what it means for God to love, let alone *be* love, I, like many, hold that love is the central attribute of God. Any other divine attribute is motivated, directed, amplified, or curtailed by love. It is most assuredly good and right to say that God is holy, wise, merciful, and righteous. These are all praiseworthy and great-making attributes. But we do not say that God *is* holiness, wisdom, mercy, or righteousness in the way we say that God *is* love. This is significant because it means God's being, nature, and character can never be disassociated from love. I am not suggesting that God can act unholy, unrighteous, unwise, or without mercy—God cannot. The reason, however, why God is holy, merciful, wise, and righteous is because God is love. Love is the genesis of those

---

[4]Alexander Campbell and W. A. Morris, *The Writings of Alexander Campbell: Selections Chiefly from the Millennial Harbinger* (Austin, TX: Eugene Von Boeckmann, 1896), 206, 451.

qualities.[5] Love entails not only that God perform loving acts but that all other attributes can be attributed to God because God is love.

God is sovereign and free to do many things, but not to coerce love. This is why faith is an imperative in love. "God can have our love only if we decide to give it. . . . God empowers but does not overpower."[6] While God loves and desires, longs for, and hopes for our love, it cannot be guaranteed we will love God in return. This means that God's love for us is not only faithful but also faith giving—trustworthy and trusting. God desires love be returned and given to others, yet we have the power to refuse. We, and not God, limit the width and depth of God's love. Without our free response God's love is benevolent (God can do good and beneficial things for us) and emotive (God cherishes each of us deeply), but without our willingness to receive and return God's love, it will always be limited and incomplete. Again, God loves all, some in greater ways than others, but God's greatest hope is surely to love all in all ways, and that means the giving of God's self, not merely beneficial acts.

To give power is to give up power. Even God cannot give us power, that is, freedom to make our own decisions, and yet guarantee that every decision we make will be exactly as God desires.[7] But the same cannot be said about love. To give love is to behave lovingly. To give control and freedom to the other out of love is to be most loving—but also most vulnerable. God's sharing of power limits God's sovereignty; to give us the power to create or destroy, obey or rebel means God cannot control who or what we love.[8]

---

[5]John Sanders, "Divine Providence and the Openness of God," in *Perspectives on the Doctrine of God: Four Views*, ed. Bruce Ware (Nashville: B&H Academic, 2008), 197n1.

[6]Clark H. Pinnock, *Flame of Love: A Theology of the Holy Spirit* (Downers Grove, IL: InterVarsity Press, 1996), 157.

[7]This is the basis of free will theodicies in their various forms. The general consensus of those affirming this argument is that God could not actualize a world of free beings and also ensure they always do what God wills. For a very tidy summary of the free will defense, see Daniel Speak, *The Problem of Evil* (Malden, MA: Polity Press, 2015), chap. 2.

[8]For a counterargument that maintains, "When an infinite Being *gives* power He does not *give away* any power. He is still infinite in power after He creates," see Norman Geisler, *Chosen but Free: A Balanced View of God's Sovereignty and Free Will* (Bloomington, MN: Bethany House, 2010), 128.

To state this in no uncertain terms: God does not limit God's self by sharing power with creation for God is not power *simpliciter*. God is love, and as love, God is most divine in giving others the power to love freely. "The nature of love is to bestow freedom on its object of love. . . . When God bestows His power upon us, therefore, He does not limit Himself, for He does not limit love."[9] Like all Christians, I trust that the Son has overcome all powers that seek to separate us from the love of God (Rom 8:39). But this is trust in the love of God, dare I say, in the weakness of God. Paradoxically, those who seek power first and foremost do so out of fear—fear and weakness. Yet, as Dietrich Bonhoeffer reminded us, Christ's help came in the form, not of omnipotence, but as weakness and suffering, for "only the suffering God can help."[10] "God is love" means that God is vulnerable, and vulnerability is more than God taking risks, it is about God embracing faith.

LOVE DEFINED

My main argument in what follows is this: because God loves, because God *is* love, God has faith. To love but not trust your beloved, or minimally, not aim, work, and hope toward building trust and making those you love trustworthy, suggests that what is being called love is something other, something less. It may be valuing the other, cherishing them, doing good and acting benevolently toward those we adore, but it is something less than love in the fullest. Love, intimate self-sharing love, means giving yourself and desiring the other give himself or herself in return. But because love is a pointedly free response, there is no assurance that love will be returned, and thus the lover is always vulnerable that love may be refused.

Love is terribly difficult to define. Much like faith, love is dynamic and irreducible—for us and for God. Love affects, or is manifest in, how we

---

[9]Nels F. S. Ferré, *The Christian Understanding of God* (New York: Harper & Brothers, 1951), 101.
[10]Dietrich Bonhoeffer, *Letters and Papers from Prison*, trans. Reginald H. Fuller et al. (New York: Macmillan, 1972), 361, quoted in William C. Placher, *Narratives of a Vulnerable God: Christ, Theology, and Scripture* (Louisville, KY: Westminster John Knox, 1994), 18.

feel, act, and think—our pathos, ethos, and even logos. Love, when whole and complete, is mutual, reciprocal, and relational. Love may not always be requited but always desires love in return. This is the telos of love: mutuality, fellowship, communion, friendship. These ideas are best expressed in the idea of relationship, more precisely, in relationships of love.

My view is that love is *best* understood in terms of reciprocal relationships. This is true of both human and divine. Thomas Oden offered, "God's love for humanity, *like all love*, is reciprocal."[11] Love is complete when the love given is embraced and met with love returned and love shared. Love certainly includes the doing of good and benevolent acts, and lovers who selflessly and sacrificially seek the well-being of the beloved are to be abundantly praised. Let's add that love means being interested in the beloved, emotionally invested, not only in the beloved's well-being but in the relationship itself. This love certainly is self-interested but in no way selfish.

If we are to love God with all our being—heart, soul, strength, and mind—it seems that love has a multidimensional symmetry to it. Love is not merely intellectual or affective or practical but ideally all three. That is, love means I feel, think, and act in affectionate and beneficial ways for the beloved and the self. Many theists who believe that God desires a relationship with humanity will tip their hat to all three elements while still emphasizing one aspect over the others. Edward Vacek, for example, emphasizes an emotive/affective understanding of love. He defines "love as an emotional participation in a valuable object."[12] But for Vacek, emotion is a "complex activity" that includes an openness to good, consciousness of value, being affected by, and responding to, the valuable object.[13] Even though the emotive element of love is highlighted it is not to the detriment of love's relational and reciprocal elements. Love is "an emotional participation," but Vacek also says, "Love is a relationship

---

[11]Thomas C. Oden, *The Living God*, vol. 1 of *Systematic Theology* (San Francisco: HarperSanFrancisco, 1992), 121. Emphasis mine.

[12]Edward Collins Vacek, SJ, *Love, Human and Divine: The Heart of Christian Ethics* (Washington, DC: Georgetown University Press, 1994), 21.

[13]Vacek, *Love, Human and Divine*, 12.

between two or more beings . . . that aims at enhancing the beloved in at least some aspect of its greater being."[14]

Thomas Jay Oord emphasizes the practical aspect of love when he says, "To love is to act intentionally, in sympathetic/empathetic response to God and others, to promote overall well-being."[15] Oord explains that love is primarily doing good intentionally, and this applies to both human and divine love.[16] "God always acts intentionally, in sympathetic/empathetic response to Godself and others, to promote overall well-being."[17] While Oord emphasizes the practical and active feature of love, he does not neglect its relational feature. "Love requires actual relations with others."[18] Furthermore, "God is omnirelational. God acts as both the ideal recipient and the ideal contributor."[19] So even those who may define love in terms other than "relationship" still see the necessity of relationship for love's fuller development.

Kevin Vanhoozer and Thomas Oord raise important cautions concerning defining love exclusively in terms of relationship. According to Vanhoozer, if love *is* the relationship, this means love can never be unrequited. Love given but not returned would not be love since love necessarily entails reciprocal relationships. He adds that if love entails reciprocity, the command to love our enemies is incoherent. "To be sure, love *aims* at generating a loving response," but love cannot have mutuality as an "essential ingredient."[20] Oord, too, is critical of defining love exclusively in terms of relationship; "few of us . . . would describe all relationships as loving. Some relationships generate evil. Some relationships are

---

[14]Vacek, *Love, Human and Divine*, 55.
[15]Thomas Jay Oord, *The Nature of Love: A Theology* (St. Louis, MO: Chalice, 2010), 17.
[16]Oord explains that his use of love is that love is best understood as *hesed*—righteousness. "When I use the word *love*, . . . I follow the practice of the love-as-doing-good tradition and therefore refer to action that engenders well-being." Thomas Jay Oord, *Defining Love: A Philosophical, Scientific, and Theological Engagement* (Grand Rapids: Brazos, 2010), 28.
[17]Oord, *The Nature of Love*, 129.
[18]Oord, *Defining Love*, 19.
[19]Oord, *Defining Love*, 193.
[20]Kevin J. Vanhoozer, *Remythologizing Theology: Divine Action, Passion, and Authorship* (New York: Cambridge University Press, 2010), 173. Vanhoozer suggests that if the goal is simply reciprocity, then "eye for an eye" is the most mutual reciprocal approach we could take.

not healthy . . . we should not equate love with mutuality, despite the necessary role mutuality plays in love."[21]

I agree with Vanhoozer and Oord; love need not be defined exclusively in terms of relationship. If love was only possible in relationship, then passages such as "We love because he first loved us" (1 Jn 4:19) would not make sense. To love one's enemies, even though it is unrequited, is still love. Love does not somehow lose its essence when it is unanswered. While unrequited love is one-directional, it is love nonetheless. But unrequited love is not all love can be or all God hopes it to be. One of the most powerful aspects of love is that it makes the most out of the situation given. God always loves without reserve, but for love to be all that it is meant to be, it involves love returned in relationship. Just as it could be said that Jesus was fully God but not the fullness of God, we can say God's love for the unrepentant sinner is fully love and yet not the fullness of love—not because God's acts of benevolence are less than loving, but because the love has not yet reached its telos. The issue then is not whether we or God can genuinely love another without having love returned, but whether that is a love God is satisfied with. As stated above, I believe the love God desires and works to bring about is a requited mutual love of communion and fellowship, and therefore the "Hound of Heaven" will be satisfied with nothing less.

In Vincent Brümmer's assessment, mutual relational love has these five characteristics: (1) Love is established and maintained in mutual freedom. (2) Love entails vulnerability. (3) Love strives to serve the interests of the other. (4) Love sees each partner as unique and irreplaceable. (5) Love is a relationship between persons.[22] These characteristics distinguish

---

[21]Oord, *Defining Love*, 27-28. I agree with Oord that love should not be defined *as* relationship. Love is certainly more than relationship itself, but even if one were to suggest "love is relationship," that would not necessitate that "relationship is love" any more than "God is love" necessitates that "love is God."

[22]These characteristics are paraphrases of Brümmer's larger discussion. See Vincent Brümmer, *Atonement, Christology and the Trinity: Making Sense of Christian Doctrine* (Burlington, VT: Ashgate, 2005), 27-30. Vincent Brümmer, *Brümmer on Meaning and the Christian Faith: Collected Writings of Vincent Brümmer*, ed. John R. Hinnells (Burlington, VT: Ashgate, 2006), 296-99.

mutually loving relationships from other kinds of relationships.[23] In the
section below, I will show that each of these five characteristics rests upon
faith, particularly trust and hope. I will discuss characteristics one and
two under eros, three under agape, and four and five under philia.
Furthermore, as I discuss eros, agape, and philia, I will show that all three
of these aspects of love depend upon or seek to establish faith.

METAPHORS OF LOVE AND FAITH

We can talk about love in different ways, highlighting its various features,
breaking down its modes, goals, and expressions. For many theologians,
love, including God's love, is best understood by exploring the three
prominent Greek terms eros, agape, and philia. I will follow suit, but I
will try to avoid suggestions that these are different kinds of love even
though I will speak of "eros love" or "agapic love" out of convention. As
I see it, however, eros, agape, and philia are differing shades of the same
love. When we shine light through a prism we do not experience different beams of light but a spectrum of colors from that single beam.
The same is true of God's love. When put through a theological prism we
do not see three different loves but one love in differing hues. The
spectrum of God's love reveals the many ways God loves, but not the
many loves of one God.

My intent is to discuss eros, agape, and philia as differing shades of
God's love, not as competing or opposing loves. While human motives,
means, and ends concerning love can be perverted, God's ways and means
are perfect. God's experiences of eros, acts of agape, and designs for philia
never compete with one another but rather complete one another.[24]

It should be remembered that in all thoughts and discussions of God we
employ analogy and metaphor along with literal and univocal statements.

---

[23]I am surprised that Brümmer did not include in this list of characteristics mutual faith and
faithfulness. Perhaps faithfulness is assumed in the fact that love strives to serve the interests of
the other, but mutual faith will need to be teased out.

[24]"To separate *eros* and *agape* or to oppose them or to set them absolutely off against each other
as alternatives . . . is to view love incompletely and to fail to understand how one dimension may
strengthen the other." Oden, *The Living God*, 119.

To say that God loves is to say something literal. God loves the church, the world, my neighbor, and even me. While these are limited statements, they are nonetheless literal. The "literal idea of love . . . is skeletal in meaning and insufficient for understanding all aspects of our experience, which is why we seek to understand topics such as love via conceptual metaphors."[25] This is especially true regarding God's love and, as I hope to demonstrate, God's faith. So, to better understand the relationship of faith and love it is helpful, perhaps necessary, to employ particular analogies and metaphors, namely, God as lover, parent, and friend. These are the most important relationships we have, and luckily, they are loves we can empirically study. By examining and contemplating these human relationships we can get a better, though certainly imperfect, picture of love. These images of love will be the windows by which we attempt to see what God's love is—but also what it is not.[26]

Eros love is desirous love. It longs to give love freely but also have love freely returned. It is a risky but hopeful love for there is no promise that the love given will be accepted and returned. Agape is a gift love that acts for the betterment of the beloved. It is selfless and sacrificial. It is a love that labors to produce virtues—in short—trustworthiness. Trustworthiness is the fruit of trust, just as faithfulness the fruit of faith. Agape is the means of love, it is the way we love the beloved. Philia is mutuality. It is the aspect of love that loves the other in relationship. Philia is not

---

[25]John Sanders, *Theology in the Flesh: How Embodiment and Culture Shape the Way We Think About Truth, Morality, and God* (Minneapolis: Fortress, 2016), 63-64.

[26]Brümmer states that the purpose in exploring human love is not merely to describe it, "but to find an adequate conceptual model for talking about our relationship with God." Vincent Brümmer, *The Model of Love: A Study in Philosophical Theology* (Cambridge: Cambridge University Press, 1993), 157. Some are critical of attempts to understand God's love by way of human love. Ron Highfield, for example, argues that to begin with human love will naturally lead us to believe God's love is risky or needy since our love is both of these. According to Highfield, by beginning with discussions of human love we erroneously judge divine love by human love instead of judging human love by the divine. While we should be mindful that all analogies break down and metaphors tell us both what something is and what it is not, this does not mean beginning with human experiences is somehow ill fated. Even Jesus makes use of human love in order to explain divine love. In Luke, Jesus helps us better understand divine love by comparing it to a shepherd who seeks after a lost sheep (Lk 15:3-7) and a father who waits for a wayward son (Lk 15:11-32). For Highfield's full treatment of God's love, see Ron Highfield, *Great Is the Lord: Theology for the Praise of God* (Grand Rapids: Eerdmans, 2008), chap. 6.

primarily about the self (eros) or the other (agape) but about the "us."
Philia love is mutuality, solidarity, harmony, unity, and fellowship. It is a
love that is dependent on a relationship of shared trust, for where there
is friendship there is faith. This is the telos of love, it is what eros and
agape each hope to realize.

Eros. The sacrificial giving love of agape is sometimes described as
"spontaneous, unmotivated, indifferent to value, nondesirous and
nonemotive."[27] Unmotivated love would mean we could not say God
loves for any reason other than God freely chose to love. I maintain,
however, that God's love is not unmotivated or indifferent. God's love is
better understood as purely motivated, interested, and passionate. We
see God's agape most clearly and dramatically in actions such as the
liberation of Israel and in the life, death, burial, and resurrection of Jesus
Christ. But when we peer behind these events, when we seek to understand the motivation for God's patience and willing humiliation, we find
God's eros—"God's desire to recover an estranged lover, child, or partner,
God's longing to reconcile and to reunite with one who has betrayed the
divine love."[28] Why? Because God cherishes us, desires us, and is long-
suffering until that love returns.

The distinction between eros and agape has been overstated, and
while there are differences there is no dichotomy, especially in God.
Anders Nygren famously pitted the two against each other, writing that
"eros *recognizes value* in its object—and loves it," while "agape loves—
and *creates value in its* object."[29] I see no reason not to affirm both
of these.

To say that God loves out of a desire for the beloved and that God
suffers when love is not returned does not mean that God's love is selfish
or egoistic. "Mutual love is inextricably linked with freedom, risk, and

---

[27]John C. Peckham, *The Love of God: A Canonical Model* (Downers Grove, IL: IVP Academic,
2015), 22. Peckham is summarizing Anders Nygren's thoughts on agape.

[28]Jeff B. Pool, *God's Wounds: Hermeneutic of the Christian Symbol of Divine Suffering*, vol. 1: *Divine
Vulnerability and Creation* (Cambridge: James Clarke, 2009), 120.

[29]Anders Nygren, *Agape and Eros*, trans. Philip S. Watson (New York: Harper & Row, 1953), 210.
For Nygren, we have no value and are not worthy of love, but we acquire worth once we are
loved by God (78).

patience, but never with selflessness."[30] If God's love were merely eros then perhaps this would be true. But God does not love by eros alone any more than God loves by agape or philia alone. Let us not be so naive to think that God has no wants or longings. If God desires nothing, has neither plans nor goals, then our love, worship, and adoration for the divine is for ourselves only. "God desires fellowship with created beings (*philia*)," and through "self-sacrifice (*agape*) God becomes more fully satisfied in love (*eros*)."[31]

"God is a serious lover who wants . . . relationships of love most deeply."[32] To call God "lover" might lead some to recoil,[33] but I find it a moving description and one supported by many biblical images and narratives.[34] God as lover is passionate, righteously jealous, overjoyed, and deeply interested. God as lover means God has hope in the beloved and trusts the beloved to breathe deep God's love. Furthermore, romantic lovers depend on one another to return the love given; they must trust the other to be faithful. This love is risky, prone to heartbreak, and so can only be founded on faith. Lovers who refuse to risk try to build relationships by controlling the beloved or maintain relationships in suspicion. Some who refuse to risk simply seek to give love while telling themselves they do not need or deserve love returned. Love given while being deeply suspicious of the other or without any desire for love returned tries to eschew vulnerability, but that is not what relationships are made of, and that is not divine love. Eros relationships

---

[30]Stephen G. Post, "The Inadequacy of Selflessness: God's Suffering and the Theory of Love," *Journal of the American Academy of Religion* 56, no. 2 (1988), 220.

[31]Paul Fiddes, "Creation Out of Love," in *The Work of Love: Creation as Kenosis*, ed. John Polkinghorne (Grand Rapids: Eerdmans, 2001), 173.

[32]Clark Pinnock, *Most Moved Mover: A Theology of God's Openness* (Grand Rapids: Baker Academic, 2001), 140.

[33]Sallie McFague says all but a fringe group of mystics have eschewed the noun "lover" for God because it smacks of eroticism and female sexuality. See McFague, *Models of God: Theology for an Ecological, Nuclear Age* (Philadelphia: Fortress, 1987), 125.

[34]Scripture is not shy in speaking of God as husband and lover, sometimes with imagery too scandalous for most Sunday sermons. For example, Ex 34:15-16; Lev 17:7; Is 50:1; 54:6-8; 62:4-5; Jer 2:2, 32; 3:6-14; 31:32; Hos 2:16, 19. The NT also uses the metaphor of husband with Christ as the groom and the redeemed as the bride. See also Eph 5:21-32; Rev 19:7-9; 21:2. For more on the imagery of God as husband, see Leland Ryken, James C. Wilhoit, and Tremper Longman III, eds., *Dictionary of Biblical Imagery* (Downers Grove, IL: IVP Academic, 1998), 414-15.

without faith are about manipulation not mutuality, about control not communion.

Consider the ways faith and trust fit into marital and romantic relationships. It is quite common to see discussions about faithfulness in marriage, but faithfulness extends beyond sexual fidelity. A partner can be unfaithful if he cares more about self than his spouse. A partner can be adulterous and unfaithful if he is an addict abusing alcohol, drugs, pornography, gambling, and the like.[35] We have a good idea about what it means to be faithful in the passive sense (not doing what damages the relationship), but marriages require we be "full of faith" in the active sense (trusting the other). That is, not only must we be worthy of trust, we must likewise, be willing to trust. Intimate relationships in which one cannot or chooses not to have faith in the other are seriously anemic—or already dead.

Picture a relationship in which one spouse has no faith in the other. When the wife leaves for work the husband goes through her things, repeatedly checks her location on his phone, and demands that she report back to him on everything she did and everyone with whom she spoke. He does not trust her with credit cards or bank information, demanding receipts whenever he gives her money to make a purchase. In all other ways he may be kind, gentle, and caring, but can we say this is a loving husband? If we can, the love must be qualified and understood to be deficient and truncated. Supposing we can say he loves her, we would surely add that he should commit to trusting her. Being faithful is more than being trustworthy. Faithfulness in relationships also means trusting the beloved.

Spouses whose relationships have suffered from infidelities, especially sexual, often find it is not their love for the other that is the problem; it is the lack of trust. A spouse whose partner has been unfaithful may still have very deep feeling for the beloved. She wants the marriage to continue

---

[35]For discussions on biblical adultery, see Patrick D. Miller, *The Ten Commandments* (Louisville, KY: Westminster John Knox, 2009), chap. 6; and Lewis B. Smedes, *Mere Morality: What God Expects from Ordinary People* (Grand Rapids: Eerdmans, 1995), chap. 6.

but finds it difficult to trust. The love may continue, but the relationship will remain broken until trust is restored. If the relationship is to be healed each spouse must take a risk and commit to trusting the other. Healthy and genuinely loving relationships can never be one-sidedly trusting any more than they can be one-sidedly faithful.

If it is right and good for us to trust our own spouses, and God's relationship with the church and Israel is articulated in lover and marital imagery, we should say that God trusts us. It seems odd to suggest that I should believe and treat my wife as trustworthy but God should not. God's trust in us is surely different than how we trust one another, but it is not absent. Husbands are called to love their wives as Christ loved the church (Eph 5:25). Does Christ love but not trust the church? God has, after all, entrusted the church with the ministry of reconciliation (2 Cor 5:17-18).

God's love for us must mean that in some sense God desires to trust us because that is the way to a deeper love. This is, in part, what it means to be a loving and faithful spouse—to trust your beloved. If it is true that God loves all in some ways, but longs to love all in all ways, then God must act in faith; that is, hope and trust in us to be faithful lovers. The relationship between God and human will never be all it can be if trust is one-sided.

The eros hue of love is vulnerability in both caring for the other and the person's well-being, in addition to entrusting one's desires into the care of the other. Divine love means not only that God acts in our best interest but also that God has entrusted us with God's own well-being. God is dependent upon others returning love for love, as well as, trust for trust.[36] This is vulnerability, to love without guarantee of love in return, to give power to those who may abuse it, to empathize and feel what the other feels.

Love can bring suffering because it seeks to be with the beloved. The separating distance between God and humanity is an existential, spiritual,

---

[36]I will say more about God's faith as a necessary pathway to God's well-being in the conclusion.

moral, and emotional distance. God's response to such separation reveals
God's faith. Authentic love means waiting, hoping, and trusting the other
to freely respond. Love is not reveling in, quietly accepting, or elimi-
nating the hurt through manipulation, but overcoming the hurt by embracing faith in the other.[37] This kind of love is only possible if one has
faith in the other. A love that becomes vulnerable to pain and suffering
without reveling in suffering is a love infused with trust that the other will
be faithful and return love in kind. If there is no faith that love will be
returned, then there can be no intimate relationship, only respect and
good will.

While engaging in faith makes real sorrow possible, it is also the only
way to make real joy possible. God risks, not only for the joy of loving
but for the joy of being loved. This may be what the author of Hebrews
had in mind when writing, "looking to Jesus the pioneer and perfecter
of our faith, who for the sake of the joy that was set before him endured
the cross, disregarding its shame, and has taken his seat at the right hand
of the throne of God" (Heb 12:2). While God desires a restored and renewed relationship with all persons, this should not be interpreted as
God being distant or wholly unrelated to us prior to such a restoration
(Acts 17:27).

In this section I have sought to demonstrate that divine love is motivated by God's cherishing of humanity and long-suffering desire to fellowship with us in the mutual exchange of love given and love returned.
Because we are free, give-and-take love is possible but so too is love
spurned and rejected, so God risks. God acts in faith, trusting us not to
slight divine acts and invitations of love but to accept and be affected by
them—to respond, not just with love for love but also with faith for faith.

---

[37]Brümmer explains that the proper relationship between faith and suffering is acceptance of
suffering by knowing that authentic love must face such possibilities. "The only response which
does not pervert love which it seeks is to accept the vulnerability, not for its own sake, but for
the sake of love itself. I long for your love, but I will restrain this longing when it tries to control
your love and prevents you from bestowing it on me freely. . . . I know that such efforts on my
part will only pervert the fellowship which they seek to establish. In other words, I value our
mutual fellowship more than the invulnerability which I can attain by denying your freedom as
a person to let me down from time to time." Brümmer, *The Model of Love*, 225.

That is the eros hue of love. Thank God for eros! Without eros agape would be nice, very nice, but hardly the fullness of love.

Agape. "Love seeks and love gives."[38] Eros is that hue of love that seeks both its own and the beloved's good. Agape is the hue that gives. "Driven by divine erotic love, God loves agapically."[39] Eros is the why—the eyes of love that see the good and the valuable, rightfully cherishing it. Agape is the how—the arms and legs of love working to obtain the beloved's best interest.

If divine love were merely eros, both God and humanity would despair since love would be powerless to effect change, able to wish for love but without much reason to hope. Agape is God's strength—the capacity to help bring about good and desirable states. Eros can be expressed as a love "because of"—because of God's cherishing and desiring us for communion. Agape can be expressed as love "in spite of"—in spite of our sin, rebellion, and selfishness God still does what is in our best interest. It is also love "in spite of" the cost to the lover. Because of God's desire to be in full relationship with creation, and in spite of humanity's failings, God does what is loving.

In what follows I will show that one thing in our best interest is to become persons of character, persons capable of fellowship and mutual love—in short, trustworthy, loving persons. It is in our best interest that God work to help us become trustworthy. It is in our best interest that God have faith in us. It is most loving for God to have faith in us.

Paul Fiddes notes that agape is often defined as "self-giving love . . . understood as a person's spending himself freely and carelessly for the other person, sacrificing himself without any calculations about gain."[40] This depiction is very close, but the essence of agape is not that it is "without any calculations about *gain*," but without any calculations about *loss*. Because eros and philia are vibrant hues of divine love, we cannot

---

[38]Smedes, *Mere Morality*, 45.
[39]Pool, *God's Wounds*, 121.
[40]Paul Fiddes, *The Creative Suffering of God* (Oxford: Oxford University Press, 1988), 170. Fiddes suggests this definition is mistaken, or misguided, given that the NT often speaks of our gain by the losing of our self (Mt 16:25).

miss that love is motivated and seeking. God does hope to gain fellowship and mutual love by loving creation. Because we are free creatures, God's love includes calculations, carefully and wisely assessing situations so that humanity and, as result, God might gain. The pain and sacrifices of love are what God refuses to consider in those calculations. "Self-giving love always *hopes* for a response," but a response is never guaranteed.[41]

The exact meaning of agape is debatable.[42] It is most often spoken of in terms of gifting or giving. The emphasis for agape is the offering to, or doing unto, another what is in their best interest. It is an intentional "effort to promote overall well-being."[43] Agape entails, more than any aspect of love, an act. It is the practical aspect of love, the means by which eros meets philia. Agape is what love *does*.

Love is most dramatically demonstrated in sacrificial acts, though common acts of kindness are aspects of agape to be sure. God's love is poured out on us moment by moment in the sustaining of creation, the giving of life and breath. God's love is not sporadic or periodic—it is constant. At no moment is the divine love inactive, resting from previous deeds or waiting for new opportunities. Yet in the constant of God's love there are spectacular and vivid punctuations, moments in which the reality of being loved washes over us and we experience God's love anew. The life and death of Jesus is the ultimate expression of God's love. In Jesus Christ we see divine love lived out physically, historically, and sacrificially. The giving of Christ for the world is God's paramount act of love (Jn 3:16).

While God's love is constant, it is also a love demonstrated passively. To love another not only means benevolence, it also means restraint, empowering, giving the beloved space to be. All relationships seem to need

---

[41]Fiddes, *The Creative Suffering of God*, 173.
[42]Robert Adams calls agape a "blank canvas on which one can paint whatever ideal of Christian love one favors." See Robert Merrihew Adams, *Finite and Infinite Goods: A Framework for Ethics* (New York: Oxford University Press, 1999), 136.
[43]Oord, *Defining Love*, 43. Oord's definition is "agape is intentional sympathetic response to promote overall well-being when confronted by that which generates ill-being." I have shortened it to highlight the active aspect of agape. The intentional aspect of love is found in my discussion of eros. For a careful but concise treatment of agape, see pp. 32-45.

boundaries. Parents, for example, can overwhelm and smother a child's growth into maturity and independence by not letting a daughter succeed on her own, or allowing a son to fail. Of course, there are better and worse ways to do this. Nevertheless, the parent who gives little to no room for the child's independence is not more loving but less.[44] Most often parents mean well when being overly protective, but children, like all persons, need solitude and privacy. This is the wisdom of friendship, marriage, or parenting—knowing when to engage and when to withdraw. Even Paul seems to wrestle with the relationship between active and passive love when he says that love "always protects" but also that love "always trusts" (1 Cor 13:7 NIV).

In part we give space and privacy because the beloved has a right to these goods. Then again, it is also out of love and care for the beloved. To withdraw or give the beloved space is not to withhold love but is an aspect of gift love. Whether it is "do unto others" or "act in such a way that your action could become a universal maxim," to love and act in the other's best interest does not always entail actively providing for them. Love can also mean refraining from acting, allowing the other the freedom and room to develop and mature or to simply let them be. This space, license to be, necessitates trust in the beloved however. To give a friend room to be is to trust he will reengage in the fellowship at a later time. To encourage a spouse to pursue interests you may not share is to have faith that the spouse knows these are good and beneficial pursuits. It seems then that part of loving others entails giving them the space and freedom to develop and grow.

We are often so entrenched in God's omnipresence and omnipotence that we fail to consider God's allowing us space and even privacy. I am unsure how much space and privacy divine love must give. But there are at least prima facie reasons for considering this. Biblically we are confronted

---

[44]Teaching my daughter to drive is a vivid example for me of when to love actively and when to love passively and the desperate search to know when to scream "Brake! Brake! Brake!" and when to quietly trust that she will figure it out. For more on this, see Wm. Curtis Holtzen, "Believe It or Not, God Has Faith in You," in *Uncontrolling Love: Essays Exploring the Love of God,* ed. Chris Baker et al. (San Diego, CA: SacraSage, 2017), 185-87.

by narratives in which God seems to give humans privacy or at least some kind of space. In the garden story Adam and Eve are alone when tempted by the serpent and only after God must ask, "Where are you? . . . Who told you that you were naked? Have you eaten from the tree of which I commanded you not to eat?" (Gen 3:9-11). God comes down to "see the city and the tower, which mortals had built" (Gen 11:5). Regarding the outcry against Sodom and Gomorrah, God says, "I must go down and see whether they have done altogether according to the outcry that has come to me; and if not, I will know" (Gen 18:21). The psalmist invites God to learn his secrets; "Search me, O God, and know my heart; test me and know my thoughts" (Ps 139:23). I am not suggesting these passages always be read literally, that God is ignorant of particular events until God empirically checks them out and learns of their truth. Perhaps, though, God knows the number of hairs on our heads but out of love God somehow "turns away" from knowing every intimacy about us until we invite God to search and know us. Maybe these narratives convey that God is not intrusive and overbearing but is willing to give us the space and freedom necessary to be and become.

If God gives us freedom, space, and even privacy, it is because God desires that we grow, develop, and mature. This is a gift, a gift however that requires and entails trust. Metaphysics may necessitate that God create humans with a significantly free will, but it is love that leads God to trust we will bring that love into partnership.[45]

Above I discussed eros and the metaphor of lovers. In discussing agape the fitting metaphor is parental love. Parents who properly love and care for their children do need to have some control of the child, watch them closely, only let them make decisions when the parent knows that their choice cannot be utterly detrimental. And yet, while this is true for the parent of the very young, loving parents seek ways to help a child become trustworthy. Love seeks to bring a child to maturity, to help him develop into a person who is dependable. Obviously, parents should not give more

---

[45]It may be that God had to create persons with freedom of the will because humans are not persons without significant freedom. But even if this is the case, God's willingness to trust is not a metaphysical necessity but an act necessitated by divine love.

trust than is due according to the child's age or development. Furthermore, it is only natural not to trust a child who has proven him or herself to be dishonest. But love calls us to seek ways to trust. To love a child is to actively help him or her into maturity, which is trustworthiness.

Agape includes "acting in ways that develop a person's virtuous dispositions, habits, and character. To promote well-being is to act to increase flourishing in at least one but often many of these dimensions of existence."[46] We love our children best when we promote and help develop them into virtuous persons. The only means by which to train up a child to be responsible is to give him responsibilities. The only way to train up a child to be trustworthy is to trust her with those responsibilities. Children learn by example. Parents want their children to be honest, so they model honesty. Parents want their children to be kind, so they model kindness. Parents want their children to be trustworthy, so they model trustworthiness. And if parents want their children to trust, especially to trust them, then they need to model trust, not merely model trustworthiness.

Modeling trust is not difficult with younger children since the tasks and behaviors we trust them with are generally safe and controlled. The older a child gets, the more difficult—and frankly dangerous—trust modeling becomes. But it also becomes more necessary. Trusting adolescents to do chores or keep up with homework evolves into trusting teens not to engage in dangerous or reckless behaviors. Parents, however, need to trust their children in the right ways at the right times, because this is part of what it means to love a child. To say we love our teenage children but then refuse to ever trust them may produce adults so stunted they cannot accomplish the simplest tasks or result in irresponsible adults who care nothing about social concerns. I am not suggesting all of society's ills are due to a lack of right-trusting parents. I am saying that parental love and agape is more than protecting a child. Agape must include producing virtues in a child that are good and noble, most notably, trustworthiness.

[46]Oord, *Defining Love*, 24.

If God is understood to be our parent, and we understand this metaphor as saying that God loves in ways only a parent can love a child (Lk 11:11-13), then we must consider God's trust in us. Parents surely want to protect their children from the world's many dangers, but withholding trust and in turn responsibility poses its own dangers. Why would we think God wants to love us fully but has no desire to trust and entrust to us? To love is to trust, but where that is not possible, love seeks to develop trust.

It is certainly possible to love and not trust. The parent of a child with a serious drug addiction will surely love that child, wanting him to get help and conquer the addiction. But that parent may have found she can no longer trust the child since addiction leads to lies and theft. Maybe a spouse has been caught having an affair, and while the other spouse still loves the partner, trust has nonetheless been severely damaged. Maybe a close friend has shared a secret he should have kept and so the friendship is fractured. In these scenarios it does not seem that because trust was broken the love has ended. Love is healthiest where there is trust, but this is because the love can be mutually fulfilling. Love does not die when trust is gravely wounded, but the relationship might if trust is not restored.[47]

All relationships have their problems. Friends will fail us, marriages grow cold, and children rebel. But the health and maturity of a relationship depends on each partner's ability to move on from past weaknesses and transgressions. Vacek sums it up nicely, "love always includes a sense of expectation and hope, a love grounds trust that exceeds legitimate inferences from past experience."[48] Out of love, despite our past sins, God trusts us. I cannot rightly make this a one-sided sense of trust, for each of us have had frustrations with God. Yet despite disappointment

---

[47]Conversely, it is obviously possible to trust without a sense or feelings of love. I trust people with whom I merely have a professional relationship. I can even trust people I've never met, like pilots or chefs. So, while love is possible without trust and trust is possible without love, both are necessary for a relationship to be loving in the fullest sense. A relationship with one of these missing could hardly be described as intimate or fulfilling.

[48]Vacek, *Love, Human and Divine*, 45.

in God's silence and hiddenness, in the midst of pain and evil, out of love, we continue to trust and hope.[49] God forgives in order to be in relationship, in order to build trust. Relationships require that we forgive the past, trust in the present, and hope for the future.

In this section I have tried to show that agape, which seeks to advance what is in the beloved's best interest, finds ways to trust the beloved. This is true not only in friendships, marriages, and families but is also true in the relationship between humans and the divine.

Philia. While eros seeks and agape gives, philia shares. What distinguishes philia from eros and agape is the "*mutuality* of the relation it creates." We love the other, not for their sake or for our sake, "but for the sake of the mutual relationship we share with them."[50] We love the other(s) in a way that transcends or completes eros and agape by bringing them to their objective. If eros is the "why" and agape is the "how," philia then is the "what." It is what eros and agape hope and work for—love united.

The goal of love is not simply to be with the beloved, as wonderful as that might be, but to be in partnership, fellowship, communion, with the beloved.[51] Eros is dependent on the beloved; the lover is dependent upon the beloved to reciprocate and return the love yearned for. Agape is independence; the lover can act on the beloved's best interest independent of the beloved's desire or ability to return love.[52] Philia, however, is interdependence. Both lover and beloved prize and appreciate one another, serving and magnifying the other for the union itself.

Consider members of an orchestra performing a musical piece. More than each musician playing well, they each need to play well *together*—not

---

[49]Notice in Jeremiah 31:33-34 that the relationship—knowing and being known by God—rests on sins forgiven and forgotten. "I will be their God, and they shall be my people. No longer shall they teach one another, or say to each other, 'Know the LORD,' for they shall all know me, from the least of them to the greatest, says the LORD; for I will forgive their iniquity, and remember their sin no more."

[50]Vacek, *Love, Human and Divine*, 281.

[51]Although a mark of love is that lovers can simply be with the other, in stillness and quiet simply enjoying the presence of the other.

[52]John Peckham explains that the differences between agape and philia are often difficult to discern and that NT writers often used the words (or word groups) interchangeably. See Peckham, *The Love of God*, 73-77.

only for their own good or the good of their bandmates but for the good of the performance. That is philia. The joy that comes from performing with the beloved is found in the other but also in the performance—the product of that partnership. It is certainly possible to cherish and do great goods for the beloved while never achieving philia. We may long for a relationship with another, do many benevolent acts, and yet not see a relationship come to life. When there is a relationship of love, however, that is more than two individuals in love and loving one another; it is individuals "creating love"—that is philia. Divine philia invites us to pick up an instrument and play along.

Philia is often lost in the theological discussions of divine love. Agape and eros tend to get the attention. But again, eros and agape are the motive and means to philia. God desires our fellowship (eros) and so God acts to forgive and win our love as well as bring us into maturity (agape) so that we can be in communion with the divine (philia). We sometimes forget that forgiveness is a relational deed. God forgives so there can be reconciliation, and reconciliation is for the purpose of mutual love. Christ's death was a means to an end, a risky act of divine faith, so that God and human might be restored in fellowship. The life and death of Christ was not an end in itself, even though it is God's most supreme demonstration of love; the cross is the means God has chosen to restore mutuality.

As discussed above, Brümmer's five characteristics of love include love's seeing each partner as unique and irreplaceable and love's being a relationship between persons. These characteristics appear most clearly in the hue of philia. Philia is for the sake of the other, self, and the relationship. It is "a relationship between two or more beings . . . that aims at enhancing the beloved in at least some aspect of its greater being. . . . It is a 'movement toward' the not yet realized value."[53] Philia means encounter with free beings, an authentic engagement "with someone whom we cannot control."[54] In part we value philia because the beloved

---

[53]Vacek, *Love, Human and Divine*, 55.
[54]Vacek, *Love, Human and Divine*, 290.

has freely found qualities in us that she enjoys. The beloved not only loves us (agape) but genuinely likes us—genuinely enjoys our company.

God is to be highly praised for unconditional love (Rom 5:8). But we misunderstand both the nature of love and God if we neglect God's conditional love. Philia is not conditioned upon divine election but upon the human. God's unconditional and universal love shines brightest in agape, but the fullness of love depends on our free response to God's invitation and our willingness to share in God's purposes. These are the conditions of love—to love the Son and do the will of the Father (Jn 14:21-23; 15:24; 16:27). To love God with all our being and our neighbor as our self (Lk 10:27). We should not see this as earned love since God's agape is unmerited and gratuitous, but philia is only possible if we submit and embrace the loving fellowship and friendship God has offered.[55] Philia, then, is partiality—for now at least. It is the feature of love that is limited by the beloved. God's hope, however—and it should be our hope as well— is that eros will be satisfied and agape see the fruits of its labor in the fullness of philia (1 Tim 2:3-4).

Philia is often described as "friendship love," but this is too narrow for it is a love marked by many kinds of special relations. Mutual love is found in both romantic and familial relationships. Where there is mutuality in love there is philia. It is true that a father or mother is not a child's friend but a parent, but this does not mean that parents cannot be friendly or have friendship with a child.[56] Parent and child can and should have a unique bond that is mutually enhancing and fulfilling. Romantic couples as well should have a mutuality uniquely developed in their mutually enriching relationship. While these relationships are different than standard friendships, each has a specialness that is the highpoint of philia. That being said, I will nonetheless discuss divine philia primarily through the metaphor of God as friend.

---

[55]For more on the conditional and unconditional aspects of divine love, see Peckham, *The Love of God*, chap. 7.

[56]This has become one of the best things about my daughter becoming an adult; our relationship has taken on a friendship aspect that could not rightly be had when she was young.

Philosophically, the roots of friendship first take hold with Aristotle. His book *Nicomachean Ethics* has two chapters devoted to the subject. Aristotle values friendship deeply, suggesting that "it is most necessary for our life" because "no one would choose to live without friends even if he had all the other goods."[57] C. S. Lewis saw friendship differently, suggesting that friendship is "unnecessary, like philosophy, like art, like the universe itself (for God did not need to create). It has no survival value." But Lewis adds that friendship "is one of those things which give value to survival."[58] For Aristotle friendship is an intrinsic good while for Lewis it is instrumentally good. Friendship, however, loses some value when only appreciated instrumentally. Certainly, we would shy away from being friends with someone if we thought the friendship was only of instrumental value to the other person. If philia (friendship, mutuality, communion, intimacy, collegiality) is the telos of eros and agape, it is intrinsically valuable. It is an end that God has paid the highest prices to obtain.

There are, of course, deeper and more intimate friendships as well as more casual and cursory friendships. As I see it, intimate friendships are marked by mutual caring, sharing, and trust. This is not only true of friendships with other people but also of friendship with God. Friends care about each other in special ways—more intensely. Hearing news of a plane crash, we would be moved by the loss of life, but upon learning a friend was one of the victims, the pain would be far more penetrating. It would not be heartache for the "loss of life" but for the loss of a friend. Friends celebrate one another more passionately. Every year at my university a faculty member is recognized for excellence in teaching. I am always happy for the instructor who is recognized, but it becomes a richer personal celebration when the award goes to a friend. When our relationship with God becomes friendship, it becomes more intimate because of the mutuality. God is able to comfort by mourning with those who suffer, and we can comfort God by consoling those whom God loves (2 Cor 1:3-5).

---

[57] Aristotle, *Nicomachean Ethics*, trans. Terence Irwin, 2nd ed. (Indianapolis: Hackett, 1999), 119.
[58] C. S. Lewis, *The Four Loves* (New York: Houghton Mifflin Harcourt, 1960), 71.

Friendship is also marked by sharing. We give to our friends—our belongings, time, and ourselves.[59] Our friendship with God is also marked by giving. We give to God when we devote ourselves and resources to building the kingdom. God's friendship is also marked by giving, when in friendship with God we get God. God is able to be present in ways beyond omnipresence (Mt 18:20; Jn 15:4). But of the three marks of an intimate friendship, mutuality is the most decisive aspect for we care about and share with others even when we cannot trust them. These are aspects of eros (caring) and agape (giving), but only in trust can there be shared mutual intimacy. "Trust is certainly possible, and actual, outside of friendship. But friendship is not possible without trust."[60]

One reason friendship depends on trust is because friends are free. As the saying goes, "you can to pick your friends, but you're stuck with your family." And this is true to a large degree. Some family members feel forced to gather for holidays and celebrations, "but friends choose to be together."[61] Trust is also necessary since there is "no determinate list of things a friend should do, no fixed role specifying just what it is to be a friend"—other than loyalty.[62] The friendship is formed and shaped as it journeys—as it discovers the friend. Philia desires the friend to be free—free to speak or be quiet, free to engage or withdraw. Friendships wither and die when one tries to control the other and their response.[63] Paul Moser uses the term "gracious friendship" to refer to relationships that are reciprocal, interpersonal, not coerced, and never against a person's will.[64] Vacek notes that we will lose our philia relationship with God if we seek to control the divine. When we attempt "to make God be our servant, the one who does our bidding, the one who must answer all our

---

[59] All three of these can happen when we participate in modern life's highest act of friendship—we help a friend move! Or slightly lesser, we drive him to the airport.

[60] Trudy Govier, *Dilemmas of Trust* (Montreal: McGill-Queen's University Press, 1998), 21.

[61] McFague, *Models of God*, 159.

[62] Govier, *Dilemmas of Trust*, 21.

[63] Vacek, *Love, Human and Divine*, 290.

[64] Paul K. Moser, "The Virtue of Friendship with God," in *Religious Faith and Intellectual Virtue*, ed. Laura Frances Callahan and Timothy O'Connor (Oxford: Oxford University Press, 2014), 141.

prayers, the one who must be concerned only for us, we lose *God*."[65]
Likewise, if God seeks to control us, coerce us to do God's bidding, force
us to obey a blueprint plan for our lives, God loses *us*. God perhaps could
gain something in controlling and coercing humans, but would as a
result lose philia. God would lose friends. To gain what God desires,
mutual fellowship of love, God must trust, not as a means to an end but
as an end. Friendship is being in a relationship of faith with someone
you love.

Although talk about "God as friend" is understood metaphorically, it
is, as I have been arguing, the "central part of God's redemptive aim . . .
for humans freely to appropriate and to manifest the power of divine
friendship."[66] Stated more succinctly, "friendship with God is the heart
of Christian life."[67] Biblically, we see the metaphor of God as friend when
Abraham is called "the friend of God" (2 Chron 20:7; Is 41:8; Jas 2:23) and
Moses is said to have spoken with God "face to face, as one speaks to a
friend" (Ex 33:11). Jesus says there is no greater love than to lay down
one's life for a friend and calls the disciples friends because he has entrusted them with everything he received from the Father (Jn 15:13-15).[68]
The hymn "What a Friend We Have in Jesus" misses the mutuality of
friendship. Our friendship with the divine is not merely about giving all
our sins and griefs for Christ to bear or for God to be willing to hear our
prayers. Friendship with God means being coworker, companion, and
colleague. Friendship with God is to share with God in the *missio Dei*.[69]

Our mutual friendship with God extends into cooperation, not only a
mutual love but a mutual mission. Our purpose is to be missional partners
with God, not simply servants or workers commissioned by God. Therefore,
we should understand our love for and relationship with God as friendship
(Jn 15:15). It is not merely the church's mission, not merely God's mission,

---

[65]Vacek, *Love, Human and Divine*, 290.
[66]Moser, "The Virtue of Friendship with God," 141.
[67]Vacek, *Love, Human and Divine*, 319.
[68]Jesus was also called a "friend of tax collectors and sinners" (Mt 11:19).
[69]"It is not the church that has a mission of salvation to fulfill in the world; it is the mission of the
Son and the Spirit through the Father that includes the church." Jürgen Moltmann, *The Church
in the Power of the Spirit: A Contribution to Messianic Ecclesiology* (London: SCM, 1977), 64.

it is our mission. God has invited us to share in this work. I have had jobs that required very hard work, long hours, and poor pay, but it was work I did with friends. I have also had jobs that were not difficult and paid well but where friendships never really developed. I would choose the former over the latter every time. Perhaps this is in part why God's yoke is easy and the burden light (Mt 11:30), because we labor with our friend.

Friendship is based on mutuality, not equality. It is not necessary that friends be equals, only that friends care about one another, share their lives with one another, and are trusting and loyal. We are in no way God's equal, but through grace we can have friendship with the divine. And while we will never be equal with God, we can, through friendship, become more like the divine. Moser speaks about this as "redemptive friendship" in which humans become friends of God in order to share in God's perfect moral character.[70] While friendship is not a means to an end but is an end in itself, it can nonetheless be a benefit.[71] In part, this is what it means to love, to help effect change in the other for the better. Our friendship with the divine is pleasing to God, beneficial to God because fellowship with humanity is what God hopes for and desires.

God labors to complete a good work in us (Phil 1:6), to make us more divine (2 Pet 1:4) and this is why God acts but it is also, in part, why God trusts. Love changes the beloved. But it is not only the beloved who is changed by love—the lover too is changed by acts of love. Edward Vacek and Raymond Brown, each drawing from 1 John, comment on how love affects and perfects both the lover and the beloved. Vacek writes:

> The relation between God and ourselves is mutual and—what is more surprising—mutually perfecting: "Yet if we love one another, God dwells in us, and his love is brought to perfection in us" (1 John 4:12), and further, "Our love is brought to perfection . . . for our relation to this world is just like his" (1 John 4:17). God's love becomes complete in our love, and we become complete in acting as God does to overcome sin and to love God's people (1 John 4:11).[72]

[70]Moser, "The Virtue of Friendship with God," 142-45.
[71]Moser, "The Virtue of Friendship with God," 143.
[72]Vacek, *Love, Human and Divine*, 90.

Brown states that the author of 1 John "dares to make divine indwelling . . . dependent on and expressed by our loving one another." Furthermore, "the love that God reveled in sending His Son to die for us and to give us life reaches perfection . . . when we love one another by that same love (4:12d)." God is love "when He is loving. His love is not *perfectly* what it should be until it begets children in His image who themselves love."[73] God, then, trusts us to perfect divine love by our loving one another. God's own perfection is dependent upon our willingness to love because God has chosen to create a world in which God is vulnerable and the divine plans rely upon our response to God's call. If Vacek and Brown are correct, God's perfect and complete love is only possible if God is a God of faith.

Friendship with God should not be taken lightly, but then again, no friendship should. God depends on us to be a good friend. Philia cannot happen with only one lover since philia is mutual reciprocal love built upon trust. Friendships (special relationships) make a difference in our lives; we are different persons because of the friends we have. God's love for us evolves into faith in us when there is desire for mutual friendship. God wants us to make a difference in the divine life. Our friendship with God gives God hope that the good work God has begun and desires for all creation can and will see its end. Our yes to God fuels divine hope that others can and will eventually respond in love to the love given— respond in faith to faith given.

CONCLUSION

God, as open and relational theists understand, cannot know the future free choices that persons will actually make. God cannot know if we will be faithful or apathetic, loving or self-obsessed, fellow builders or wayward destroyers, or something among the many positions between.

---

[73]Raymond Edward Brown, *The Epistles of John* (New Haven, CT: Yale University Press, 2008), 555. Brown adds, "The objection that God's love, since it comes from Him, must already be perfect independently of human beings is based on a philosophical conception of God quite foreign to Johannine thought. The fact that the Word was with God already before creation implies a God who is outward-looking, for a word needs an audience."

But God still desires, and commands, that we love one another, advance mutuality, and develop into virtuous and Christlike beings. Given that we are persons that God cannot control and yet has chosen to partner with in the development of the kingdom, it is necessary that God not only employ but also embrace faith. God hopes, trusts, and even believes in us to do what God cannot do alone. There may be several reasons for God to have faith in us, but as I have sought to demonstrate in this chapter, love is the ultimate reason.

Because God is love and loving, God seeks mutuality, fellowship, love returned, and love increased. Because God is love and loving, God acts to restore fellowship through sacrifice, justification, and forgiveness. Because God is love and loving, God seeks to lead us all into mature and honest fellowship with the divine, raising us up to be trustworthy—in character and in competence. Love is what motivates God to trust, and faith is what God wills as the telos of this divine and human work.

In examining what it means to be loving—as romantic partner, parent, or friend—we see that faith constitutes an essential element of each of these. The romantic lover cherishes the beloved and longs for her love in return, but because the beloved is free that cannot be forced. Thus, the lover must trust the beloved to requite her love. God as lover not only desires that we return God's love because God enjoys our love but also because it is in our best interest to be lovers of God. Divine eros hopes and trusts that the beloved will freely love because God has loved.

Parental love is self-giving and sacrificial, acting for what is in the best interest of the child. Loving parents adore but also discipline, all in the hope that the child will grow into a mature adult. Loving parents sacrifice their own interests for the good of the child, not merely so the child will be happy, but in order that the child grow into a trustworthy and faithful person.

Divine agape sacrifices for the sake of the beloved, in spite of sins, to restore fellowship and help the child show herself approved. Agape does not mean that God always trusts, but it does mean that God always works toward trust. God may trust when we are genuinely trustworthy, or God may trust in the hope of eliciting and developing us into trustworthy beings. Parents take risks in order to raise upright children, and that will often entail showing faith in the child and "acting on the assumption of their trustworthiness," even if "not actually believing it."[74] God wants us to be worthy of faith and trust and so takes the risk of trusting in order to produce that desired end.

Friends, intimate and mutually enriching, seek the good of the relationship. They love one another because they enjoy one another but also because they enjoy the relationship itself. Couples will weather rough times "for the sake of the marriage," and families will come together because "that's what families do." Friendships are unique, however, for they, more than any other relationship, depend on trust. In relationships there is always at least one who trusts and one who is trusted, but in healthy relationships both serve this roll—both are trusting and trustworthy.[75] Philia is a friendship love, though it extends to all special relationships that seek to complete what eros and agape yearn and work for—relationships of mutuality, communion, and fellowship. God is friend, for God is loyal, authentic, caring, sharing, and trustworthy. Friends accept us, they appreciate and nurture our positive qualities. Friends do not love us for who we might be but for who we are. God too loves us for who we are (Rom 5:8), as strange as that might sound to some, but God also seeks through mutual friendship to develop us into who we can be—Christlike. But all of this takes faith, the kind of faith found among friends.

Love can cause a person to do many foolish things, most notably trusting those who are simply not trustworthy. God is no fool. God knows better than anyone who to trust and when to trust and with what

---

[74]John Bishop, "Trusting Others, Trusting in God, Trusting the World," in *Religious Faith and Intellectual Virtue*, ed. Laura Frances Callahan and Timothy O'Connor (Oxford: Oxford University Press, 2014), 167.

[75]Govier, *Dilemmas of Trust*, 12.

to entrust them. God will rightly distrust at times, perhaps even be suspicious, but God will continually love without end. To love without end means God will never cease to hope in our faithfulness and never cease to work for our trustworthiness. Love leads to trust, and trust is the ground of mutual love.

4

GOD BELIEVES

If you find it hard to believe in me, maybe it
would help you to know that I believe in you.

Oh God!

WHEN PEOPLE SPEAK ABOUT BELIEF as it relates to faith, they express a curious mixture of *belief that* and *belief in*. To be a believer might simply mean one believes *that* God exists—nothing more. The belief about God may be no different than the belief that Saturn has fifty-three moons.[1] Others, however, are intending to say much more than "God exists." On these occasions the believer is saying that she believes *in* God, meaning that she has placed her trust and hope in God.

In this chapter I address how each delineation of belief might apply to God, that is, to God's *belief that* and to God's *belief in*. The first half of the chapter I explore four different ways in which open theists understand God's omniscient beliefs regarding an indeterminate future. From there I discuss how it is that God has *belief in* us. It is not just that God holds beliefs about what is true, but also that God has a confidence in us to become the partners God desires us to be. Finally, I address divine doubt as hesitations that give God pause regarding our faithfulness.

GOD BELIEVES *THAT*

I suggested in chapter two that faith is possible without belief. It is not necessary to mentally affirm that God exists in order to have faith. To

---

[1]This is the latest estimation and does not include what counts as Saturn's rings.

have faith may only require hoping that God exists and acting as if God exists. Applying this standard to divine belief, however, is unnecessary since God both believes and knows we exist. When I speak about my faith it does include *belief that* statements such as, I believe that God exists, that Jesus was resurrected to new life, that God is unrelenting love, that God will pour out justice and right all wrongs, and that I will one day be caught up in the beatific vision. My beliefs here are a mix of statements about the past, present, and future. But what are God's beliefs concerning the past, present, and future? Past and present will not be much of an issue. The important and difficult question concerns humans having libertarian freedom and the future being open to contingent possibilities. Open and relational theists argue that God may not know, for example, whether I will break my diet on Saturday and have a piece of cake at the party or whether I will demonstrate self-control and resist. But what does God believe about my future free choice to eat the cake or not? What does God believe about possibly indeterminate propositions?

In order to address these questions properly, it is necessary to unpack how open theists understand God's relation to the future, specifically to propositions describing contingent future free acts. To do this, I will begin with the problem of omniscience and divine foreknowledge.

The problem. The enduring discussion on divine foreknowledge and human freedom was given new life by Nelson Pike's 1965 essay, "Divine Omniscience and Voluntary Action."[2] Pike's argument is forceful and it has generated considerable literature. In the essay, Pike takes an incompatibilist position, concluding that any philosopher who holds that God is essentially omniscient and that God at no time holds any false beliefs about future human actions "is committed to the view that no human action is voluntary."[3]

The standard argument is that if "God knows X" is true, then "God believes X" is true and "X" is true.[4] That is, if it is the case that God knows

---

[2] Nelson Pike, "Divine Omniscience and Voluntary Action," in *God, Foreknowledge, and Freedom*, ed. John Martin Fischer (Stanford, CA: Stanford University Press, 1989).
[3] Pike, "Divine Omniscience and Voluntary Action," 73.
[4] Pike, "Divine Omniscience and Voluntary Action," 58.

"Blair has 10,000 hairs on his head" then God believes "Blair has 10,000 hairs on his head" and it is true that "Blair has 10,000 hairs on his head." What is included in "X" is the second part of the problem. Pike notes that it is generally held that God's omniscience, which must include no false beliefs, entails that God knows all past, present, and future truths. "X" then is any statement that happens to be true. However, key to this discussion, is whether statements about the future are always either true or false.

I am less interested in Pike's incompatibility argument than in the way he frames omniscience. In particular, the following two claims are crucial:

1. "God existed at $t1$" entails "If A did X at $t2$, God believed at $t1$ that A would do X at $t2$."

2. "God believes X" entails "'X' is true."[5]

With these claims in mind, the basic argument can be simply restated: if in fact God has always believed that Curtis would break his diet on Saturday, then (since God cannot believe something false) Curtis cannot do other than what God has always believed Curtis would do—that is, break his diet.

Open theists have generally agreed with Pike's basic incompatibilist conclusion, that human freedom and exhaustive divine foreknowledge are incompatible. However, open theists have—and rightly, by my lights—sought to demonstrate that the first claim is false, by suggesting that God need not have believed at $t1$ that A would do X at $t2$. That is, regarding my future diet breaking, God may not believe that "Curtis will break his diet Saturday" is either true or false. In this spirit, Pike himself writes, "although I doubt if any Christian theologian would allow that an omniscient being could believe something false, he might claim that a given person could be omniscient although he did not hold beliefs about the outcome of human actions *in advance* of their performance."[6] And this is the approach many open theists take. If this is the case, then my

---

[5]Pike, "Divine Omniscience and Voluntary Action," 63.
[6]Pike, "Divine Omniscience and Voluntary Action," 73.

question is, *what kind of beliefs, if any, does God hold about the future if God can only hold true beliefs?*

Open theism(s) and true propositions. Open theists take very seriously biblical statements that speak of God's authentic and dynamic relationship with humanity. Key tenets are that God regrets (1 Sam 15:10-11, 35), repents (Gen 6:6; Ex 32), relents (Jon 3:10), is surprised (Is 5), tests to know character (Gen 22:12), has changes of mind (Jer 18:8-10), hopes (Jer 26:3; 36:3), and even, quite shockingly, believes falsely ("I thought, 'After she has done all this she will return to me'; but she did not return" [Jer 3:7; see also 3:19-20]).[7] In my estimation, most of these are examples of divine changes of mind. God appears to have believed that it was good to have created the world and to have made Saul king, but these beliefs apparently changed. God appears to have believed that Israel would return, but Israel did not. In light of these passages, how is one to make sense of a standard definition of omniscience that "a person is omniscient just in case he believes all and only true propositions"?[8] In this sense then, God's knowledge is composed of beliefs,[9] but only *true* beliefs, putting God's beliefs in a wholly distinct category from that of human beliefs.[10]

This all leads me to wonder how an open theist might make sense of God's changes of mind. Even if the open theist follows Pike's suggestion and insists that "a given person could be omniscient although he did not

---

[7]I know of no open theist who argues that God holds false beliefs. Most, I imagine, would argue that this statement is meant to convey, quite dramatically, that God desired and even hoped for Israel's return to faithfulness. But Israel did not return, and God's disappointment is expressed in this announcement.

[8]John Martin Fischer, introduction to *God, Foreknowledge, and Freedom*, Stanford Series in Philosophy (Stanford, CA: Stanford University Press, 1989), 4.

[9]Not all philosophers define omniscience as God having only *true beliefs*. William Alston instead claims that God's knowledge is intuitive, "that knowledge of a fact is simply the immediate awareness of that fact" and not a belief about the fact. In this sense God does not hold true beliefs about reality as a kind of psychological state, but God intuits the "actual existence of the object." For more, see William P. Alston, *Divine Nature and Human Language: Essays in Philosophical Theology* (Ithaca, NY: Cornell University Press, 1996), 178-93 (originally published in *Religious Studies* 22 [1987]: 287-306). For a response to Alston, see William Hasker, "Yes, God Has Beliefs!" *Religious Studies* 24, no. 3 (1988): 385-94.

[10]Whatever God believes, God believes it infallibly. The same cannot necessarily be said for human knowledge.

hold beliefs about the outcome of human actions *in advance* of their performance," this does not solve the problem of divine changes of mind.[11] To change one's mind is, it seems, to change what one believes. So again, if much of the future is open, and thus does not yet exist, what can God believe about it?

APPROACHES TO OPEN THEISM AND THE QUESTION OF FUTURE CONTINGENTS

Contingents are statements about future states or events that are possible but not inevitable. So, my example, "Curtis will break his diet on Saturday," is a contingent statement since it is possible I break my diet but not inevitable. The question is, if this statement, "Curtis will break his diet on Saturday by eating a piece of cake," is uttered prior to Saturday, does it have a truth value prior to the event? If it has a truth value, that is, if the proposition can be said to either be true or false, then God should know (and thus believe) its truth value since God is omniscient and believes all and only true propositions. But open theists allow that God may not know ahead of time if I will or will not break my diet since it is a future free act on my part. What do open theists think about the truth value of future contingents of this kind, specifically regarding free choice? Furthermore, if God cannot know what our future free acts will be, what does God think or believe about those future acts? I hope to give plausible answers to both of these questions.

Before I explain the different ways in which open theists understand the truth value of future free contingents, it might be helpful to add an additional example to my possible diet failure—a statement about God's own future free acts. My test passage will be from Exodus 32. After the Israelites cast and bow down to the golden calf, God tells Moses that God intends to consume Israel and make a new nation from him. Moses, however, intercedes on behalf of the people, "And the LORD changed his mind about the disaster that he planned to bring on his

---

[11]Pike, "Divine Omniscience and Voluntary Action," 73.

people" (Ex 32:14).[12] This being the case, what was the truth value of God's statement, "I will consume the people and make a great nation out of Moses"? Furthermore, what did God believe about this statement? Did God believe that the people would in fact be consumed and that a Mosaic nation would be formed, even though neither of these events occurred? Or did God perhaps make the statement knowing it was false? Another possibility is that God made the statement knowing it was neither true nor false. Or maybe there is some other explanation.

Open theists take a few different approaches to the truth status of future contingents, each of which is closely connected to open theism's view on divine omniscience.[13] The approaches can be usefully categorized in terms of the acceptance or rejection of bivalence. Those who accept bivalence insist that all statements, even those about future free contingents, are either true or false (with some caveats), while those who reject bivalence allow that some statements, namely future free contingent statements, are neither true nor false. Bivalence, as expressed by open theists, has three different approaches (I have titled them "standard," "preventative," and "contrarian") while non-bivalence, as I will discuss it, has only one. Space does not allow for a thorough discussion of the merits and challenges of each of these, so I will simply survey the first three and spend the bulk of my time on the non-bivalence approach since this is the one I find most plausible.

Standard bivalence. Standard bivalence affirms that all statements, even future free contingent statements, are either true or false. So, "I will break my diet on Saturday" is now (prior to Saturday) either true or false. Other examples could include that "humans will walk on Mars by 2050,"

---

[12]It should be noted that the NRSV says, "Now let me alone, so that my wrath *may* burn hot against them and I *may* consume them; and of you I will make a great nation" (Ex 32:10 emphasis added). Context denotes that *may* should be read to mean *can* or *will* and not *might* or *perhaps*. The word is not being used to denote possibility but intentionality.

[13]Alan R. Rhoda makes a helpful distinction between "causal openness" and "epistemic openness." Causal openness means that some future state is not already settled. It is possible that X obtain or that X not obtain. Epistemic openness refers to a person's inability to know whether a future state will obtain or not. See Rhoda, "Generic Open Theism and Some Varieties Thereof," *Religious Studies* 44, no. 2 (2008), 225-34.

"Japan will win the 2030 World Cup," or "my great grandchildren will not
be American citizens." These are all statements that are likely to be uncertain for us but are, according to standard bivalence, either currently
(perhaps eternally) true or false. Some open theists affirm standard bivalence by adding that some propositions about the future are logically
impossible even for God to know. This is because God's knowledge is
limited to logically knowable truths. William Hasker defines divine omniscience with such logical impossibilities in mind when he states, "It is
impossible that God should at any time believe what is false, or fail to
know any true proposition such that his knowing that proposition at that
time is *logically possible*."[14] Richard Swinburne advocates something
similar by limiting God's knowledge to propositions that are "logically
possible" for God to entertain.[15] Any open theists who affirm standard
bivalence would seem to be committed to the view that certain propositions about the future are true or false, but are nonetheless unknowable,
even for God, given that they are propositions about future free choices.

Standard bivalence proponents face the challenge of explaining why
true "will" or "will not" propositions about future contingents are beyond
God's ability to know.[16] Why is God unable to know some presently true
statements? There is also the question of how I am free to stay on my diet
this coming Saturday if it was true on Monday that I would break my diet.
This seems to suggest I am somehow able to change the past.

How does the advocate of standard bivalence handle divine mind
changing? Was the statement "God will not consume Israel" a logically
unknowable truth at the time God declared that God would consume
the people of Israel and make a new nation from Moses? It is problematic for God to make a statement about God's own intentions, a

[14]William Hasker, *God, Time, and Knowledge* (Ithaca, NY: Cornell University Press, 1989), 187.
Italics mine. I do not know if Hasker does affirm standard bivalence, but given his definition of
omniscience he could affirm this standard form of bivalence.
[15]Richard Swinburne, *The Coherence of Theism* (Oxford: Clarendon, 1993), 181. As with Hasker, I
do not know if Swinburne holds to standard bivalence, but his definition of omniscience lends
itself to this approach.
[16]Rhoda, "Generic Open Theism and Some Varieties Thereof," 8. Rhoda uses the term "limited
foreknowledge" for what I am calling the open approach to standard bivalence.

statement that is either true or false, and yet God not know if the statement is true or false. It is even more problematic since what God stated was indeed false, according to standard bivalence.[17] Also, what did God believe about the statement, I will consume the people and make a great nation out of Moses if God holds no false beliefs? So, on this view, we get to keep bivalence, but we are left with God not knowing whether certain statements—some about God's own intentions—are currently truth or false.

Preventative bivalence. Preventative bivalence maintains that statements concerning future free contingents are either true or false but also that their truth value can change from true to false or false to true, and even back again. Preventative bivalence builds upon P. T. Geach's "logic of prevention." The logic of prevention looks like this: at $T1$ it is true that P will happen at $T3$, but at $T2$ it is true that P will not happen at $T3$. That is, something happened at $T2$ that *prevented* the (previously true) statement, "at $T1$ it is true that P will happen at $T3$," from obtaining. It is not the case that it was never true that "at $T1$ it is true that P will happen at $T3$"; rather, this statement changed its truth value from true to false. The future, under this view, "is *mutable* in a particular way."[18] It is important that preventative bivalence (or *Geachianism* as it is sometimes called) is understood as saying something much more radical than simply, "*P might*" or "*probably will happen.*" The approach is saying that "*P* can go from being true to being false, and from being false to being true, but must remain false when $T10$ [the time of the actual event] is present or past."[19] In other words, the truth of a proposition at $T1$ concerning a future state at $T10$, can move from being true to false or false to true *until* $T10$ obtains. From that moment on the truth of the proposition is fixed.

Our common language example understood through preventative bivalence might go something like this, "although it was true that I was

---

[17]If Hasker or Swinburne has dealt with such questions I am unaware of their answers.
[18]Patrick Todd, "Geachianism," *Oxford Studies in Philosophy of Religion* 3 (May 2011): 226.
[19]Todd, "Geachianism," 228.

going to break my diet, Phil prevented this from happening by success-fully diverting my attention from the cake, allowing me to regain control."[20] The real force of preventative bivalence over other approaches is demonstrated when particular biblical narratives are examined. For example, the story of Hezekiah's prayer, in which Hezekiah is told by the prophet that his death is imminent (Is 38:1-5). Hezekiah prays for healing, and subsequently has fifteen years added to his life. This "plain reading" neatly fits preventative bivalence since it would mean that it was true that Hezekiah was going to die, but his prayers prevented his death. The truth of, "Put your house in order, because you are going to die; you will not recover" (NIV) changed from being true to false. "Curtis will break his diet" is true, but when I am thankfully distracted by Phil, "Curtis will break his diet" becomes false.

How is it that God might experience preventable truths? For the pre-ventative bivalence theist, it seems that God must experience truths about the future differently than truths concerning the past and present. God knows whatever was or is cannot change for it is now an immutable truth. Certain truths about the future, without being any less true, are pre-ventable, and so God must know these future truths as true and yet po-tentially false because of prevention. God, therefore, must have greater confidence concerning past and present truths than about beliefs re-garding future preventable truths. Geach, however, says, "What God knows is simply what is so,"[21] but what *is so* concerning the past and present is different than what *is so* concerning the future. Thus, can we say that God simply knows what is so, or should we add that God knows what is so but also knows that not everything that is so will necessarily be so?

How might preventative bivalence explain God's change of mind? Perhaps some of God's declarations are immutable truths and others

---

[20]I have reworked an example given by Fischer, Todd, and Tognazzini: "although the plane was going to crash, the pilot prevented the disaster by successfully performing some action that helped him regain control." For more on this approach, see John Martin Fischer, Patrick Todd, and Neal Tognazzini, "Engaging with Pike: God, Freedom, and Time," *Philosophical Papers* 38, no. 2 (2009): 263.
[21]P. T. Geach, "The Future," *New Blackfriars* 54, no. 636 (1973): 214.

preventable. When God said, I will consume the people of Israel and make a new nation from Moses, God must have known this was a preventable truth and therefore God knew it might not happen. But it was a true statement nonetheless. God believed that and thus knew that God would destroy Israel. This was a true statement even though God did not destroy Israel. But this leads to the question, does God ever believe, and therefore know, that some preventable truths will not be prevented?

On this system we again get to keep bivalence, since statements are either true or false. But we are left with the awkward approach that statements are both true and false, though perhaps at different times.

Contrarian bivalence. Contrarian bivalence suggests that definitive statements concerning future free actions are never true prior to the event. This approach, held by those like Greg Boyd and Alan Rhoda, takes the position that "for future contingent X, both 'X will obtain' and 'X will not obtain' are false and, instead, 'X *might and might not* obtain' is true."[22] It is argued that "will" and "will not" statements are contraries, not contradictions, since both can be false. It retains its bivalence in that the falsity of "will" and "will not" are contradicted by "might" or "might not" statements.[23] So the statement "Curtis will break his diet on Saturday" is false, but so too is the statement "Curtis will not break his diet on Saturday." The true statement is, "Curtis might and might not break his diet on Saturday."

Contrarian bivalence has much going for it. First, like both standard bivalence and preventative bivalence, there is no clear departure from formal logic (unlike, as we will see, with non-bivalence). There is also the fact that when someone says, "Curtis will break his diet on Saturday," what he intends to say is that "it is exceedingly likely" or that "there is a very strong *probability* Curtis will break his diet on Saturday." The primary challenge to contrarian bivalence is defending why "will" and

---

[22]Rhoda, "Generic Open Theism and Some Varieties Thereof," 11.

[23]There is question concerning just how "will" and "will not" statements are merely contrary. For a careful defense of contrarian bivalence, or simply "bivalence," for these writers, see Alan R. Rhoda, Gregory A. Boyd, and Thomas G. Belt, "Open Theism, Omniscience, and the Nature of the Future," *Faith and Philosophy* 23 (2006): 432–59.

"will not" statements are not contradictories, but contraries. For example, assume that the statement "I will break my diet on Saturday" is false and yet, I do in fact break my diet on Saturday. It feels rather odd to be able to say that even though I broke my diet the statement uttered on Monday, "I will break my diet on Saturday" was false. Perhaps it would be easier to accept this if we were to eliminate all *will* and *will not* statements and simply spoke in terms of *might* and *might not*.

Back to divine mind changing. The advocate of contrarian bivalence does not think that God believed that God actually would consume the people of Israel and make a new nation from Moses. That would mean God believed something false. But it also means God did not believe God would not consume the people of Israel. What God must have believed and thus knew was that "I might and might not consume the people of Israel" even though it was stated in "I will" language. Contrarian bivalence also raises questions about God authentically having changes of mind when "I will consume the people of Israel" actually means "I might and might not consume the people of Israel." This reads more like God finally makes up God's mind, not that God changes God's mind. That may be the case, and if so, we should stop speaking about divine mind changing.

Non-bivalence. Non-bivalence holds that future free contingent statements are neither true nor false until the event occurs, or the future event is inevitable. This view preserves omniscience because God still believes every true proposition and God does not believe any false proposition. The future is genuinely open since statements about future free contingents are subject to being either true or false once the event occurs. This is the approach I find most plausible in affirming human freedom as well as understanding God's true beliefs concerning an open future.

Non-bivalence, like the other views discussed, has its criticisms, primarily that it breaks with classical bivalent logic. For many it seems odd that a statement like, "Curtis will break his diet on Saturday" is neither true nor false—especially when Curtis will do one or the other. But the non-bivalentist holds that while either may become true, neither is true prior to the event.

If the statement "Curtis will break his diet on Saturday" is neither true nor false and God only believes what is true, what can we say God believes about the statement? As I see it, God believes and thus knows one of the statements is more likely to be true than the other. That is, God knows neither statement about my diet breaking is true or false, but God believes (and thus knows) the potential truth of each statement. My example will be rather wooden, but I think it will illuminate nonetheless. Let's say, on Monday there is a 70 percent chance I will stay on my diet Saturday and a 30 percent chance I break my diet. God has a belief about my future free actions, but God's belief is actually about the present. God knows our history, our wants and desires, our dispositions and abilities. This is how God knows the chances of my being successful. Now, as the week goes on and all the varying factors come into play, that percentage will likely change. Perhaps I had a frustrating week at work and it turns out the host of the party, unbeknownst to me, has bought my favorite cake specifically with me in mind. And so, by Friday the percentages may have changed to a 10 percent chance I stay on my diet and a 90 percent chance I break it. The non-bivalence open theist could say that God's beliefs about my staying on or breaking my diet have changed but that at no time did God believe something false. It was true on Monday that I had a 70 percent chance of staying on my diet, while on Friday it was true that I had a 10 percent chance of staying on my diet. God believed one thing on Monday and something other on Friday. God has a change of mind yet all the while believing only what is true.

This sort of discussion is not all that different from how we ourselves approach future free contingents. When I believe "I will stay on my diet Saturday," it is not that I believe this statement is now and has always been true. I am saying something to the effect of, "based on my current mindset I believe I will have the fortitude to stay on my diet this Saturday." But if I do not stay on my diet I will not be shocked to learn my statement on Monday was false. When a non-bivalentist says "Curtis will break his diet on Saturday," he is not saying he believes this statement is true, that it is already settled, but is saying that given everything he knows about Curtis and the situation it is most likely the diet will be broken.

Let's apply non-bivalence to God's statement, "I will consume Israel and make a new nation of Moses." God did not utter something false even though God did not consume Israel. But God also did not utter something true since Israel was not consumed. But like the other approaches, this is not without its oddness. Not only does it sound odd to say God made a declarative statement that was neither true nor false, but it raises the question of how it can be said that God had a change of mind. The simplest explanation is that what God uttered was a kind of shorthand that expressed both God's inclinations and the likelihood of those inclinations happening. Given the situation of Israel erecting the golden calf and God's own state of anger, disappointment, frustration, and even doubt about Israel being a faithful covenant partner, God willed to start again with Moses. Unless we want to say God lied we need to see the statement as conditional, given that God did not wipe out Israel and begin again with Moses. What God communicated to Moses was that it was true that there was an 80 percent (for argument's sake) likelihood that God would consume Israel. But this also means it was just as true that there was a 20 percent likelihood that God would not consume Israel.

This is not all that different from how we communicate. If I were to say to my students that because of low test grades we were going to start having pop quizzes each week, I would be speaking the truth of my intentions. And yet, if there was a reason for me to not follow through on this, say the test results were wrong due to a faulty key or perhaps the quizzes were taking too much of class time, it would be incorrect to say I lied about the pop quizzes. It would be that I changed my mind because new information became available to me. It seems the very same can be said about God. God intended to consume Israel and begin anew with Moses. God believed and thus knew this was likely, and yet, the less likely alternative transpired, apparently due to Moses' intervention, and thus God had a change of mind.

God then has beliefs that concern our futures. God's beliefs are entirely about what is presently true, but these truths concern our future free actions. I suggest this is how we can say that God believes that you or I will be faithful in trying times. This is how God can believe that we will be trustworthy. This is how God can believe that I will be faithful, even though I fail. God has many beliefs that concern the future (huge understatement), but all of these are beliefs concerning present truths.

Conclusion. I have tried to explain how we might understand God's beliefs, specifically propositional beliefs regarding future free contingents. While I have not sought to demonstrate that the three variations of bivalence are wrong, I do believe that the non-bivalence approach makes the most sense. In this way it can be said that God holds true beliefs about the past and present that can be translated in ways that reveal God's mental states about future free contingents. This means God holds beliefs about our future states, our choices, and their outcomes. And what God believes about that future state is what God knows about the likelihood of that state obtaining. Pike's incompatibilist argument does hold, but it is no trouble since what God believes to be true or false does not include future free contingents since they are neither true nor false.

I also demonstrated how this applies to divine changes of mind. The Exodus 32 example shows how God could make a statement about God's own future action and yet it be contingent and even mutable since what God revealed was the likelihood of that future event. Many examples of God's change of mind could be discussed, but the key point is that we can discuss these changes of mind in a way that does not diminish God's omniscience and also allows for real human freedom.[24]

Understood in this way, we can speak about God believing some individuals or groups to be basically trustworthy even though they may still let God down. Likewise, God may believe and thus know that some are not trustworthy, but God can still hope that their character will

---

[24]Here is an incomplete list: Ex 32:14; Deut 9:13-29; 1 Kings 21:21-29; 1 Chron 21:15; 2 Chron 12:5-8; Jer 3:7; 26:2-3; Ezek 4:9-15; Amos 7:1-6; Jon 3:10.

change and mature. All this holds while God can still be said to be omniscient since God believes only and all true propositions.

BELIEF *IN*

To *believe in* something is rather different than *believing that* something
is true. Said another way, believing some statement is true is different
than believing someone is true. We can believe in a great number of
things. We can believe in persons, organizations, laws, policies, proverbs,
and even ourselves.[25] It makes just as much sense to say, "I believe in God"
as it does to say, "I believe in being prompt." However, *believe in* means
something rather different in these two uses.

Defining what it means to *believe in* is difficult for a few reasons: first,
because of the many ways in which we use the phrase. To *believe in* may
mean nothing more than believing that something exists ("I believe in
aliens"). It may mean that one is exceedingly confident in the abilities
of another ("You will set a new personal best in this race—I believe in
you"). *Belief in* can express approval of a plan or policy ("I believe in
the ACA") or allegiance to an organization ("I believe in the GOP"). To
believe in can equate to hope in ("Even though they are down by six
runs I believe in my Dodgers"). All of these examples (except mere acceptance of something's existence) express a positive attitude and confidence concerning the object of belief. But *belief in* can also express a
feeling or attitude too difficult to define as mere mental assent, trust, or
even hope. A mother whose son has been sentenced to life in prison
can say to him, "I believe in you." This pronouncement need not express
that she believes he is innocent or that she trusts him in any particular
way. But it also means more than she simply hopes he will change his
ways. Belief in her son is less than trust, but more than hope. As I see
it, at its most basic, this is an expression of her belief in her son's worth.
"I believe in you" can say more than "I love you," though I am not entirely sure how. To follow "I love you" with "and I believe in you" says

---

[25]J. J. MacIntosh, "Belief-In," *Mind*, New Series, 79, no. 315 (1970), 395-407.

exceedingly more than "I love you" alone. But just what it means is hard to locate.

To believe in someone is to experience a particular positive attitude or outlook about the person. While all instances of *belief in* cannot be reduced down to a single basic sentiment, they all express a positive mindset about the object of belief. It may be a very robust positive attitude about the person's abilities or character—or it may be a very thin positive feeling about one's being or potential. To *believe in* is always to express a positive attitude. I cannot believe in the dishonesty of my students or in the duplicity of my congresswoman. I may *believe that* my students are being dishonest or *believe that* my congresswoman is duplicitous, but this is rather different than believing in those vices.[26]

Many cases of *belief in* assume some *belief that*. To believe *in* God is to believe *that* God exists, *that* God is good. To believe in democracy is to believe that democracy is a better means of governing. But *belief in* need not always express some *belief that*. If a friend is off to an audition, I may rightly express that I believe in him, even though I do not believe that he will get the part. In this way *belief in* is a kind of approval, a form of support for my friend. To believe in, as I will be using the term, is to say, minimally, "I value what this or these persons can offer or become."[27] Again, *belief in* can mean much more than this, but I struggle to see how it can mean less.

God's belief in. There is a persistent worry I have about discussing God's belief in persons, specific and general. I fear that this idea conjures up notions of self-help books filled with questionable psychology and sermons spouting dubious theology. I offer my treatment of God's belief in us not so we might "believe in ourselves." While I do not think self-help books are inherently wrong or that theology should never make people feel good about themselves, I am suggesting something quite different. I am proposing that it makes sense to consider that God actually believes in those who God partners with, and perhaps even those who

[26]H. H. Price, "Belief 'In' and Belief 'That,'" *Religious Studies* 1, no. 1 (1965), 5-27.
[27]MacIntosh, "Belief-In," 398.

refuse God's invitation. God as a being of maximal love and we, co-creators[28] in whom God has chosen to share power with, leads me to conclude that God actually believes in us. It's not just that God believes we will or might be faithful partners, but that God believes in us as partners. Even though this is not about self-help or the power of positive thinking, I nonetheless imagine that a theology of divine *belief in* can and should lead to positive changes in how we think and live.

As I hinted at above, God's belief in us is not the same as God's trust. I will say more about God's trust in the next chapter, but it might be helpful to differentiate *belief in* from trust at the start. Even though *belief in* and trust can be used synonymously, they are not always the same since I can trust someone without believing in him, and I can, likewise, believe in someone without trusting him. When I step onto any kind of public transportation I am trusting the driver or pilot to do their very best to get me to my destination safely. However, without knowing the driver or pilot I cannot say I believe in him or her. *Belief in*, minimally, requires we know something about a person's character or abilities. Perhaps I know something about, and thus, believe in the hiring policies and pilot review practices of an airline. But without knowing the pilot I cannot say I believe in her even though I am trusting her to get me to the next airport safely. Likewise, I can believe in someone without trusting him. If I am watching a key baseball game on television and it is the bottom of the ninth and the home team puts in their closing pitcher, I can rightly say, "I believe in him, he'll get us the win."[29] But I am not trusting this person with anything. I have not risked, nor have I chosen this pitcher, so it cannot be said I am actually trusting him in any way.[30]

---

[28]By "co-creator" I mean that we cooperate with God's work of bringing about the kingdom. We are not passive spectators but active participants sharing in God's work (Jn 14:12; 1 Cor 3:9).

[29]To trust another person is to willfully enter into some kind of risk. It cannot be said I am trusting the pitcher because I had no say in whether he pitches or not. Furthermore, if he lost the game and I met him one day I could not rightly say he betrayed me by breaking trust. I can say he disappointed me, but not that he morally failed me.

[30]Maybe it could become an instance of trust if I make a sizable bet on the pitcher. By my willfully choosing to risk money on this pitcher's ability I act in trust that he will get the necessary outs. Even as stated, though, if I do trust the pitcher, it is the thinnest of trust.

In what follows I will offer examples and ways in which God might believe in us. Some of the examples may be cases in which belief in leads to trust, but it is not necessary that it does.[31]

As argued earlier, because God is a being of maximum love, God seeks a way to trust us, but more than that, love leads God to believe in us. It would be concerning to find a parent who claimed to deeply love her child but refused to say she believed in the child. The parent may have significant doubts about the child's abilities or maturity, but she would still tout her belief in the child. What this will mean to each parent is again, hard to say, but at the very least it will express an encouragement that a statement of love alone may not. Belief in, for God at least, is an extension of love. God values what we are capable of doing and who we can become. But this is something God loves about us now, not later. "God believes in us" means God values us—as us. God values what we have to offer, actually and potentially, as being other than God—beings free to embrace God's love and invitation. God loves us both in spite of our being sinful but also because of our being valuable. God believes in us because we have potential. We may be fallen, but we are not hopeless!

Pragmatic relationships are dependent upon one's belief that the other will be responsible. Intimate relationships, however, are dependent upon one's belief in the other. Relationships are never perfect. They include missteps and misgivings. There may be love but also doubts. The commitment to remain in the relationship shows, minimally, that there is belief in the relationship partner.

While belief in the other might be the bare minimum for a relationship, it can also express a maximal aspect of a relationship. The success of a several decades-long marriage might have the couple not only confess their love for one another but also their deep and unyielding belief in the other. A child may hear a parent regularly say that he loves her, but the

---

[31]I disagree with Robert Audi when he argues that "you cannot have faith in a person you do not trust." Faith or belief in a person can be prior to trust and minimally mean one believes that the person can one day be trustworthy. Audi, "Belief, Faith, and Acceptance," in *Ethics of Belief: Essays in Tribute to D. Z. Phillips*, ed. Eugene Thomas Long and Patrick Horn (Dordrecht: Springer, 2008), 95.

relationship enters a new dimension when the parent says he believes in her. I have heard so many times that God loves me that I am almost numb to the real meaning and depth of this statement. Maybe it is time to say that part of God's love for us is God's belief in us, God's longing to have faith in and with us.

Both the Old Testament and New Testament contain examples of God taking a chance on an individual. God called on these persons and acted in ways that lead me to think God believed in them. In some cases, God's belief in leads to trust in. I hold that the following examples are not simply acts of trust, but acts motived by God's belief in the person.

Abraham. The "binding of Isaac" is one of several stories in which God tests, either individually or corporately, the character of those for whom God has future plans.[32] In this difficult story Abraham is commanded to bind and sacrifice Isaac (Gen 22). At its conclusion the angel of the Lord stops Abraham from killing his son and declares, "Now I know that you fear God" (Gen 22:12). There are many interpretations of this story, many of them, understandably, trying to protect God's moral character.[33] I will, however, follow the traditional Christian reading that identifies this event as God testing Abraham's faithfulness (Heb 11:17-19).

A plain reading of the story leads the reader to suppose that God did not know what Abraham would do or the extent of his character, so the test was necessary. Once God saw that Abraham would not spare his son God believed Abraham feared God. Prior to the event, again given the nature of an open future, God did not know and thus did not believe that Abraham would show himself trustworthy. Yet while God could not *believe that* Abraham would be obedient, it seems to me that God

---

[32]Other texts of God's testing in order to know character include 2 Chron 32:31, in which "God left him [Hezekiah] to himself, in order to test him and to know all that was in his heart," and Deut 8:2, "God has led you these forty years in the wilderness, in order to humble you, testing you to know what was in your heart, whether or not you would keep his commandments."

[33]For alternative readings, see Terence E. Fretheim, "God, Abraham, and the Abuse of Isaac," *Word & World* 15, no. 1 (1995): 49. Howard Moltz concludes, "Abraham, in questioning the promise, had undermined his role as covenantal partner; and God, uncertain of Abraham's devotion, had devised a brutal test. It is in this loss of trust and thereafter in the absence of any genuine 'I-Thou' relationship, that the sadness of the story lies" (68). See "God and Abraham in the Binding of Isaac," *Journal for the Study of the Old Testament* 96 (December 2001): 59-69.

nonetheless *believed in* Abraham. If God did not have reason to believe that Abraham might be faithful there would be little reason for God to administer such a horrific test. Most often, by testing persons, God demonstrates an expectation of their success. God not only hopes they will succeed but believes they will likely prove faithful and worthy of God's trust.[34] But this all rides on God's beliefs *that*. I'd like to add that God also believed *in* Abraham.

The horror of this story suggests, even requires, we advance that God believed in Abraham. God must have surely known the torment such a command would cause. It is hard enough for a parent to know that they will soon lose their child to illness, but to be commanded to kill your own child is simply too grim to fathom.[35] What would make the narrative even worse is picturing God as indifferent about Abraham's success. If God simply needs information about Abraham, and nothing more, this narrative feels especially cruel. But what if when God tests Abraham God hopes he succeeds? What if we assume that God values who Abraham is and what he can offer? If that is the case, then we can say God believed in Abraham. God chose Abraham because God believed in him even if God was unable to believe (or disbelieve) that Abraham would be obedient.

The "binding" is often told and considered from Abraham's vantage. We seek to know his thoughts and beliefs. We contemplate the emotional state of this soon-to-be "knight of faith." However, we should also ponder God's thoughts and contemplate God's emotional state, deliberating if God too is a "knight of faith." Is it possible that God wrestled with the horror of such a demand? God needed to know the character of the person to whom God would entrust the progeny who would become

---

[34] I am not suggesting that in every case of testing God believes or expects that the ones tested will succeed. For example, Exodus 16:4 states that God will test whether Israel will follow God's instructions. Yet this test is in the midst of a complaining Israel. Israel at this point is giving God very little to believe about their obedience and character, and so it is unlikely that, given the context of this situation, God expected or believed it was likely Israel would pass the test.

[35] Søren Kierkegaard's classic, *Fear and Trembling*, dramatically explores the anxiety and dread Abraham might have experienced. See *Fear and Trembling*, trans. Alastair Hannay (London: Penguin, 1985).

the nation that would bless all the nations. If God is a God of love, then such a horrific demand could only be placed upon an individual that God believed had a character to likely rise to the occasion. God needed to know if Abraham was trustworthy, a person who feared God.[36] But if God believed him to be easily swayed, a person of unthinking blind subservience, then to demand the life of his child is neither the act of an omnisophic being nor is Abraham's obedience a virtue. No, it would be unwise and even cruel for God to demand such a thing if God did not believe in Abraham. God believed in the person of Abraham. Perhaps it was Abraham's faith (Gen 12:1-9) that motivated God's faith (Gen 22).[37]

Abraham had shown himself to be a fitting partner for God. Earlier Abraham had shown himself willing to stand toe to toe with God questioning divine plans for the destruction of Sodom and Gomorrah (Gen 18:16-33).[38] When God made known plans to destroy the cities, Abraham took the risky path of challenging God's justice in possibly destroying the righteous with the wicked. God, it seems, was not looking for a person who would timidly or recklessly obey but a person of integrity and contemplation. Given Abraham's past experiences with God, there was reason to believe Abraham was the right person. God's belief in Abraham was justified by Abraham's prior acts.

However, Abraham had given God reason to question. Over the twenty-five-year journey Abraham had shown both faith and faithlessness. Abraham had twice passed off Sarah as his sister, had fathered a son through Hagar, and was impatient with God's timing about an heir.

---

[36]Fear in this sense should not be associated with anxiety or terror. Rather, in this context to fear God is to have "a deep reverential regard for God's character as a provider." Paul Borgman, Genesis: The Story We Haven't Heard (Downers Grove, IL: InterVarsity Press, 2001), 96. Borgman notes that Abraham had demonstrated fear many times given his wife's attractiveness. But does God want Abraham to simply replace one fear with another? Unlikely. The progression of God and Abraham's relationship was leading toward "friendship, not fear; dedication, not dread; trust, not trembling" (97).

[37]Thanks to K. C. Richardson for helping me work out this section.

[38]The text states that "Abraham stood before the LORD," and this is surely a place of subordination. Some early texts read, "The LORD stood before Abraham," possibly revealing a part of Abraham's character (a heart for justice?) not revealed earlier. For more information, see Walter Brueggemann, Genesis, Interpretation: A Bible Commentary for Teaching and Preaching (Atlanta: John Knox, 1982), 168.

This certainly justifies God's need and motivation for the test. But I would also add that God had reason to believe in Abraham and hope he would be faithful. Yet in the end, God could not know until the binding of Isaac. Perhaps it could be said that just as Abraham believed and thus said to Isaac, "God will provide"; God too believed and said, "Abraham will provide."

Job. Once again, we are presented with a story that stretches the limits of our ability to think of what a good God would do or allow to happen. I am not interested in the historicity of this story; in fact I firmly hold that this is a moment of poetic narrative. I am interested, however, in what the narrative communicates about God, our predicament, and what we might hope for. Again, I will make my comments based on a plain reading of this story.

This story as well is set up as a testing narrative. Yet from there, the stories are quite different. While Abraham had a history of faith mixed with failures, Job was "blameless and upright." Job feared God and turned away from evil (Job 1:1). And while Isaac was spared, Job's children and servants were not so fortunate. The Abraham story is neatly and quickly wrapped up once Abraham raises the blade; Isaac is saved, and a proper sacrifice provided. Yet the modern reader (and possibly the ancient as well) is left feeling less than satisfied at the conclusion of Job's narrative with God's speeches that hardly comfort Job or justify his suffering.[39] Finally, Abraham was tested so God could learn if he was trustworthy, yet it is suggested that Job is trustworthy, and this is why he is tested. It seems that testing took place in both situations in order for God to learn, but perhaps the level of faith God has in Job is greater than that of Abraham prior to the testing. God tests Abraham to learn if he is trustworthy, but tests Job because he is trustworthy. Among these differences, however, I think the story of Job, like that of Abraham, portrays God as one who believes in these persons and hopes they are faithful. The book

---

[39]Fretheim humorously, yet rightly, adds that these speeches would "provoke a failing grade in most pastoral counseling classes." Terence E. Fretheim, *God and World in the Old Testament* (Nashville: Abingdon, 2005), 220.

does not set out to teach that God believes in Job; it is not an argument found in the book but a necessary assumption, certainly for this drama to make sense.

The divine-human relationship is a theme that arises in the prologue. Job 1:6-12 sets up the remainder of the book when God calls the heavenly court together, most especially the satan.[40] When the satan informs God that he has been going "to and fro on the earth," looking for one to accuse, God asks him to consider Job. God proudly confesses that there is none like him for he is "a blameless and upright man who fears God and turns away from evil" (Job 1:8).[41] It is at this point that God is forced to ponder a question asked by the satan, "Does Job fear God for nothing?" What kind of relationship does God have with Job?[42] Like all relationships, in happy times there is comfort, but what about times of trial? What happens to the relationship if one fails to be true to the partnership? God knows Job is faithful when God is faithful, but God does not know the depths of Job's faithfulness in times of despair? Does God know if Job will remain faithful, even if God is not? Perhaps this is the internal dialogue we are to assume God having as God ponders the satan's question. It is ultimately a question posed to both God and, through the author, to all humanity. Is Job (and anyone else in relation to God) faithful only for the blessings?

Terrence Fretheim raises questions concerning this story being read as a testing story. Theologically it is problematic because the test would not be given in order for God to learn something about Job and thus deepen the divine-human relationship. Rather, Job would be tested to prove something to the satan. Fretheim believes "testing" is a poor term to be used if Job's trials are to settle a "celestial dispute."[43] However, if the question posed by the satan and the ensuing "wager" are understood as literary

---

[40]In the book of Job, the accuser (the satan) is this character's job and title, and thus it is inappropriate to capitalize "satan" as if it were a proper name. For further information concerning the satan in the book of Job, see David J. A. Clines, *Job 1–20*, Word Biblical Commentary 17 (Dallas: Word, 1989), 18-23.

[41]The reader is first informed of Job's righteousness in 1:1, even before God's statement.

[42]J. Gerald Janzen, *Job*, Interpretation: A Bible Commentary for Teaching and Preaching (Atlanta: John Knox, 1985), 38-42.

[43]Fretheim, *God and World in the Old Testament*, 223-24.

devices, then this might be read as a test of their relationship. It must be remembered that because this is poetic literature, it allows great freedom in the imagery. Fretheim notes that the portrayal of God is troublesome and raises the question of whether God can be trusted. But, given that the book is a "didactic tale," perhaps we might also ask, "Can God trust Job?"[44]

From a relational theology, this story is demonstrating the narrator's belief that God did not know exactly how Job would respond. With the fact of Job's faithfulness as an open question and with God accepting the accuser's challenge, it should nonetheless be obvious that this story only makes sense if God believes in Job—not only that Job will succeed and prove trustworthy, but also that God believes in the person and character of Job. If the story requires the reader to presuppose God believes in Job, can the reader then also conclude that when she is tested that God also has faith in her?

I am not offering a theodicy. I do not have a full-fledged theory of divine goodness in light of sentient suffering. But if Job is meant, in part, to offer some comfort to the afflicted, then we should consider God's belief in Job. Just as it is comforting to know that God is not causing your pain and suffering due to some sin, would it not also be comforting to affirm that God believes in you? In the midst of trials, I not only want to see my suffering come to an end, I want to show that I have persevered. I want to show that anyone who believed in me was right to have such faith. It is one thing to assert that our personal sins are not the cause of our suffering. It is a greater good to know that in the midst of suffering God believes in us—not just that God loves us, but that God believes in us. It is encouraging that even in spite of our success being an open question, God still believes in us—hopes for us, affirms us, and values us.

In the movie *Trading Places*, we see two very rich brothers, Mortimer and Randolph Duke, argue over whether it is nature or nurture that determines whether a person can rise above life's tragedies. In order to settle the dispute, they destroy a wealthy man's life, Louis Winthrope, by

---

[44]Fretheim, *God and World in the Old Testament*, 220-21.

taking away his job, house, fiancée, and reputation. Even worse, he had to watch as everything that was his be given to a con artist, Billy Ray Valentine, who was seemingly not deserving of such riches or accolades. These brothers, however, did not care anything about Winthrope. In fact, the bet was a mere dollar. It would be hard enough knowing my life was turned upside down over a $1 million bet, but one dollar?! There are key parallels between *Trading Places* and the story of Job, but I'd like to believe that God is not like the Duke brothers. God doesn't enter into the wager to simply prove a point to the satan. The Duke brothers care nothing about the people they hurt or help, such people are but pawns in their game. But if we are to retain some semblance of divine goodness, we need to think that God enters this wager believing in Job. The question at hand is not God's reputation but God's hope and belief in Job.

God trusted that Job would not "curse God, and die" (Job 2:9) and that Job would continue in relationship with God in spite of the trials, that is, continue a relationship that is hardly idyllic. Yet among questions and doubts, both Job and God pursue the relationship. God believes that Job will remain faithful in spite of Job living in a world that often harms the faithful and rewards the unjust. It is a world all the more tiresome given God's hiddenness and silence. The irony of the story is that Job does not know of God's belief and confidence in him.[45] If only Job had known of the heavenly dialogue between God and the satan, perhaps he would have faced the trials with greater confidence knowing God believed in him. Perhaps this is an aspect of the message of Job. If only we could know that God believes in us when we face such heartbreaks and tragedies. I have no final answer on why the world is filled with the evils it is, but I am sure that if we knew that God not only hoped that we would triumph but also believed in us, perhaps such trials could be overcome with even greater success.

Peter and Paul. Unlike Abraham and Job, the New Testament does not suggest Peter or Paul were tested by God. There is no event divinely

[45]John E. Hartley, *The Book of Job*, The New International Commentary on the Old Testament (Grand Rapids: Eerdmans, 1988), 183.

orchestrated, as far as we are told, in order for God to specifically learn something about their character. Instead, each man was called to give up his present life and follow the leading of God and the example of Christ. Peter and Paul may not have been wealthy men, but each had vocations that would be sidetracked if they were to heed God's call. To heed the call meant real sacrifice for each, so there is reason to think either could have eschewed the call or retreated from it when difficulties and persecutions arose. Again, I am not suggesting these narratives set out to teach that God acted in faith when calling these men, but given my thesis that God is a God who trusts, I am considering the callings of these men through this hermeneutic. I hold that these narratives suggest that God believed in Peter and in Paul prior to their callings, especially given that Paul "had been entrusted with the gospel for the uncircumcised, just as Peter had been entrusted with the gospel for the circumcised" (Gal 2:7).

The Gospels speak of Peter more than any other apostle, but the portrayals are not always flattering. Peter is an impetuous character, quick to act and speak, sometimes to his detriment. Nonetheless Jesus believes in him enough to include him in his inner circle. Jesus trusts Peter to not speak of his transfiguration "until after the Son of Man has been raised from the dead" (Mt 17:9). But it is not simply Jesus who trusts and believes in Peter, God the Father too believes in Peter.

In Matthew chapter 16 Jesus asks his disciples "Who do people say that the Son of Man is?" and then asks, "But who do you say that I am?" (Mt 16:13, 15) Peter answers, "You are the Messiah, the Son of the living God" (Mt 16:16). Peter is praised by Jesus but not for being especially clever or insightful; no, Peter is blessed because God has seen fit to entrust him with the truth of Jesus' full identity and nature as well as the keys to the kingdom (Mt 16:18-19). Despite Peter's flaws and shortcomings, God has chosen him to hold an office and play a role that is "unique and unrepeatable . . . in the foundation of the church."[46] If Peter's future faithfulness is indeterminable and the church's foundation, in part, contingent on that

---

[46]Eugene M. Boring and Fred B. Craddock, *The People's New Testament Commentary* (Louisville, KY: Westminster John Knox, 2004), 69.

future faithfulness, then God must be acting in faith. God believes in Peter, trusting and hoping that he will be an unyielding foundation. This does not mean that God is wholly and utterly dependent upon Peter; God surely has countless ways to deal with our failings. It does mean, however, God was willing to risk and entrust Peter with this role.

Perhaps even more radical than God's belief in Peter is God's belief in Paul. To entrust the gospel for the uncircumcised to Paul is, to say the least, an unconventional choice. Paul was a Jew with a clear "love for his ancestral race (Rom 9:3)."[47] Not just a Jew but, as Paul said, he "belonged to the strictest sect of our religion and lived as a Pharisee" (Acts 26:5), a group who had deep separatist and exclusivist tendencies.[48] Paul witnessed, was likely responsible, and certainty approved of Stephen's execution (Acts 7:58; 8:1). While this comparison is a bit unfair, by today's thinking, Paul would have been seen as a radicalized fundamentalist who approved and even engaged in activities meant to terrorize Christians (Acts 9:1-2). God's belief in Paul must have been great since God chose a man who worked to kill the very church he would be an instrument in birthing. God chose a man from the strictest separatist group to share the gospel to the Gentiles.

Paul's acceptance of Christ's call may have been swift and immediate (Acts 9:18-20), but this does not mean his personal transformation did not take time.[49] Paul himself speaks of maturing in Christ (1 Cor 13:10-12; Phil 3:15), and there is no reason to think Paul excluded himself from this process. He had particular character traits that justified God's

---

[47]Ralph P. Martin and Carl N. Toney, *New Testament Foundations: An Introduction for Students* (Eugene, OR: Cascade, 2018), 379.

[48]Martin and Toney, *New Testament Foundations*, 66.

[49]In Gal 1:15-16, Paul says that he was "set apart" and called before his birth. Nancy Elizabeth Bedford suggests that understanding this as a statement about predestination is a less compelling reading than seeing it as a statement about vocation. The statement is about God's call being one of grace, and by moving it to Paul's birth no one would confuse God's calling with the idea that Paul earned his vocation. See Nancy Elizabeth Bedford, *Galatians* (Louisville, KY: Westminster John Knox, 2016), 34. Even if Paul meant this literally, this does not mean God preordained Paul's entire life or that God ordained and approved of Paul's persecution of Christians prior to the Damascus road experience. In fact, this may even further show God's faith, in that God set him apart for this ministry, and despite Paul's persecution of Christians, God still risked entrusting him with this calling.

calling (courageous, persistent, uncompromising), but he also had traits and demonstrated behaviors that highlighted God's call as an act of faith. Despite the presence of the Holy Spirit in Paul's life and ministry, he made mistakes. Paul comes across as inflexible in his falling out with Barnabas over giving John Mark a second chance (Acts 15:36-41). Furthermore, Paul's youthful approval of violence toward those who understood God, Christ, and obedience differently than he reappears when he wishes those who promote circumcision would "castrate themselves" (Gal 5:12).[50] Despite Paul's shortcomings, God believed in Paul and saw fit to entrust him, and all Christians, with the ministry of reconciliation (2 Cor 5:19).

God's choosing and using of both Peter and Paul gives us reason to marvel at God's influence and ability to use the foolish, weak, low, and despised—"things that are not"—to accomplish God's purposes (1 Cor 1:27-28). God is also to be praised and we are to rightly boast that we worship a God who believes in us and is willing to entrust impetuous fishermen, stubborn Pharisees, and the many of us in between to partner with God in the advancement of the kingdom.

Conclusion. I suspect that many will find it too radical an idea to think that God believes in humanity, corporate and individual. We are quite versed in passages that rightly speak of human failings. There is no doubt that all have sinned and fallen short of God's glory (Rom 3:23). We are sinners, enemies of God deserving of wrath (Rom 5:8-10). But the truth of our sinfulness does not eliminate God's belief in us any more than sin utterly destroys the *imago Dei*. As argued in chapter three, God's love for us is an actual love *for* us, motivated in part by God recognizing our value. Christ died for us because we were lost, but not a lost cause. God is not willing to give up on us and this mission. God's belief in us began at creation. It did not end with the fall, nor does it end with our

---

[50]It is understood that Paul's statement here is more complex than simply wishing harm on those who have a different theology. Paul was right to oppose those preaching and performing circumcision but to so crudely wish castration upon them hardly measures up to Paul's own standards of excellence in Phil 4:8. For more on Gal 5:12 see Craig S. Keener, *Galatians*, New Cambridge Bible Commentary (Cambridge: Cambridge University Press, 2018), 241-43.

persistent falls, but it continues today and every day. We do not earn
God's love and we cannot earn salvation, but we can earn God's trust,
which begins with God's belief in us. Just as good parents do not require
their children to earn their love, even though children can earn their
trust, God's love for us will never increase or decrease, but God's trust is
more dynamic and situational (more on this in chap. 5, "God Trusts").
The life of the Christian includes many points in which God's faith may
increase—most notable is our conversion. With every Eucharistic meal,
moral victory, and confession of sin, God's faith and belief in us grows
because in those moments we demonstrate our fidelity to God and commitment to the kingdom.

There are good arguments that the chances of personal success increase when a person believes (whether this is real or perceived) others
have confidence and trust in them.[51] Parents have a moral obligation to
affirm and build up their children. This does not mean false praise or
insincere accolades but genuine affirmation for the child as *their* child.
A fortiori, it is imperative that we consider the value of God's belief in
us. I can say this no better than Paul, "If God is for us, who is against
us?" (Rom 8:31).

GOD DOUBTS

Norman Lamm writes, "In a word, God had, or has, faith in man; He
trusts him, believes in him. . . . But faith always implies the possibility of
doubt. If, then, God has faith in man, he can also doubt man."[52] Given
what was said above, that God has only true beliefs and that God believes
every proposition that is true, can we say that God has doubts? God

---

[51]To trust another person who is believed to be less than trustworthy for the purposes of affecting
the trustee's behavior is known as "therapeutic trust." For more on therapeutic trust and related
issues, see Philip Pettit, "The Cunning of Trust," *Philosophy and Public Affairs* 24, no. 3 (1995),
202-25; Trudy Govier, *Dilemmas of Trust* (Montreal: McGill-Queen's University Press, 1998),
170-74; Victoria McGeer, "Trust, Hope, and Empowerment," *Australasian Journal of Philosophy*
86, no. 2 (2008), 237-54; Victoria McGeer and Philip Pettit, "The Empowering Theory of Trust,"
in *The Philosophy of Trust*, ed. Paul Faulkner and Thomas Simpson (Oxford: Oxford University
Press, 2017), 14-34.
[52]Norman Lamm, *Faith and Doubt: Studies in Traditional Jewish Thought* (New York: KTAV, 1971), 32.

surely has no doubts about what is true. But because, according to open theism, much of the future is open to contingent choice, God may have real doubts about our future choices based on our past and present choices and intentions. Divine doubt, it seems, occurs when God knows the likelihood of some desired state is less than 50 percent. God may desire that I spend several weekends building homes in Mexico. But God may also know it is only 25 percent likely that I will commit to this. So, God rightly doubts I will build houses in Mexico. Now, I may have a change of heart and surprise God, but at this point God rightly doubts, but does not disbelieve, I will work in Mexico.[53]

Doubt is pervasive because faith requires we act even when the truth of the situation is still unsettled. This is why doubt and faith are natural elements of relationship. Relationships in which both parties have power always entail doubts and questions about the other's use of that power.[54] If God is relational and has beliefs and trust, then it is necessary to discuss God having doubts.

It is an attitude of suspicion, not mere doubt, that colors how one sees another and ultimately taints the relationship.[55] While doubt makes faith and trust necessary, suspicion, cynicism, and despair hold one back from exercising faith and trust. God certainly questions and hesitates concerning divine action and human response, but this form of doubt never brings an end to divine faith. In fact, it makes faith that much more necessary. Romans 8:38-39 reveals that God's doubt is never utterly destructive concerning relationships because God is ever seeking fellowship and communion, and that is why nothing can separate us from the love of God, not even God's own doubts.

God does not doubt or lose faith by simply being unsure of what we will do, for if that were the case, God would never trust. Doubt, on God's part, results from what we have done and what God knows of our

---

[53]Maybe God has more faith than that since I have built several homes in Mexico with Amor Ministries.
[54]Trudy Govier, *Social Trust and Human Communities* (Montreal: McGill-Queen's University Press, 1997), 86.
[55]Govier, *Social Trust and Human Communities*, 238.

character. It is a doubt born out of knowledge not ignorance. God doubts whether we will continue the relationship after we have betrayed God and trusted in another. The narratives of God's doubt are all born out of betrayals, which lead God to question the future of the relationship's intimacy and fellowship. Humans hurt the relationship when they turn from the one who is trustworthy and faithful and instead trust in the idols of power and self-glory.

Narratives of divine doubt and lament. The Bible contains stories of God's belief, trust, hope, and love but there are also stories that depict God's questioning and doubting. While no language plainly states, "God doubted," these narratives reveal the actions of one who is unsure about the faithfulness of another.

We can see evidence of divine doubt in the laments attributed to God. A lamentation is an expression of sorrow, grief, or regret—a complaint or voice of distress.[56] In these various Scriptures God suffers, certainly only as God can, because of the unfaithfulness of God's relational partners.[57] The statements convey not only God's suffering but also concerns and doubts regarding the state of the relationship due to Israel's unfaithfulness and increasing rejection of God and God's plans.[58] God rhetorically asks what to do in light of such unfaithfulness. While always seeking to preserve the relationship, God expresses doubts about its future health.

The flood. The flood epic communicates not only the depths of human sin but also the passion of God.[59] The narrative portrays the divine as a God with high hopes for a creation that refuses to be what God intends. Instead of order and good will, creation is fraught with rebellion, disobedience, chaos, and disorder. The sin and disorder reach a point that

---

[56]"Lament," in *The Eerdmans Bible Dictionary*, ed. Allen C. Myers (Grand Rapids: Eerdmans, 1987), 638.

[57]In this section I will focus on how some of these lamentations can be understood as expressions of divine doubt, but they are certainly more than that. God's lamentations are expressions of suffering, but divine suffering is not always suffering *due to* the other. God also suffers *with* the other and *for* the other. For more on divine suffering, see Terrence Fretheim, *The Suffering of God: An Old Testament Perspective* (Philadelphia: Fortress, 1984), 107-48.

[58]Fretheim, *The Suffering God*, 108-9.

[59]Like the book of Job, I am not assuming this narrative is historic; it is likely mytho-poetic. Nonetheless, the narrative can reveal important truths about God's relationship to a sinful world.

causes God to lament having made such a world because "the LORD saw that the wickedness of humankind was great in the earth, and that every inclination of the thoughts of their hearts was only evil continually" (Gen 6:5-6). While this statement reveals much concerning God's thinking and nature, it cannot be overlooked that this also expresses God's doubts concerning the future goodness of creation. God laments having ever created such a world, perhaps in ways I can imagine a parent mourning having a child who has become a mass murderer. God is a troubled parent grieving over the kind of being humanity has become.[60] God's beliefs concerning creation have changed. God now has doubts, that is, God's beliefs about the creation's future have changed significantly. Where God had once believed the creation to be "very good," God now believes creation to be wicked and evil.

While it was God's will that creation follow the pattern of order announced for it, creation was not compelled to obey. God trusted humanity would follow the plan set before it, but humanity refused. God's doubt leads to the decree that God is sorry humankind was made. In rather dramatic fashion, God is looking back and wishing that humankind had never been created. Can this statement be understood in any way other than expressing reservation, concern, and doubt about humanity's future faithfulness? God's looking back has caused God to have grave doubts about the world's future.

In the end, the epic reveals more than God's doubt and judgment. It also reveals God's hope and faith, for humankind. The epic ends with God seeking to restore after judgment, to heal after the effects of evil. The story is not about the flood per se but about a "change wrought in God which makes possible a new beginning for creation."[61] And new beginnings bring with them faith that past failures might be avoided and hope for a renewed relationship. God "will not let the rebellion of humankind

---

[60]Brueggemann, *Genesis*, 76. Brueggemann explains that the language used denotes God's grief, not anger. The word used is the same as found in Gen 3:16 when the woman is cursed with increased pain. Once again, we see this story depicted in parental terms and not in that of a distant or unrelated manufacturer. God is creator in the way a mother "creates" her child.

[61]Brueggemann, *Genesis*, 73.

sway him away from his grand dream for creation."[62] The flood epic then is a story in part about God's doubts concerning humankind, doubts that are overcome by faith, even if it is a cautious faith.

Hosea. The book of Hosea is a metaphoric treatment of Hosea's family life[63] that reveals the inner life and ponderings of God's relationship with Israel.[64] This book reveals that God is angry, frustrated, feels betrayed, and yet God is still hopeful Israel will return. By discussing the sins of Israel through the metaphor of a marriage, the book highlights God's doubts concerning the future of the relationship. God's cry reveals that God is hesitant and undecided concerning Israel's love:

> What shall I do with you, O Ephraim?
>   What shall I do with you, O Judah?
> Your love is like a morning cloud,
>   like the dew that goes away early. (Hos 6:4)

God is depicted as conflicted: "Now I will uncover her shame in the sight of her lovers, and no one shall rescue her out of my hand" (Hos 2:10), but hopeful, "And I will take you for my wife forever; I will take you for my wife in righteousness and in justice, in steadfast love, and in mercy" (Hos 2:19). It is the juxtaposition that reveals the nature of faith and doubt. God is suffering because of Israel's acts of betrayal. God is doubtful, but God ultimately has faith in a reunion.

Jeremiah. The prophet Jeremiah also uses imagery of marriage, and even divorce, in communicating divine doubt regarding Judah.[65] The question is asked, "How can I pardon you? Your children have forsaken me, and have sworn by those who are no gods. . . . Shall I not punish

---

[62]Brueggemann, *Genesis*, 81. Brueggemann just as easily could have said that God will not allow the rebellion to sway God away from *belief in* creation without changing the meaning of the statement.

[63]While it is not always clear what pertains to God's relationship with Israel and what concerns Hosea's marriage with Gomer, Hosea's marriage is certainly to be understood as symbolically "participating in the realities of God's life." See Fretheim, *The Suffering of God*, 155-56.

[64]Abraham J. Heschel, *The Prophets*, 2 vols. (Peabody, MA: Prince Press, 1962), 1:47. Heschel notes that it is interesting that the focus of the book is not on the apostasy of the people but rather on the pathos of the abandoned God.

[65]Jer 3:8, "She saw that for all the adulteries of the faithless one, Israel, I had sent her away with a decree of divorce; yet her false sister Judah did not fear, but she too went and played the whore."

them for these things?" (Jer 5:7a, 9a; see also Jer 9:9). God had once be-
lieved Judah would return after following other gods: "And I thought,
'After she has done all this she will return to me'; but she did not return"
(Jer 3:7). Again,

> And I thought you would call me, My Father,
>   and would not turn from following me.
> Instead, as a faithless wife leaves her husband,
>   so you have been faithless to me, O house of Israel (Jer 3:19b-20)

These passages show a God who "suffers the effects of the broken relationship at multiple levels of intimacy."[66] Can we expect anything less
than God having reservations, concerns, and doubts about continuing
the relationship?

While such statements and questions reveal God's hurt, frustration,
and doubt, they do not constitute God's being unfaithful. In the end, God
never forsakes those who have betrayed God but is ever hopeful of their
return. As Fretheim states, while passages such as these indicate that,
"God is indeed a vulnerable God, touched and affected in the deepest
possible way by what people have done to the relationship, God's grief
does not entail being emotionally overwhelmed or embittered by the
barrage of rejection."[67] It could also be said that God is not overwhelmed
by doubt and questions. This is the faith of God made real—God overcomes doubts that come with being in relationship with fallible beings.
God remains faithful—trustworthy and trusting. Summing up Jewish
history, Gerald Shapiro says, "Jews doubt God, and God doubts the
Jews—it's been part of our relationship since the golden calf."[68] While
Shapiro is being a bit tongue in cheek, he nonetheless has captured the
logical effects when humans mistrust: divine doubt.

While I used the testing narratives of Abraham and Job as stories of
God's *belief in*, these could also be read to suggest God had doubts. It
is possible that the testing stories reveal not only a God of faith but also

---

[66]Fretheim, *The Suffering of God*, 116.
[67]Fretheim, *The Suffering of God*, 111.
[68]Gerald Shapiro, *Bad Jews and Other Stories* (Cambridge: Zoland Books, 1999), 185.

a God of doubt. This is the approach Howard Moltz takes regarding these two particular narratives. "I would suggest God had come to doubt Abraham, as in time he would come to doubt Job. And as he would soon test Abraham, so eventually he would test Job (Job 2.5-6)."[69] While I believe these stories are better understood as suggesting that God believes in these persons, it is important to remember that doubt often accompanies faith. It makes sense to speak of the testing stories as God having both faith and doubt because "where there is doubt, faith has its reason for being. Clearly faith is not needed where certainty supposedly exists, but only in situations where doubt is possible, even present."[70]

It is no more human than divine to doubt, it is simply the nature of relationship. Where there is trust, there is doubt born of risk. Yet where there is doubt there is fertile ground for trust. "Man's trust in and doubt of *Elohim* is paralleled by God's trust in and doubt of the *tzellem Elohim*, the divine image. Wherever a relationship involves at least one free agent, there are immediately implied the possibilities of both faith and doubt in that free agent."[71]

CONCLUSION

A significant aspect of faith is belief, not only propositional beliefs that are true or false, but also positive attitudinal beliefs that are expressed in terms of *belief in* another. I have sought to demonstrate how God might *believe that* and *believe in* given the openness of the future.

I have also argued that God has doubts, that because of our weaknesses and failings God has reason to be conflicted and hesitant in the ways in which God partners with us. It is not that God simply disbelieves we will be faithful or successful in some endeavor. That would mean God knows we will fail. Doubt means that the question is open, that God has

[69]Moltz, "God and Abraham in the Binding of Isaac," 67.
[70]Daniel Taylor, *The Myth of Certainty: The Reflective Christian and the Risk of Commitment* (Downers Grove, IL: InterVarsity Press, 1992), 81.
[71]Lamm, *Faith and Doubt*, 32.

reason to vacillate, but in faith, God takes a risk. Doubt, even divine doubt, is not the end of faith but is that which makes faith necessary.

Finally, I discussed the difficult notion of God believing in us. This kind of belief is difficult to define, but I have suggested that, minimally, it is valuing the person for who the person is, may become, and can offer. While God knows our sinfulness thoroughly, God also knows and believes in our value and potential. This is a status not independent of God but founded on being *image Dei*. Certainly there are many blinded by their own self-worth who fail to recognize the depth and damage of their sin. But there are others who are blinded by their own self-deprecation who fail to recognize what God sees—our value and potential as co-creators and faithful followers of Christ.

I will end with these words regarding the Christian religion written over a century ago by New Testament scholar Henry Nash:

> Its entire body of doctrines—Creation, the Incarnation, the Atonement, the Trinity—moves toward this end. Saving faith in God is the faith whereby man takes fast hold on God's faith in humanity. To be believed in is the deepest necessity of our nature, and the conviction God believes in humanity and puts his whole being and purpose at the back of his belief is the very marrow of Christianity. . . . The whole mass and body of Christian dogma comes to the conclusion that God believes in humanity.[72]

---

[72]Henry S. Nash, *Ethics and Revelation* (New York: Macmillan, 1899), 6-7, 149.

5

GOD TRUSTS

Oh the bravery of God in trusting us!

OSWALD CHAMBERS, *MY UTMOST FOR HIS HIGHEST*

ANYONE WHO IS WHOLLY SELF-SUFFICIENT has no need for trust. If one has power to control all in existence—to govern the movement of each particle of the universe and sovereignly decree every human affair—that being has neither trust nor mistrust. This, however, is not the picture of God I see in Scripture. Nor is this a God who can be relational in any meaningful way. As I have already argued God has chosen to be dependent upon this created world. God has chosen to be dependent in order to bring about goods otherwise impossible, goods such as reciprocal love, cooperation, and perhaps, even trust itself. These goods should not be seen as necessary evils that are the result of a world gone bad but as valuable states God sought to give ground. Just as one plus one has always equaled two and squares have always been four-sided, so too love, cooperation, and trust have always been valuable. In creating a world in which these goods could become realized, God became dependent on others by means of willfully choosing to trust. As discussed in chapter three, a person who loves fully is a person who trusts, and God is no exception. Every relational metaphor we have for God (parent, spouse, friend, even king) involves trust.

It is certainly true that God desires our faith and trust. God acts to elicit trust (Ex 14:31), commands trust (Jn 14:1), punishes failures to trust

(Num 20:12), praises trust (Jer 17:7), comforts those who trust (Is 28:16), protects those who trust (Nah 1:7), and even acts so others will trust God's prophets (Ex 19:9). God desires our trust because God desires our love.

To be in steadfast relationship with God it is indispensable that we trust God. I am not suggesting that God refuses to be in relationship until we trust, which hardly seems loving, but that *intimate personal relationship* is dependent upon trust. Without trust I can most assuredly fear God, act to satisfy God's demands, or somehow escape wrath. Without trust I can submit to divine regulations and commands, but I may be left wondering if God will repay obedience with misery. Trust, though, fosters intimacy. Trust overcomes temptations to be guarded, suspicious or fearful of vulnerability.

This all makes sense from a human perspective, for we are by nature limited and dependent, but to speak of God having trust may be a whole other story. Some will surely be uncomfortable or unnerved by the idea of God having trust: God's being vulnerable and dependent undermines the very notion of what it means to be God. The divine, they suggest, is by nature independent (totally free), above the risks associated with relationship, the frustrations of being failed, and the pains of rejection. For others, however, the notion of God's vulnerability and dependence means that God is with us, sharing our pains and joys as we work together. As God invites us to trust in God's promises, God also seeks to trust us. The divine project means God longs to find those worthy of divine trust, individually and collectively. As creative relational love, God's very nature moves God to trust humanity, especially those proven trustworthy, but also to take a risk on those who have not. Those who commit and are obedient love and trust God, but we must not forget that God's giving of the gospel reveals, at least in part, God's love and trust in all humanity. As long as we speak of God as relational, we must speak of God as trusting, for trust is a necessary element and logical consequent of each of these.

As stated in chapter two, it is best to understand our trust of objects metaphorically. Even if we can literally trust objects like a seatbelt or medication, there is no doubt that objects do not trust us in return. There can be no reciprocal trust between a child and her toy or between a man and his car. This is because the relationship is not between persons— subject to subject. To suggest that we can trust God but that God cannot trust us is to flirt with the objectification of God—to think and speak about God not as a personal being but as object. Furthermore, as seen in chapter three, relationships of love are more than having one who trusts and one who is trusted. Mature and dynamic relationships of love mean each is trusting, not merely trustworthy. Said another way, "Both, fidelity and trust, exist in the actual realm of relationship between two persons. Only in the full actuality of such a relationship can one be both loyal and trusting."[1] Humans are called to trust God as a loyal and faithful covenant partner. Likewise, humans are called to be faithful and loyal to God. Reason requires that we include God as a trustor and not merely trustee if God is authentically loving and relational. Just as relationships require not just one party but both to be faithful, relationships require not just one but both to be trusting.

In this chapter I lay out my case for God's trust in humanity, general and particular. My point here is not that God is always perfectly vindicated in these divine acts of trust (though I see no reason to think God is never vindicated in trusting), but that God is a genuine lover, which means God willingly takes a chance on us, with us, and for us.

PRELUDE TO DIVINE TRUST

Trust is personal, volitional, and risky. In fact, trust is a subcategory class of situations involving risk—risk that depends on the performance, character, and intentions of another.[2] Russell Hardin explains, "To say we trust you means we believe you have the right intentions towards us and that you are competent to do what we trust you to do."[3] Trudy Govier

---

[1] Martin Buber, *Two Types of Faith*, trans. Norman Goldhawk (New York: Harper, 1961), 29.

[2] James Samuel Coleman, *Foundations of Social Theory* (Cambridge, MA: Belknap Press of Harvard University Press, 1990), 91.

[3] Russell Hardin, *Trust* (Malden, MA: Polity Press, 2006), 17.

offers, "Trust is in essence an attitude of positive expectation about other people, a sense that they are basically well intentioned and unlikely to harm us. . . . A trustworthy person is one who has both good intentions and reasonable competence."[4] These depictions of trust all point to the fact that trust involves at least two parties, one or both of whom risks injury or disappointment by exposing needs and vulnerabilities in the belief or hope that the other will act in such a way that the trustor's best interests are cared for.

It should be clear that simply because we use the word *trust* in conveying an idea or sentiment that does not mean we are actually trusting. If I have a guest who stays the night and upon seeing him the next morning say, "I trust you slept well," I am hardly expressing an actual act or attitude of trust. I may be saying I assume you slept well or even that I hope you slept well, but there is no risk in this event. There is also no object of trust other than trusting my own imagination or assessment of the sleeping area. Likewise, a football coach might explain why he called for a particular play saying, "I trusted the other team to run a blitz." An army general may strategize while "trusting that the enemy will attack from the west." In each of these examples the word trust is used but is better understood to mean something closer to believe, assume, or plan.

Trust can be conceived in a variety of ways. Some approach trust as a means of self-interest, what might be called a "benefits model." Trust is given, withheld, or sought based on perceived benefits. It is assessed by a risk versus reward analysis. This does not mean trust in these cases is necessarily selfish, it simply means that trust, in this sense, is strictly a means to an end.

Another approach conceives of trust as a moral category. Morality demands that in right circumstances we trust, not simply that we be trustworthy, but also that we trust well. There are moral questions tied to being both trustee and trustor. It seems that we are to be trustworthy persons to both acquaintance and stranger. But the more difficult

---

[4]Trudy Govier, *Dilemmas of Trust* (Montreal: McGill-Queen's University Press, 1998), 6.

question is, who am I obligated to trust? Who am I to trust, not merely for my benefit but for theirs? Minimally it is anyone we are in relationship with. As discussed in chapter three, friends, family, and coworkers certainly deserve our trust in the right circumstances. Where there is mechanical reliance or, even worse, suspicion where there should be trust, relationships are in danger. This is true whether it be God or a human who fails to trust.

Trust, as I argued, is volitional. Trust is much more than mere reliance. It is not uncommon, for example, to see statements made about an infant trusting his mother for care.[5] Ethicist Daryl Koehn says, regarding a child's reliance on its mother, "At some point we are driven to trust other persons . . . the young, the old and the vulnerable have no option but to trust a helpmate, a parent, or fellow citizen to show them good will."[6] But this seems to be something less than trust, even if there is reliance. If trust is to be praiseworthy or foolish, it must have a mindful and volitional component.[7] This is why trust is reliance plus. God's trust as well is not mere reliance, but a willful and mindful event.

In relationships of love trust is a vital element of the relationship's health. Relationships are built upon trust, for when we trust, "we are more likely to let ourselves be vulnerable to others, to allow ourselves to depend on others, to cooperate, to confide."[8] Thus, there is no intimacy without trust. In fact, I don't believe I am overstepping when I say intimacy is trust. In business, trust is a means to an end, but in loving intimate relationships, trust is the means *and* ends. I trust for the sake of relationship and I commit to the relationship in order to increase the trust.

---

[5]Annette Baier, for example, discusses infant trust mostly as a means of discussing trust in relation to disproportionate power. See Baier, *Moral Prejudices: Essays on Ethics* (Cambridge, MA: Harvard University Press, 1994), 105-7.

[6]Daryl Koehn, *Rethinking Feminist Ethics: Care, Trust and Empathy* (New York: Routledge, 1998), 82.

[7]Although trusting is an act of the will, being trusted is not always a choice. That is, we do not always get to choose who or what is in our care. Thus, while other drivers on the road have not necessarily chosen to trust me, they are nonetheless reliant on my skill and conscientiousness as a driver. By law and by God I have been entrusted with the care of those around me.

[8]Govier, *Dilemmas of Trust*, 6.

Trust can be defined as *willful actions that reflect the belief or hope that one will seek my good will and not exploit my vulnerabilities*. As I demonstrate, God has willfully chosen to trust humans (corporately and individually) for both God's and our own good. If God loves the world and has given humanity the power to act over against God's plans and desires, then God has entrusted us with God's own good will. God has no use for a benefits model of trust. God trusts out of, and for the purposes of, love and fellowship. If God seeks loving relationships with humanity (Jn 14:23), has given the church the ministry of reconciliation (2 Cor 5:18), and has chosen to partner with us on this grand divine project (Phil 2:13), then trust is necessary. By entering into relationships of mutual trust with autonomous beings, God not only risks rejection but also risks many of God's plans being thwarted. Trust, then, is a risk even for the divine. If God desires cooperation, then God cannot exist risk free. Even God cannot have the proverbial cake and eat it too. To be a God of love is to be a God of trust.

One final caveat. Divine trust is more analogous to the trust between humans than the trust we place in God. It is the object of trust that brings about uncertainty for God. Our trust in God is never misplaced. It is never the case that we put our trust in God only to have mistakenly chosen an untrustworthy deity.[9] However, because humans are fallible in matters of knowledge and morals, we often mistrust, mistakenly place trust in those who are ultimately not trustworthy. We put trust in individuals and communities that let us down by seeking their own interests above our own interests. We have trusted these persons to be concerned about our welfare, but because of our limitations and sin, our trust is at times wrongly given.[10]

God's trust is not wholly immune to such situations. Given that humans are free but fallible, God's acts of trust are sometimes frustrated. Not that it was wrong for God to trust, in fact it was the right thing to do.

---

[9]This is not to suggest that faith and trust is never a risk for Christians. It is impossible to escape the fact that we may simply be wrong on many levels.

[10]Govier discusses varying accounts of disturbing cases of trust. One such example is of prisoners in Nazi death camps who, in hopes of survival, trusted and entrusted themselves to Nazi guards only to face betrayal. For more information, see *Dilemmas of Trust*, 13.

Nonetheless, the object of God's faith was regrettably unfaithful. Because humans are prone to selfishness and their knowledge of future free choices is limited, it is a risk to trust another person, for us and for God. It is safe to say, however, that God never mistakenly puts trust in essentially untrustworthy persons or groups. Nor does God entrust persons with tasks they are wholly unable to accomplish. Yet because of free will and sin, it is still possible for us to fail to meet God's standards and requirements and thus cause God to lose faith.

God does not trust every individual in every situation even though God loves every individual in all situations. Love is born out of God's essential nature, while trust is an act born out of God's freedom and wisdom. Divine trusting means that God engages in risk, and even though God wisely chooses who and when to trust, that trust at times ends badly. God, however, never trusts wrongly. God trusts abundantly, but never foolishly.

TRUST AND OMNIPOTENCE

> O wonderful omnipotence and love! A human being cannot bear this that his "creations" should be something directly over against him; they should be nothing, and therefore he calls them "creations" with contempt. But God, who creates out of nothing, who almightily takes from nothing and says "Be!" lovingly adds, "Be something even over against me." Wonderful love, even his omnipotence is under the power of love! . . . Thus love which made a human being to be something (for omnipotence let him come into being, but love let him come into being over against God), lovingly demands something of him. Now that is the reciprocal relation.[11]

Kierkegaard sums up wonderfully the tension between God's power and love. God has called us into being while at the same time calling us to become something other than God. God has the power to call us into

---

[11]Søren Kierkegaard, *Samlede Vaerker*, ed. A. B. Drachmann, J. L. Heiberg, and H. O. Lang, trans. Paul Sponheim, 15 vols. (Copenhagen: Guldendals, 1901–1936), 10:132-33. Cf. Søren Kierkegaard, *Christian Discourses*, ed. and trans. Howard v. Hong and Edna H. Hong (Princeton, NJ: Princeton University Press, 1997), 127-28; quoted in Paul R. Sponheim, *Speaking of God: Relational Theology* (Philadelphia: Fortress, 1988), 42.

being but not the power to make us become the being God ultimately desires. For this, loving patience and trust, among other virtues, is necessary. In order for us to be what God desires, we must be empowered with the ability to act over and against God because that is the only way our ability to act for and with God can be of real worth. Control must be given up and autonomy gifted. God has not begrudgingly given us power to act over and against God's self but has done so out of love and for love. In fact, the giving of power *is* love.

If one is to love, then one must trust for love entails the other has power over you. To love another is to be dependent upon the power of the one who is loved. In many of her works, Dorothee Soelle has reflected on love as shared power.[12] This is a power that is not aggressive, it does not dominate or control, but a power that, out of love, gives itself away. Many Christians are fascinated by God's power. God is praised and worshipped for mighty acts. Yet what is often missed is that God's most powerful act is to give power away. One should not think of this in ratios, however, that somehow the more power God gives the more loving God is. It is no more necessary for God to give away all power in order to be all loving than it is for us to give all power to our children out of a love for them. This is sentimentality without wisdom. Under Soelle's model, God's love is dependent upon God's power, for without power to share there is no love to give. Conversely, power without love means God is the puppeteer who controls risk free, from above and beyond in the safety that absolute power provides. The point is not about the amount of power God has, the issue is that authentic love never seeks to hold on to power. "Power can do everything but the most important thing: it cannot control love."[13] God, the source of all power, gives us power to act in partnership with God, but this comes with the risk that we may act over and against God.

---

[12]For example, see Dorothee Soelle, *Theology for Skeptics: Reflections on God* (Minneapolis: Fortress, 1995), 14; *The Silent Cry: Mysticism and Resistance* (Minneapolis: Fortress, 2001), 128; *Of War and Love* (Maryknoll, NY: Orbis, 1983), 40.

[13]Philip Yancey, *Disappointment with God: Three Questions No One Asks Aloud* (Grand Rapids: Zondervan, 1988), 75.

Out of love and a desire for authentic relationship, God shares power with creation, gives up absolute control, and trusts that God's partner(s) will be faithful to the relationship and its objectives. By sharing power, God can then do more than act; God can *interact*.[14] For God to include humanity as co-creators, authors, and partners in the creation of goods, God acts with us and not simply upon us. Love means power is shared, and those who have power have power over us. Power is not truly power if there is not the capacity to oppose. But if relationship is the desired end, then trust is necessary.

The power shared is the power to work with or work against. Because God created a world in which a loving relationship is the goal, God cannot control all that happens because love is not controllable. Love requires, and even is, the giving of power, a clear act of trust. When we trust we give power to the other to decide our welfare. It is also a restraint of power in relation to time and history. For God to act in trust is to be patient, to wait, to have faith in spite of mistakes on the part of the trusted. Trust gives powers to the trusted and requires the one who trusts to delay accounting and be willing to wait and see.[15]

It could be said, "The advantage of creating free beings is that they are thereby nearer to the Divine nature, and can respond to God's love and interact with him in a way not possible to necessitated beings."[16] The giving of power and thus a divine nature means that God cannot have the only say in the relationship. God may command but God cannot control—at least not if God desires our faith and not mere compliance. It must be remembered that "each party to the relationship must give up any monopoly on power for the sake of the relationship. . . . Any relationship of integrity will entail a sharing of power."[17] Partnership means that neither party is totally free or independent of the other.

---

[14]Anna Case-Winters, *God's Power: Traditional Understandings and Contemporary Challenges* (Louisville, KY: Westminster John Knox, 1990), 143.

[15]Annette C. Baier, *Trust: The Tanner Lectures on Human Values*, https://tannerlectures.utah.edu/_documents/a-to-z/b/baier92.pdf (accessed February 28, 2018), 117.

[16]Keith Ward, *Rational Theology and the Creativity of God* (New York: Pilgrim Press, 1982), 82.

[17]Terence E. Fretheim, *The Suffering of God: An Old Testament Perspective* (Philadelphia: Fortress, 1984), 36.

Christianity has never been shy about paradox, and that is good because God's power is paradoxically limited by giving freedom, which enables us to relate with God or turn from God. At the same time, God's giving away of power results in the creation of even greater total power, for freedom given is love, and love is nothing less than power and strength. In short, the idiom, "there is power in numbers" is true. When we love God, we return our power to its source. Here relationship hits its highest note as power is given, power is returned, love is perfected.

Giving power can be seen as risky behavior, but when it is done—in love—it is not merely being risky but faithful. The surrendering of power and control may seem like a reckless move on God's part. But it equally looks foolish for a God of immeasurable power to willingly become human, weak, and vulnerable, even unto death. Are Reinhold Niebuhr's sentiments correct that humans, because of sin, are to be loved but never trusted?[18] I certainly hope not. There simply is no relationship without trust. Radical responses see God giving up power to the point of dying on the cross. Paradoxically, God's strength was revealed in pure weakness. God's ways in matters of love and human freedom are mysterious. This is not a dodge; I have made the argument for trust, but in the end, I cannot say I fully understand God's love or God's acts of trust. In fact, I often do not understand my own acts of love and trust. I take comfort in the words of Isaiah:

> For my thoughts are not your thoughts,
>   nor are your ways my ways, says the LORD.
> For as the heavens are higher than the earth,
>   so are my ways higher than your ways
>   and my thoughts than your thoughts. (Is 55:8-9)

And yet, while God's ways are too often a mystery, I trust them nonetheless. I believe there is reason to trust God's love and wisdom, including God's willingness to trust this creation and, even more radically, to trust me.

---

[18]Stanley J. Grenz and Roger E. Olson, *20th-Century Theology: God and the World in a Transitional Age* (Downers Grove, IL: InterVarsity Press, 1992), 103.

This all leads to the question at hand: Does God, especially as open and relational theists understand, act in trust? I see no other answer but *yes*. If God's power is either necessarily or voluntarily limited, and if God partners with those who are also beings of power, no matter how diminished in comparison, and if there is an open-ended aim for those who share power with God, then trust is necessary. To will something while at the same time give others the power to frustrate that will is to enter into relations of trust. It is absolutely necessary that God trust the creation and those who have been created for relationship. To speak of God as one who risks and is in relationship infers a God who enters into relationships of trust. God is vulnerable, hoping, and trusting that creation—God's relationship partners—will not ultimately fail but will do and become what God desires us to be.

PARTNERSHIP AND TRUST

Understandings of divine power hold weighty control over our greater theological positions. "If two philosophers were to take as their presuppositions the contrasting ideas of 'Power is God's greatest attribute' and 'Restraint of power is God's greatest attribute,' and each followed those assumptions down their respective paths, those two thinkers would never meet again. One assumption leads to determinism. The other leads to covenant."[19] Concerning power and control, it is not a question of how God partners but whether God partners at all. Partnering is not possible without self-limitation and a sharing of power. God's power is necessarily restrained, limited, shared, or in some cases given up in order to achieve God's purpose of creating values and sharing in the giving and receiving of love.

Partnership is a distinctive kind of relationship that can take many forms. For example, coworker relationships, friendships, marriages, and so on. Communities and societies are partnerships, which, in the best of occasions, work together, partnering for justice and peace. Partnerships

---

[19]Mont W. Smith, *What the Bible Says About Covenant* (Joplin, MO: College Press, 1981), 68.

exist when two or more parties agree to work for a shared interest. But these partnerships need not be equal. There are partnerships in which one party holds considerably more power than the other. Political leaders, ideally, partner with the *polis* in order to establish a functioning state. Parents must partner with children to make a cohesive family. And God must partner with humans to achieve the desired ends of fellowship, communion, and creativity.

There are also partnerships of inequity concerning what is entrusted. There are business partnerships in which one partner invests 70 percent while the other only 30 percent. Some partnerships involve time or effort being distributed unequally among the partners.[20] So, while it is true that there are relationships that do not require any partnership, relationships of partnering do require trust to varying degrees.[21]

God as king. Depictions of God's relationship with humans can be seen explicitly in a variety of biblical metaphors including king, judge, parent, and creator—all of which depict real partnering between God and a variety of persons. Some of these metaphors may not immediately cause us to think in terms of divine partnering. For example, many understand the metaphor of God as king implying that God has and exercises total sovereignty over humanity. This can be described as the "monarchical model" of God. In this sense, God is understood primarily, if not exclusively, as authorial lawgiver. There is relationship, but no partnership. Humans are basically subjects who must serve and obey in order to win their desserts.

Theologian Sallie McFague believes the king metaphor promotes ideas and images of a distant God who rules and controls from afar.[22] Biblical scholar Marcus Borg, basically agreeing with McFague, adds that the king metaphor does not eliminate talk of God's love but ultimately

---

[20]It should be remembered that fair and equal are not the same thing.

[21]Examples of such relationships without partnership are those of very casual acquaintance, for example, the relationship between me and my mail carrier, though I do need a minimal amount of trust in him or at least in the USPS who in turn trusts him.

[22]Sallie McFague, *Models of God: Theology for an Ecological, Nuclear Age* (Philadelphia: Fortress, 1987), 63-68.

frames such talk in terms of legalism and wrath appeasement.[23] But the king metaphor in no way demands such interpretations. The Bible is quite good at capsizing our precontrived notions. Theologians Clark Pinnock and Robert Brow argue that, when understood through a hermeneutic of love, God's kingdom involves a sharing of power for the goodness of the kingdom. "When creative love theists think of monarchy, we do not picture an all-determining power but a Davidic king who protects and shepherds his flock and delegates power to others."[24]

While kingly metaphors point to God as final authority, they need not suggest that God always rules alone. The institution of a monarchy in Israel signals that God rules through and also with human agents. The kings of Israel were not simply puppets for the divine, but neither were they replacements for Yahweh. The kings were servants of God, working in and for partnership. Psalm 78:70-72 portrays David as having skills and character right for ruling with God: "He chose his *servant* David, and took him from the sheepfolds; from tending the nursing ewes he brought him to be the shepherd of his people Jacob, of Israel, his inheritance. With *upright heart* he tended them, and guided them with *skillful hand*" (emphasis added). If partnership was unnecessary, the character of the king would be a nonissue. However, because God seeks trustworthy persons, character is key.

God as judge. Judge is another divine metaphor that may lead some to uncritically dismiss aspects of partnership. This is probably due to the fact that contemporary images of a judge are strongly associated with the courtroom and the handing down of sentences to the accused on trial. This model of judge not only dismisses partnership but all aspects of relationship. Today it is necessary that a judge be one who is objective and uninvolved. A judge must recuse herself if there is any relationship with the plaintive or defendant. This modern picture of a judge, however, is not the biblical image. The biblical idea is not of a judge over the people

---

[23]Marcus J. Borg, *The God We Never Knew: Beyond Dogmatic Religion to a More Authentic Contemporary Faith* (San Francisco: HarperSanFrancisco, 1997), 63.

[24]Clark H. Pinnock and Robert C. Brow, *Unbounded Love: A Good News Theology for the 21st Century* (Downers Grove, IL: InterVarsity Press, 1994), 29.

but for the people—one who seeks to restore and save. God as judge is relational and compassionate. God is not "cool and detached," unaffected and unknown by the courtroom parties, but has a "binding relationship with those at whom the divine anger is directed." God is "personally caught up in the situation" for "the judge behind the bench is the spouse of the accused one in the dock."[25]

Also concerning judge and partnership, it is helpful to keep in mind that what applies to king applies to judge. The two images overlap "due to the fact that in the ancient world judges also carried governing responsibilities."[26] Imagery of God as judge, given the bigger biblical picture, should be formulated in salvific and relational terms.[27] God judges with an eye toward trust based upon one's trustworthiness and for the sake of faith restored. As Fretheim writes, "judgment is understood fundamentally in relational terms; a relationship is at stake, not an agreement or a contract or a set of rules."[28]

God as parent. Lastly, God as parent also makes room for partnership. A parent is primarily caregiver when the child is young, but as the child develops so does the relationship. A child's relationship to the parent grows from simple dependence and obedience into a relationship of mindful honoring and mutual caring. Whereas a parent once acted *for* the child, the parent now acts *with* the child in order to foster growth and bring maturity, but also for the good of the relationship itself. The relationship between parent and child is dynamic, requiring mutual trust if the relationship is to continue to develop beyond childhood. The image of parent as partner would have been even clearer in the ancient world in which a child was often coworker with the parent and eventually entrusted with the family's wealth and future.

Images of God as a parent do not exclude or render incoherent the image of God as partner. Even the image of God as parental partner

---

[25]Terence E. Fretheim, *God and World in the Old Testament* (Nashville: Abingdon, 2005), 159-60.
[26]Allan Coppedge, *Portraits of God: A Biblical Theology of Holiness* (Downers Grove, IL: IVP Academic, 2008), 212.
[27]See Pinnock and Brow, *Unbounded Love*, chap. 6.
[28]Fretheim, *God and the World in the Old Testament*, 159.

makes sense when we note that God does not forever want infants for children. God desires growth and maturity so the child can serve and aid God's mission for the flourishing of the family. Philip Yancey says it well, "'Take me seriously! Treat me like an adult, not a child' is the cry of every teenager. God honors that request. He makes me a partner for his work in and through me. He grants me freedom in full knowledge that I will abuse it. He abdicates power to such an extent that he pleads with me to such an extent not to 'grieve' or 'quench' his Spirit."[29] We will, thankfully, never stop being God's children, but God desires we mature from our childishness into partners God can trust with the "family business."

If God's only desire is fixed obedience, then trust is not necessary. Political leaders know this to be true when they utilize power, coercion, and force to obtain social compliance. Parents and spouses at times use dominance or manipulation to achieve their desired ends. Power, dominance, and coercion can possibly bring order or obedience, but can never foster communion, fellowship, and certainly not mutual love. While our own obedience to God is best when born out of trust, God demanding only obedience necessitates no trust on God's part. Failed obedience in a world-divine relationship made up solely of command and response would bring divine anger and perhaps wrath, but hardly sorrow, grieving, and empathy. God's acts of trust bring with them the possibly of disappointment and lament. But they also bring surprises of joy and reassurances. God has freely entered into a relationship in which God needs a partner. The invitation to work with God means God is dependent upon the partners in the project.

All creatures, of course, are utterly dependent upon God for their existence and continuing life. At the same time, God has freely chosen to establish an *interdependent* relationship with the creation since both are responsible and necessary for the goods and values God intends. God has become *dependent* upon humans in the furtherance of these purposes in

---

[29]Philip Yancey, *Reaching for the Invisible God: What Can We Expect to Find?* (Grand Rapids: Zondervan, 2000), 182. Changing metaphors, Yancey concludes, "God does all this because he wants a mature lover as a partner, not a puppy-love adolescent."

the world. All creatures have a God-given vocation within God's creation-wide telos. Therefore, God has freely chosen to rely on that which is not divine to engage and accomplish divine purposes.[30]

God and creation have a codependent relationship. While the word "codependent" has negative connotations in today's nomenclature, it nonetheless gets to the heart of God's project. This is authentic relationship. Each needs the other to achieve the purposes, plans, and projects set out by God. Partnerships, when they are mature and intimate, are relationships of trust, relationships of faith.

COVENANT AND TRUST

Covenant is a key biblical concept that necessarily entails carefully considering God's restraint of power and willingness to self-limit for the sake of community and cooperation. The model of covenant shows God's partnering prominently. A prevailing biblical image, covenant provides a means of God entering into agreements with individuals (Abraham, David), nations (Israel), communities (the church), humanity (i.e., the Adamic covenant), and creation itself (i.e., the Noachian covenant).[31] At its simplest, a covenant is a treaty or formal agreement between two parties.[32] Parity covenants are binding agreements made between two equals. But covenants need not be between equals. Suzerainty covenants included a greater and a lesser party.[33]

The covenants between God and various persons certainly fit the suzerain image. God is the greater power who conceives and initiates the

---

[30]Fretheim, *God and World in the Old Testament*, 270.

[31]The Noachian covenant (Gen 9:1-16) seems to be an exception to the typical triad of parties, terms, and promises. There are no terms of agreement but only the parties (God and every living creature) and promises (God will never destroy all flesh by flood). There is not the threat of human failure with this covenant because God does not lay out terms for it, only an unending promise.

[32]Covenant is a subject too large to cover adequately. For more extensive studies, see Walter Eichrodt, *Theology of the Old Testament*, trans. J. A. Baker, vol. 1 (Philadelphia: Westminster, 1961); M. Smith, *What the Bible Says About Covenant*; Delbert R. Hillers, *Covenant: The History of a Biblical Idea* (Baltimore, MD: Johns Hopkins Press, 1969); Steven L. McKenzie, *Covenant* (St. Louis, MO: Chalice, 2000).

[33]Historically, when a stronger population (tribe, nation, city-state) would overpower a weaker, it would sometimes offer the dominated people life in exchange for obedience—protection in exchange for goods and services.

covenant with the weaker.[34] God freely establishes the covenant because God is under no obligation to enter such an agreement. Yet while God is the one free to initiate the covenant, human partners must be free to enter into partnership or not. Without human autonomy there would be no point to the promises that come with compliance. Why establish terms and promises if neither party is free to keep or break such promises? Humans need to be free for they have "responsibility, a task to fulfill and a contribution to make."[35]

When one really thinks about it, it is rather odd for an omnipotent and wholly sovereign God to enter into covenant. What possible reason could there be to employ communities and individuals to do what God could do alone and do infinitely better?[36] But it seems that covenants and partnership are necessary for God to accomplish what is of ultimate worth.

God takes great risks by entering into covenant. God's power, self-sufficiency, immutability, and freedom are curtailed for the covenant. God's story is forever altered by this relational act. If we are to think of God as one covenanting with Israel, the church, and various individuals, then we must proclaim God's trust in the covenant partner.

While it is an open future that allows the covenant to be authentic, God is not foolish in this risky partnership. God's omnisophic nature can discern whether it is a covenant worth entering. God trusts, bravely but not blindly, for even in the depths of human egoism, God still knows what kind of beings humans we were created to be. God trusts the covenant partners to be true, not only to God and the covenant itself, but to the person God created them to be. It is not too much to consider that God is wise enough to know when to risk and when to wait. God knows when to commit in trust and when to act alone. The risk of covenanting reveals God's trust because there is no means of entering into covenant

---

[34]Adrio König conceives of this kind of covenant relationship as "monopluralistic" because "it is one-sidedly ('mono'-) established by the Lord, but involves obligations on the part of both the Lord and his people ('pluralistic')." Adrio König, *Here Am I: A Believer's Reflection on God* (Grand Rapids: Eerdmans, 1982), 128.

[35]König, *Here Am I*, 128.

[36]As one author asks, why partner with humanity and risk "becoming the laughing stock of heaven" if it is not necessary? M. Smith, *What the Bible Says About Covenant*, 49.

without real faith. I can imagine God desiring to enter into covenant with certain individuals, but God, knowing in those cases the risk was too great, refused. And even when the risk is too great to partner and trust, divine hope that situations will change always remains.

It might be objected that Christ coming as the fulfillment of the old covenant means that humanity was utterly unfaithful and could not, and still today cannot, be trusted. It is certainly the case that humans—collectively and individually—fail to be faithful covenant partners with God. But this should not imply that humanity could not be trusted. God certainly knew the possibility of our unfaithfulness, maybe even probability, but nonetheless took the chance. God seemingly anticipated our failure and had other plans and covenants in the works (Jer 31:31-33). But human faithlessness does not mean God soured on covenant or partnership but renewed that commitment with a new covenant. It could even be said that God doubled down, not simply ending but extending the covenant beyond Israel to include all humanity. The new covenant is better than the old for we have a perfect mediator and better promises (Heb 8:6-13), but it is still a covenant with terms and promises that imply and necessitate mutual trust between God and humanity.

Not all covenants are agreements entered into for some distant or external telos. Relational covenants have the relationship itself as its end. Relationship, community, and fellowship are the means and ends of divine covenant. From what we see in Scripture, God seems to love partnership, community, and covenant.[37] If God loves covenants, then God must also love trusting the community partners. Simply being trusted is not enough; God loves to trust. Trusting and being trusted are the bones of true relationship. Trust is not a necessary evil of relationality. Trust is a good and essential aspect of expressing love and self-giving. This means that God, by loving relationships of all kinds, loves to trust.

It is understandable to miss the embeddedness of trust in the covenant model. For some, covenant is understood under the category of forensic

---

[37]Clark Pinnock, *Most Moved Mover: A Theology of God's Openness* (Grand Rapids: Baker Academic, 2001), 5.

theism in which God's covenantal relationship is exclusively law driven. In this view, God does not covenant for the sake of relationship but enters into covenant for the sake of order. The covenant is a contract more than a vow of love. Federal theology uses contractual language and legal imagery when depicting the divine-human relationship.[38] Sin is not estrangement in the relationship but a breach in the contract, a breaking of the law. Of course, a covenant can be both, but while relational theism emphasizes love and trust, forensic or Federal theism emphasizes law and judgment (wrath and satisfaction).[39] If God requires satisfaction before relationship, then God's love has little connection to trust. However, if for God the cross was an act of divine love and trust for the purpose of re-establishment of relationship, then this certainly changes one's perspective.

Covenant is thoroughly about trust. Covenant made it possible for Israel to trust God and not fear the capriciousness of Near Eastern gods.[40] But can't we imagine the same for Yahweh? Isn't God concerned about human capriciousness? The covenant is two-sided, and God has freely made promises to the covenant partner. Those who enter into the covenant make promises that are only as good as the partner is good. If humans refuse to trust God, then the covenant is rife for curses. If God refuses to trust, the covenant is void and useless because the blessings and curses would not be based on the fidelity of the partner but simply upon the capricious preordaining of God alone. The entire institution of covenant rests on the premise that trust is a living reality for each covenant partner.

Covenant then is one type of partnership in which God has made known God's willingness and active *co*-operation with humans in the accomplishing of divine plans. Without both human and divine trust,

---

[38]Federal theology emphasizes the contractual nature of covenant. Taken from the Latin term *foedus* (*covenant*), federal theology sees Christ, the last Adam, meeting the obligations of the contract that the first Adam failed to live up to. In this theology the covenant was with the two Adams (Adam and Christ), and each serves as the federal head of humanity.

[39]Pinnock and Brow, *Unbounded Love*, 24-34.

[40]William Dyrness, *Themes in Old Testament Theology* (Downers Grove, IL: InterVarsity Press, 1983), 125.

covenant becomes merely a façade. Likewise, trust is better with a covenant. Trust between parties gives life to a covenant. How can persons genuinely enter and remain in any covenant, especially covenant with God, if they do not trust the other? They can't. Neither can God, for God has given up unilateral power in exchange for cooperation, fellowship, and community. And in this exchange God gives up control, but gets something better: faith. To covenant and cooperate is to share power and enter into a relationship filled with trust and hope, that is, faith.

While covenant is a pervasive metaphor throughout Scripture, it does not exhaust the many ways God relates. Relationship is the model; covenant but one example.[41] God is perhaps best understood as one who invites others to partner with God for the good of each. This is what truly distinguishes Yahweh from the other gods of the Old Testament and ancient mythologies: "The God of the Bible distances himself from the other gods who are preoccupied with their rule, their majesty, their well-being in the plush silence of heaven."[42] Sadly, these false gods of history sound a lot like the kinds of humans God has chosen to partner with. We have shown ourselves to be distant from God, preoccupied with our own rule and autonomy. We desire the comforts of heaven not the mission on earth. Yet, in spite of this, God has still chosen to partner with humanity.

This is the heart of passion. God in partnership has suffered for humanity. God has moved beyond covenant and has sought companionship and friendship to preserve the relationship even when humanity shows itself to be an unfaithful partner. God has remained in relation and partnership while history is littered with broken covenants. This is a supreme

---

[41]Mont Smith argued that "every major philosophic and theological idea in the Bible is related in some way to covenant" (*What the Bible Says About Covenant*, 29-30). Fretheim, however, argues that God's relationship with Israel preceded any formal covenant; the covenant was to formalize a vocation for Israel within an already established relationship. Fretheim, *God and World in the Old Testament*, 15. He also argues that theologically, the relationship that exists between Israel and God is more personal than contractual. Terence E. Fretheim, *Exodus*, Interpretation: A Bible Commentary for Teaching and Preaching (Louisville, KY: John Knox, 1991), 255-61.

[42]Walter Brueggemann, "Covenant as a Subversive Paradigm," *Christian Century*, November 12, 1980, 1094.

act of trust as God continues to be faithful and trustworthy when persons have not. God continues to trust and have faith when God's partners have not. It appears that not only is divine love beyond reason, but so too is divine trust.

THE BIBLE AND HUMAN TRUSTWORTHINESS

While I have made use of philosophical and theological arguments, the Bible is not quiet on divine trust. Paul says that he "had been entrusted with the gospel for the uncircumcised, just as Peter had been entrusted with the gospel for the circumcised" (Gal 2:7).[43] In 1 Corinthians 4:1-2 Paul speaks of himself and Sosthenes "as servants of Christ and stewards of God's mysteries," adding, "Moreover, it is required of stewards that they be found trustworthy." Paul speaks of the Jews being "entrusted with the oracles of God" (Rom 3:2). Furthermore, that the Roman Christians themselves were set free from sin and entrusted with "the form of teaching," that is, a new way of living patterned after the tradition of the church (Rom 6:17).[44]

I am sure it is quite common for readers to gloss over such statements. When we read that Paul, Peter, Sosthenes, the Jews, or the Roman Christians were entrusted by God, we don't stop and think about the meaning and implication of this. And while Paul is the most forthright in speaking of God's entrusting, dozens of stories and narratives make most sense when read in the light of divine trust.

The Bible contains stories and passages that speak of God's regret and frustration, testing and changing of mind. These biblical passages are generally used by open and relational theists as examples of God's genuine relatedness to humanity, but little to nothing is said in regard to these events being cases of divine faith. Each one of these dealings,

---

[43] Also see 1 Cor 9:17; 1 Thess 2:4; 1 Tim 1:11; and Titus 1:3, each of which speak of Paul being entrusted by God with the gospel.

[44] What this "form of teaching" means is debated, but Boring and Craddock suggest this church received instructions that aided them in being servants of God rather than servants of sin. See Eugene M. Boring and Fred B. Craddock, *The People's New Testament Commentary* (Louisville, KY: Westminster John Knox, 2004), 484.

however, presupposes a God who trusts. First Samuel 15 speaks of God regretting (1 Sam 15:10) and being sorry (1 Sam 15:35) for making Saul king after Saul fails to obey God fully. When told to "utterly destroy" the Amalekites, he instead captures their king.[45] Saul did not obey, and that puts a considerable strain upon trustworthiness. The narrative implies that God desired a king in whom God could trust, perhaps with even the harshest of commands. God's regretting making Saul king means that God regretted that he could no longer trust Saul to rule Israel.

The various testing stories also presuppose that God tests for the purposes of learning the trustworthiness of those tested. Why else would God test? Idle curiosity? Divine wagers? It makes most sense that these stories presuppose that God tests in order to know one's character for the purposes of entrusting with a mission. Abraham, it seems, was tested to see if he had the character necessary to be a trustworthy patriarch and a symbol of trustworthiness for generations to follow.

Throughout Scripture God repeatedly calls for human faithfulness and trustworthiness. But what do "faithful" and "trustworthy" mean to a God who cannot not trust? The message is clear. When God is called trustworthy or faithful, it means that God is reliable, dependable—a being we can commit to without fear of abandonment. God's being faithful means we can rightly put our faith in God because God was, is, and will be true to us and the divine promises. This does not mean trust is risk free. Because of epistemological gaps, trust is always a risk. But we are called to trust God because God is trustworthy. We are to put our faith in God because God is faithful. As Deuteronomy 7:9 states, "Know therefore that the LORD your God is God, the faithful God who maintains covenant loyalty with those who love him and keep his commandments, to a thousand generations."

The Bible does not simply speak of God being faithful or trustworthy, it also declares we have been called to faithfulness and trustworthiness. Scripture says God placed faith and trust in Moses. God may speak to

---

[45]Even though the divinely ordered ban raises theological difficulties, these do not alter the point made that God trusts.

prophets in dreams and riddles, but God spoke to Moses face to face because "he is entrusted with all my house" (Num 12:7). First Samuel 2:35 says that God desired to raise up "a faithful priest, who shall do according to what is in my heart and in my mind." Second Chronicles speaks of the reforms brought about by Jehoshaphat that included righteous judges: "Consider what you are doing, for you judge not on behalf of human beings but on the LORD's behalf" (2 Chron 19:6). Jehoshaphat reminded the judges that they have been entrusted with justice because they represent God in their judgments. They were acting on God's behalf. The various leaders, be they judges, kings, or prophets, were those who God entrusted to do right, obey, and act as God's spokespersons. Sometimes they were faithful and proved God right in trusting them; other times they failed and showed themselves to be untrustworthy.

The New Testament also speaks of human faithfulness and trustworthiness. Matthew 24 contains Jesus' eschatological discourse that concludes with a call for trustworthiness:

> Who then is the faithful and wise slave, whom his master has put in charge of his household, to give the other slaves their allowance of food at the proper time? Blessed is that slave whom his master will find at work when he arrives. Truly I tell you, he will put that one in charge of all his possessions (Mt 24:45-47; cf. Luke 12:35-48).

Matthew uses this parable as a call (or warning) for trustworthiness for the church leaders of his day.[46] These leaders have been put in charge of (entrusted with) God's "possessions." The ones who have shown themselves trustworthy will be entrusted with even more. The point of the parable is not necessarily to teach that God operates in a relationship of trust with the church leaders, but this is a necessary condition for the parable to be meaningful. If God does not have faith, then a call for faithfulness loses its meaning.

This call for faithfulness or trustworthiness is continued in Matthew 25 with the parables of the ten virgins and the talents. The parable of the ten

---

[46]Boring and Craddock, *The People's New Testament Commentary*, 92-93.

virgins focuses on being prepared for the coming Son of Man (Mt 25:1-12). The parable does not seem to focus on issues of trust, but they are there. To be a bridesmaid was a great honor and held great responsibility for making the bride's day truly special.[47] But the virgins who did not bring oil with the torches proved themselves foolish and ultimately untrustworthy to be bridesmaids.[48]

The parable of the talents, however, is unmistakably and prominently about trust and trustworthiness (Mt 25:14-30; cf. Lk 19:12-27). This parable, like the eschatological discourse, speaks about slaves being given a portion of the master's possessions. As we learn by the end of the story, the slaves entrusted with the "talents" (very large sums of money) were expected to use the money and give back to the master more than was given to them.[49] It was not simply that the master entrusted them to hold and return the talents, but that the servants were expected to use them and, in the process, possibly increase his riches. The first two slaves, one given five and the other two, risked the talents and in the process doubled the master's investment. But the third slave buried the talent. When the master returned, he praised and rewarded those who returned more than was given. The good and faithful servants, surprisingly, were the ones who risked the master's talents! Those who risked the talents acted in faith and recognized the master's faith in them. The last slave, however, did not risk because he did not trust the master, but only feared. The slave who buried the talent did not understand that the master had entrusted it to him. The master had given him the talent in trust with the intended

---

[47]Craig S. Keener, *Matthew*, The IVP New Testament Commentary Series (Downers Grove, IL: InterVarsity Press, 1997), 357-58.

[48]Oil in this parable most likely represents deeds of love, justice, and general obedience. See Boring and Craddock, *The People's New Testament Commentary*, 93. I believe Stanley Hauerwas may be right in understanding the talents to simply represent continued obedience in the absence of the master. The obedience, for Hauerwas, is the good work of love, mercy and justice. See Stanley Hauerwas, *Matthew*, Brazos Theological Commentary on the Bible (Grand Rapids: Brazos, 2006), 208-12.

[49]The exact meaning of "talent" in the parable is unclear. Some believe the talents represent "personal gifts and abilities rather than the gospel itself" given the fact that the amounts differed for each slave. See Donald Hagner, *Matthew 14–28*, Word Biblical Commentary 33b (Dallas: Word, 1995), 734. Daniel J. Harrington offers that the talent is "a reference to the gift of the Spirit." See *The Gospel of Matthew*, Sacra Pagina 1 (Collegeville, MN: Liturgical Press, 1991), 352.

purpose of being trusted in return. This slave, however, understood the relationship as one based in fear, not faith. When he returned the talent to the master, his failure to recognize the master's trust in him was an insult to the master.[50] While the other slaves said, "Master, you entrusted . . . me . . ." (Mt 25:20, 22 NASB), the third slave stated, "Master, I knew that you were a harsh man . . ." (24). Hardly a response expected from one who has been trusted. The master responded to the slave's lack of trust and faithfulness by chastising him, calling him wicked and lazy, breaking all ties, and finally pronouncing him—as he was—"worthless."

While the parable at times feels callous and unfair from a modern vantage point, it also denotes tremendous praise for those who acted faithfully and proved themselves trustworthy when the master's trust in some of them was not in vain. The story has a relational application. Those who trust are in return trusted even more. When they show themselves faithful, the master then entrusts them with very much. They are expected to live the kind of faith that is risky but productive, knowing that they have been first trusted by the Father. Those who are trusted by God are given great gifts with which to produce even more. However, those who seem to be untrustworthy are still given talents, or at the least a talent, to use and show themselves worthy of God's faith. God had little faith but not no faith at all in the last slave and gave the slave opportunity nonetheless. Yet in this parable the slave entrusted with little proves the master correct because he was "wicked and lazy." This verdict came not because he stole what was not his but because he failed to trust the one who trusted him. The parable, given its literary context, is certainly speaking about how those who are patiently awaiting the parousia should live. It is a call for faithfulness and obedience. But this should not overshadow the clear and remarkable statement of divine trust conveyed in this story.

The point behind considering these passages is that each speaks of humans being called to trustworthiness. To speak in terms of God being the master and us being trustworthy slaves makes no sense if God does

---

[50]Craig S. Keener, *A Commentary on the Gospel of Matthew* (Grand Rapids: Eerdmans, 1999), 601.

not entrust something to us, acting in trust and faith. The call to faith-fulness and trustworthiness further demonstrates God's partnership with persons in doing God's will and carrying out God's plans.

DIVINE TRUST IN THE CREATION NARRATIVES

I would like to finish this discussion by going back to the start. The cre-ation narratives set the tone for the rest of the long and grand story that makes up the Old and New Testaments. So, let's end at the beginning.

Reading the Bible with an eye toward divine trust will allow the reader to see what may have been missed in past readings. Sometimes divine trust is subtle, such as in Genesis 1:28-30 in which God blesses the humans, entrusting them with the responsibility to subdue and exercise dominion over the earth. The creation account of Genesis chapters 2 and 3, however, takes leave of subtleties in portraying God as a creator who trusts the first humans to care for the garden and to heed God's warnings. It is a story of trust—trust given, trust betrayed, and the way to trust regained.

John Caputo sees the second creation narrative as a story of a God who hasn't the stomach for trust or the patience for faith.

> What interests me about this Yahweh is that he has little taste *for the risk of creation, for the risk of parenting.* He does not so much give the first couple life as he gives them a *test* to see if they are worthy of life; he gives them life on a kind of conditional trial loan to see if they are going to abuse it and try to become like him, in which case he is prepared to withdraw from the deal and wipe—or wash—them out.[51]

I could not disagree more with this reading. This is not the story of a God who fears risk and tests for worthiness. Risk and faith lie at the heart of this narrative. It is the story of God's faith and the couple's lack of faith—of God's trust and human distrust and mistrust. But the story ends with the work of restoring trust.

Divine trust given. Genesis 2 begins with an earth or land devoid of plant life since God had not caused it to rain for "there was no one to till

---

[51]John D. Caputo, *The Weakness of God: A Theology of the Event* (Bloomington: Indiana University Press, 2006), 68.

the ground." The earth is not yet, in this narrative, what it is meant to be, and the divine plans for that earth will require someone to partner with God. Just as creation reached its apex in the first story of creation (Gen 1:1–2:4) with the introduction of the *imago Dei* in whom God could share faith with, this narrative begins with God knowing that if the earth is to be what is intended, then God needs a trustworthy coworker. Terence Fretheim rightly notes that "responsible human beings are said to be as important to the development of creation as is rain!"[52] God has created humans in both stories (Gen 1 and Gen 2–3) to be coworkers with the divine in the continuation of creation. The partnership is further shown in God first "tilling" ground in order to form the man, and then the man, in the likeness of God, will till the ground to care for the garden God has planted. Thus far this is hardly the image of a God with no taste for risk.

The narrative continues with God instructing, perhaps warning, the man, "You may freely eat of every tree of the garden; but the tree of the knowledge of good and evil you shall not eat, for in the day that you eat of it you shall die" (Gen 2:16-17).[53] Walter Brueggemann sees the story containing vocation, permission, and prohibition.[54] The man is given the *vocation* of tilling the ground, *permission* to eat of nearly all trees, and the *prohibition* of eating from the tree of the knowledge of good and evil. There is far more permission than prohibition, and yet permission has little meaning without prohibition. Prohibition is not a lack of trust, for trust is only possible if there is prohibition. To say all things are lawful removes any need for trust. The vocation and permission are examples of God's faith only because there is a prohibition. As Brueggemann states, "The primary human task is to find a way to hold the three facets of divine purpose together. Any two of them without the third is surely to pervert life."[55]

---

[52]Fretheim, *God and World in the Old Testament*, 53.

[53]The words of God here lack the language of threat. The man is not told that if he eats of the tree he will be "put to death" but that he will surely die. See Gordon J. Wenham, *Genesis 1–15*, Word Biblical Commentary (Waco, TX: Word, 1987), 67-68.

[54]Walter Brueggemann, *Genesis*, Interpretation: A Bible Commentary for Teaching and Preaching (Atlanta: John Knox, 1982), 46.

[55]Brueggemann, *Genesis*, 46.

The first words of God are not a demand for obedience but a call to trust. The tree, along with the prohibition of eating its fruit, "indicates that, for all the creative power God entrusts to human beings, the human relationship to God provides an indispensable matrix for the proper exercise of power. . . . The tree is a concrete metaphor for the limits of creatureliness."[56] Human freedom and divine faith only make sense in light of real limitations and warnings. Without the tree and the prohibition of eating its fruit, freedom becomes meaningless and faith unnecessary. God's faith in granting freedom is real because of the risks symbolized in the tree of the knowledge of good and evil, and, without the tree, the relationship is stale because relationship without trust is never intimate.

The first account of the creation of humankind focuses on a relationship between God and humans that is not seen in the rest of creation. God gives humans the responsibility of caring for the creation God has lovingly fashioned. God gives responsibility to humanity, which is to be understood as God trusting, having faith in, humanity. John Sanders states it well:

> Not only does God choose to share existence, the fact that God delegates responsibility implies that God is willing to share power with humans. God sovereignly decides that not everything will be up to God. Some important things are left in the hands of humanity as God's co-creators such that we are to collaborate with God in the achievement of the divine project.[57]

Human distrust and mistrust. The story of the first couple eating the prohibited fruit is not so much a story of pride and rebellion but one of first mistrusting (the serpent) and then distrusting (God). The serpent raises doubts in the woman about God's character and motives. The words of the serpent depict God, not as a trusting giver of life and freedom, but as a petty deity fearful of losing what is God's alone—knowledge of good and evil. When the man and woman eat, they

[56]Fretheim, *God and World in the Old Testament*, 59.
[57]John Sanders, *The God Who Risks: A Theology of Providence* (Downers Grove, IL: InterVarsity Press, 2007), 43.

demonstrate that they misplaced their trust in the serpent and distrusted God. They doubted God, the giver of life and so much liberty, and instead trusted the serpent—a grave miscalculation. So often distrust leaves us vulnerable to mistrust and vice versa. The woman and the man eat the fruit they were prohibited from eating and immediately their distrust in God escalates because of fear and shame. Thankfully the story does not end here.

The restoration of trust. The relationship of God and the human couple had been damaged by their mistrust, but the text itself gives no reason to conclude that God's trust shown in chapters 1 and 2 is replaced by suspicion and distrust. The couple will continue as co-creators even though there will be consequences. Adam is still entrusted to till the ground even though it is now cursed, and the woman will give birth, though with greater pain. In an act of grace, God clothes the couple in garments[58] made of skins so they would not be put out of the garden in a vulnerable state.[59] The fact that the couple did not die the day they ate the fruit could be a sign of God's willingness to "adjust his project in response to the horrible turn of events."[60] This would mean that God did not give up on the plan of creation being a joint project. Human sin, selfishness, and faithlessness do not mean God has given up faith. In fact, it seems that God's desire to trust has greater resolve because of the distrust in the garden. The story reveals a God who is frustrated, but not faithless. God's trust of humanity is tested, but not thwarted.

While God is surprised, these events were not wholly unanticipated.[61] God gave the humans room to be free and exercise their autonomy. The interchange between the serpent and woman demonstrates that God

---

[58]The Hebrew word used here for "garments" is *kuttōnet* and is the word used for priestly robes in Ex 28:39 and 39:27.

[59]Victor P. Hamilton, *The Book of Genesis: Chapters 1-17*, The New International Commentary on the Old Testament (Grand Rapids: Eerdmans, 1990), 207.

[60]Sanders, *The God Who Risks*, 48.

[61]Fiddes argues that sin and evil were either something strange to God or were part of the divine plan. I see no reason for this dichotomy. Sin, while never part of God's plan, was recognized as a possibility if not a probability. For more on his view, see Paul Fiddes, *The Creative Suffering of God* (Oxford: Oxford University Press, 1988), chap. 8.

created a world in which it is possible to question divine wisdom. "God leaves enough space for trust to develop, but this also allows space for doubt."[62] By placing humans in a world in which doubt is feasible, and by giving them the freedom to question and even doubt divine commands and wisdom, God knew that sin was possible. God does not have to rethink this whole project because of human faithlessness but does have to respond differently. The garden story is fundamentally a trust story.[63] It is not simply a story of a "fall" into sin or of human pride.[64] It is first and foremost a story of trust given, trust tested, trust betrayed, and trust continued.

The story of the garden begins with God entrusting the couple to keep the garden and to heed God's warning about eating the fruit from the tree of knowledge of good and evil. God does not hover over the couple or dictate their actions but trusts them to do what they were created for and to obey the divine words. Tragically, the couple does not trust the words of God and betrays God's trust in them. What follows is what happens in all relationships when trust is betrayed: estrangement and alienation. The man and the woman first hide themselves from one another and then from God.

God's exchange with the couple seems to depict God looking for reasons to keep trusting. When Adam explains his fear was due to his nakedness, God responds with the questions, "Who told you that you were naked? Have you eaten from the tree of which I commanded you not to eat?" God is giving the man the opportunity to trust again. If only Adam were to confess and return to trusting God, it seems the events that followed may not have been so profound. But the opportunity for trust becomes an occasion for blame. Adam blames God for giving him the woman. Likewise, the woman blames the serpent. Neither accepts

[62]Sanders, *The God Who Risks*, 47.
[63]Terence Fretheim, "Is Genesis 3 a Fall Story?" *World & World* 14, no. 2 (1994): 151.
[64]Christian ethicist Kyle Fedler writes, "There is something in the human pair that leads them to disobey. While most people identify this as pride, I think it is more accurate to say that it is pride mixed with independence and *lack of trust*." See Fedler, *Exploring Christian Ethics: Biblical Foundations for Morality* (Louisville, KY: Westminster John Knox, 2006), 85. Italics Fedler's.

responsibility for their unfaithfulness. Estrangement between man and woman and between human and God is not the full effect; there is even estrangement between man and the soil.

The story does not end in complete tragedy, though; the reader is given glimpses of hope. God, while angry and frustrated, does not give up on the couple. God resolves to trust in spite of not being trusted. God does not utterly destroy the creation, nor does God go back on the pronouncement of it being very good. Chapters 4 through 11 give a picture of a God who must face serious challenges to the divine plan of mutual fellowship, but these challenges do not stop God from having faith.

The creation narratives in general, and the garden story specifically, are not simply stories about human faith and failure. They are stories of human struggle, sin, and divine faith. They convey not simply what went wrong but what is right in God's not giving up on humanity and continuing to trust and hope that all will come to faith in and trust with God. Mike Mason rightly states:

> Such faith is not a religion but a relationship. In other words, it is not one-sided but two-sided, being comprised not merely as our faith in God but His in us. It is our faith that behind all the fear and pain of life in a fallen world lies a loving and all-sufficient God, and it is God's faith that behind our corrupt nature lies a being with a capacity for perfection and everlasting life.[65]

God's trust in humanity is the basis for relationship. Genesis 1–11 reveals a God who longs for and seeks ways to trust the creation God loves so deeply.

A final note on the Bible's treatment of divine trust. I must confess that there is a place in the Bible in which it says that God trusts no one—not even the angels. In Job 4, Eliphaz, one of Job's "comforters," arrives claiming to speak under the influence of divinely given wisdom. Eliphaz says of God, "Even in his servants he puts no trust, and his angels he charges with error" (Job 4:18).[66] What should be done with such a statement? This would be a very problematic proclamation were it not for the fact that "we

---

[65]Mike Mason, *The Gospel According to Job* (Wheaton, IL: Crossway, 1994), 158.
[66]Eliphaz basically repeats the statement in Job 15:15: "God puts no trust even in his holy ones, and the heavens are not clean in his sight."

must keep in mind that the overall purpose of the book [of Job] includes the concept that the counselors were basically wrong even though their words were often right."[67] The friends of Job are to be read with suspicion. And while it need not be suggested that all of their advice is blatantly wrong, Eliphaz's revelatory experience is presented as near parody.[68] His statement in Job 4:17, that no mortals are righteous before God or pure before their maker, contradicts what God says about Job in the book's opening chapter. Given the contradiction, should the reader conclude Eliphaz is speaking for God? Gerald Janzen suggests that Eliphaz is speaking, not on behalf of God, but ironically on behalf of the satan.

> What Eliphaz, of course, does not know is that in imputing to humankind the qualities of inevitable untrustworthiness and inevitable error, he (or his "revelation") is speaking on one side of the issue already joined in the heavenly meeting between Yahweh and the Satan. . . . The "inspiration" of Eliphaz derives, not from God, but from the Satan. . . . Insofar as Eliphaz claims to speak by heavenly inspiration, we see here one of the many instances in Job where the author ironically subverts a speaker's intended meaning.[69]

If Janzen is correct, we should not see Eliphaz's statement as counter to my argument but as a backhanded agreement. It is the satan who is raising the issue of human untrustworthiness, and in light of this question it was "Yahweh who was willing to risk the test in hope of Job's vindication."[70] To declare that God trusts no one is to side with the satan, not with the divine.

CONCLUSION

Trust is an attitude and action that denotes positive expectation concerning the other.[71] Relationships of love and care, let alone those of

[67]Elmer B. Smick, "Job," in *The Expositor's Bible Commentary*, ed. Frank E. Gaebelein, vol. 4 (Grand Rapids: Zondervan, 1992), 894.
[68]Norman C. Habel, *The Book of Job*, Cambridge Bible Commentary: New English Bible (New York: Cambridge University Press, 1975), 123.
[69]Gerald J. Janzen, *Job*, Interpretation: A Bible Commentary for Teaching and Preaching (Atlanta: John Knox, 1985), 73-74.
[70]Janzen, *Job*, 73.
[71]Govier, *Dilemmas of Trust*, 6.

partnership and mission, are not possible without this positive, or at least hopeful, expectation. Relationships born out of love and care will always have at least one who trusts and at least one who is trusted. But as philosopher Trudy Govier explains, it is ideal when "each person trusts *and* is trusted in turn."[72] By God working with humanity, God shares in the life of humanity. The two, in a sense, become one. It is God's desire that humanity and God become one in mission, purpose, and love, and this can only happen in a relationship of mutual trust.

Trust creates a particular reality. The future is created and shaped by who we trust and how we trust, and this is no different for God. Trust brings about a positive expectation and hopeful relationship. God's relationship with humanity is in effect created by God's willingness to trust. God creates a reality of intimate relationship by trusting humans to be actual partners with the divine.

In her book *God the What?*, Carolyn Jane Bohler says that one of her favorite metaphors for the divine is "God the Jazz Band Leader." This metaphor, according to Bohler "connotes God's power and responsibility as persuasive and shared."[73] The metaphor creatively speaks to both human and divine power "in concert" with one another. God exhibits power and responsibility in leading the band. God cares about the music being played and the musicians playing, guiding the band as a whole and individually. God is not a conductor of an orchestra leading each member to play the notes as composed to its final completion.[74] God wants jazz, and for this, God must allow each musician to play her own notes. God leads but allows and even encourages improvisations. Bohler argues God is not indifferent to what music is played, but desires themes of beauty, love, and peace and that God enjoys our creativity upon those themes. This metaphor wonderfully depicts a God of trust who invites us to be a part of the band, to play our part with great freedom and creativity, all

---

[72]Govier, *Dilemmas of Trust*, 12.
[73]Carolyn Jane Bohler, *God the What? What Our Metaphors for God Reveal About Our Beliefs in God* (Woodstock, VT: SkyLight Paths, 2008), 74.
[74]Bohler, *God the What?*, 74-75.

while God trusts us not to ignore our parts or "get carried away with our own powers and abilities."[75] Though this metaphor has its limits, it nonetheless gives us a vision of God who leads us in our creative processes and yet trusts us to make our own music, to thrill and surprise God with our improvisations but not detract from the song. God has entrusted us to follow the divinely crafted melody but with our own creativity. God has trusted us to do what is beautiful, lovely, and right in concert with God. God has empowered us to be other than God. God has entrusted us to be other with God.

---

[75]Bohler, *God the What?*, 75.

6

GOD HOPES

Remember, Hope is a good thing, maybe
the best of things, and no good thing ever dies.

THE SHAWSHANK REDEMPTION

I CAN THINK OF NO GREATER REASON to despair than to love without hope. To desire, for example, health for a loved one all while also knowing that what you want for them will never come to realization can only bring heartache and despair or possibly a cold stoic fatalism. When we hope, we believe the future is open to certain possibilities, that the good we desire is possible—even if the chances are slim. The Christian God of unsurpassable love also hopes! God hopes because God desires what is good for us, what will bring us life and flourishing. If there is possibility, there is hope. Therefore, the God of the possible is the God of hope.

Unlike divine trust, it is not so unusual to find authors speaking about divine hope, many of whom, however, do not necessarily identify as relational theists. For example, Jane Regan, who writes that by carefully interpreting our experiences we can get a "sense of who God is and what God hopes for us."[1] James Smith writes, "God hopes and believes—he sees our potential even when we doubt and despair of ourselves."[2] Even in the Blackwell Companion to Catholicism we find James J. Buckley, in the

---

[1] Jane E. Regan, *Where Two or Three Are Gathered: Transforming the Parish Through Communities of Practice* (New York: Paulist Press, 2016), 142.
[2] James B. Smith, *Embracing the Love of God: The Path and Promise of Christian Life* (New York: HarperCollins, 2010), 46.

discussion concerning "heaven, hell, and universalism," speaking of God's hope: "The key question for Catholics has less to do with whether you or I or our neighbors are saved than with what God intends and whether God's intent—the goal on which God has set God's hopes—will come about."[3]

Unsurprisingly relational theologians also make mention of God's hope. Jürgen Moltmann says that God "hopes for us and expects us along his ways. He promises to go with us and bear us when we start out and seek his future."[4] John Sanders offers, "God's love is patient and God hopes for the transformation of his fallen creation."[5] Terence Frethiem says, "The heart of God hopes against hope" that Israel will respond positively to the prophet's message.[6]

A rare exception is H. Richard Niebuhr, who asserts God's faith but denies God's hope:

> Love and faith must be ascribed to God . . . for without activity that is counterpart of our desire for the good and of our fidelity the Ground of Being is just that and not God. But to ascribe hope to him seems too anthropomorphic. Whatever his relation to time, it is hard to think of time being in him as in us. So far as I know, the Scriptures never speak of the hope of God though they do speak of his love and his faith.[7]

I will have more to say about God's relation to time and about Scripture in fact speaking of God's hope.

Even though authors, pastors, biblical scholars, and theologians speak of God's hope rarely, if ever, do they give reasons to think that such statements are anything more than mere figures of speech. Rarely, if ever, do they explain why God can (or must) hope. In this chapter I build on open and relational theological sensibilities and make explicit what has been

[3]James J. Buckley, "The End," in *The Blackwell Companion to Catholicism*, ed. James Buckley, Frederick Christian Bauerschmidt, and Trent Pomplun (Oxford: Wiley-Blackwell, 2011), 382.
[4]Jürgen Moltmann, "Control Is Good—Trust Is Better: Freedom and Security in a 'Free World,'" *Theology Today* 62, no. 4 (2006): 10.
[5]John Sanders, "Divine Suffering in an Openness of God Perspective," in *The Sovereignty of God Debate*, ed. D. Stephen Long and George Kalantzis (Eugene, OR: Wipf and Stock, 2009), 114.
[6]Terence E. Frethiem, *The Suffering of God: An Old Testament Perspective* (Philadelphia: Fortress, 1984), 123.
[7]H. Richard Niebuhr, "Reflections on Faith, Hope, and Love," *The Journal of Religious Ethics* 2, no. 1 (1974): 155.

implicit. Relational theists argue that God faces an open future with some suspense because God experiences the passing of time. To add to that, God wants and desires what is truly in our (God and human) best interests but because humans are free to either accept or reject God's call, God's desires are not a forgone conclusion. Being that it is both good for us and pleasing to God if we accept God's call, God hopes—hopes that we will unite with God and God's purposes of love and justice.

The Old Testament contains a considerable amount of conditional statements attributed to God. God speaks in terms of *if* and *might*.[8] These passages, along with statements of divine mind changing and regret, make a strong case for much of the future being open and un- settled. An unsettled future, coupled with divine plans that God does not unilaterally bring to fruition, means that God does not control what happens and yet has desires about how the future unfolds. Given this reality, what is God's disposition toward the future? Is God cynical re- garding partnership with humanity? Is God anxious about what might or might not happen? The reality of human failure throughout history would make it perfectly natural for God to be cynical or in despair, yet it seems that God is neither. God is in fact hopeful. God waits patiently for the actualization of the divine project while constantly working toward its good and wonderful end. While God is not naive about the future, God nonetheless faces the future with hopefulness of a full and thorough union of the divine and human.

Hope is a necessary element of God's relationship with creation. Just as God believes in and trusts, God also hopes. One quality of belief is that it makes trust steadier for when one believes that another will be true it is generally easier to commit to that person. However, when there is little reason to trust and yet the relationship necessitates trust be found, hope becomes a necessary element of faith. God hopes that the trust given will not be in vain. God hopes humanity will respond to the divine call for communion and that we will become what God desires humanity to be.

---

[8]See Greg Boyd, *God of the Possible: A Biblical Introduction to the Open View of God* (Grand Rapids: Baker Books, 2000), 69-71; Fretheim, *The Suffering of God*, 47-49.

David Basinger writes, "The God of FWT [free will theism] hopes that individuals will always freely choose to do what he would have them do. But for the free will theist there can be no assurance that they will do so."[9] Because God has created significantly free beings, there is never complete assurance that these free agents will do what God has decreed or become what God has intended them to become. God, nonetheless, remains committed to the relationship being forged between divinity and humanity. This commitment is fostered and fueled by divine hope, for without hope a relational God could only foresee wrath and destruction. Hope delays judgment, meaning that God patiently awaits pure fellowship with the creation. God waits for love given to become love returned.

HOPE DEFINED

In the simplest of terms, hope is a positive attitude—a disposition—about how one faces a crisis. Some have equated hope with optimism and confidence, but this may be saying more about hope than is necessary. It seems that one can be hopeful without being optimistic, encouraged without being confident. It is easy to say what hope is not—it is not outright knowledge or even presumption that a good outcome will obtain. What exactly hope is and how hope might apply to God will prove a bit more difficult.

Adrienne Martin is critical of what she calls the "orthodox" definition of hope. According to Martin, the "orthodox" view is "a combination of the desire for an outcome and the belief that the outcome is possible but not certain."[10] Martin argues that this approach is far too reductionist, suggesting that quite often our experiences of hope are "more profound than is typical of desire; hope seems to color our experience in a way that

---

[9]David Basinger, *The Case for Freewill Theism: A Philosophical Assessment* (Downers Grove, IL: InterVarsity Press, 1996), 36.

[10]Adrienne M. Martin, *How We Hope: A Moral Psychology* (Princeton, NJ: Princeton University Press, 2014), 4. Martin argues that this "orthodox" view is a modern Western development that reduced hope to a single motivational power such as "desire" or "passion." This was in opposition to the medieval view in which Aquinas understood hope as part of the bifurcated subrational appetite. Aquinas saw hope as an irascible passion that gives us the ability to overcome obstacles.

is richer and more specific than does desire."[11] I agree, hope includes desire but cannot be reduced to a particular kind of desire. Whatever it is we feel when we hope, we seem to feel something more than simply attraction plus the possibility of getting what we want.

Romanus Cessario, in assessing Aquinas's writings on hope, says we find four characteristics of hope. In this section I will show that, while Cessario is only speaking about human hope, these characteristics can apply to divine hope as well. Let us begin by listing the four characteristics:

> First, hope concerns only the movement towards what perfects the human person, toward good objects or ends that enhance personal dignity of the one endowed with spiritual powers. . . . Second, hope looks toward the future, for a person never hopes for what he or she already possess. . . . Third, one speaks of hoping only when the attainment of the good, future object involves some difficulty or an element of arduousness. . . . Finally, only something that is attainable elicits hope; a person must judge that the hoped for reality lies within the realm of possible options.[12]

In what follows I will unpack a bit more of what each of these characteristics might entail and then argue how they each can apply to the open and relational understanding of God. As I apply each of these to God, remember that I am not suggesting there will always be an exact correlation between human and divine hope.

Hope looks to the good. Hope is a virtue, that is, "something that perfects us, what we must practice as a habit, be trained in, and work properly to preserve."[13] Like all virtues, hope is an act or disposition that aims at an individual good or excellence. In Aristotelian terms, virtues constitute the agent's happiness or flourishing. Aquinas too speaks of

---

[11]Martin, *How We Hope*, 5. Martin's own view could be called "orthodox plus" since she says that to hope for an outcome is more than to be attracted to the outcome and believe the outcome is possible but also includes how the hopeful person sees the probability as "license" for feeling hopeful. Also, the hopeful person uses the desire for the outcome as reason for certain activities (see chap. 2). Since Martin's treatment seems to be more about *how* we hope than what hope is, I will set this discussion aside.

[12]Romanus Cessario, OP, "The Theological Virtue of Hope," in *The Ethics of Aquinas*, ed. Stephen Pope (Washington, DC: Georgetown University Press, 2002), 232-33.

[13]Charles Pinches, "On Hope," in *Virtues and Their Vices*, ed. Kevin Tempe and Craig A. Boyd (Oxford: Oxford University Press, 2014), 349.

hope as that which is good for the agent since it is God that hope helps one attain. Virtues need not be limited to self-flourishing. Robert Adams discusses moral virtue as "persisting excellence in being *for* the good. . . . A virtuous person, a morally good person, will of course be *for* good things and against bad things—and not in just any way, but excellently."[14] If we think of virtue as Adams does, in terms of being *for* the good, then I believe we can easily apply this to God.

The author of the book of James says that every good and perfect gift is from God (Jas 1:17). Paul says that in all things God works for the good of those who love God (Rom 8:28). A being of perfect love surely only works for the good. If God works only for the good, we should have no doubt that God too hopes for the good. God never desires that we sin. God never desires meaningless suffering. God never desires that evil remain unredeemed. Thus, God only works and thus hopes for the final good, which is, at least in part, our perfect union with God. Does it not sound strange to say that God as perfect love desires the good and works for the good but does not hope for the good?

As we have seen in the previous chapters, God as pure, unsurpassable love is a vulnerable God who has willingly become dependent on us in the sharing of power. By way of the cross, God gives all for us. Does this mean that God as pure love cannot also hope and work for God's own good? The writer of Hebrews says that Jesus, "for the sake of the joy that was set before him endured the cross" (Heb 12:2). God's hope in us is not merely a hope for our good alone but also for God's good. While it might sound strange to hear, we are God's hope—just as God is ours. The human and divine hopes are not exclusive of one another but in concert. We hope in one another. Letty Russell, when discussing the meaning of human and divine partnership, writes, "It is an anticipation of a new reality breaking in as we, like Israel, hope against hope. We hope in God

---

[14]Robert Merrihew Adams, *A Theory of Virtue: Excellence in Being* for *the Good* (Oxford: Oxford University Press, 2006), 15, quoted in Kevin Tempe and Craig A. Boyd, eds., *Virtues and Their Vices* (Oxford: Oxford University Press, 2014), 8. Italics mine, though Adams does italicize "for" in the title of his book.

because God hopes in us and we can celebrate God's hope as we respond to the call to live out the promise in our lives."[15] Russell, while quoting Moltmann, goes on to discuss that we wait and trust in God because of a shared hope: "'We are hoping for God, because [God] hopes for us.' Because of God's hope for us we search out the meaning of partnership, not as a new ideology, but rather out of trust in God's promised future, and we are willing to live with poverty of knowledge about our future because of that trust."[16]

Hope looks toward the future. It would be strange to hope that I one day go to Disneyland while actually riding Space Mountain. I could hope to return to Disneyland, but that is quite different than hoping to get there. Hope is about the future. More specifically, as I will show, hope is about an open future. Aquinas also argues that hope looks toward the future, for it would be odd to hope for a state that one is currently in. For Aquinas, this means that those already in the beatific vision no longer have hope for they now have what they could previously only hope for. Those who are still in their mortal state look forward in hope to that future day. Hope looks forward toward the attainment of some good. As a theological virtue, the good that one hopes for is God, but we can see this characteristic of hope in examples other than the theological.

There are many sorts of things we hope for on a daily basis, some rather sobering while others quite trivial. We might hope that our child's future spouse will be faithful, and we can hope not to gain weight during the holidays. When running late for work one might specifically hope that traffic will be lighter than normal, though the general hope will be to somehow get to work on time. Alternatively, when diagnosed with cancer and facing a long and painful treatment, one's hope will be that the cancer will be destroyed and the treatment not in vain. In each of these cases hope is for a future good, something we do not already possess. On some accounts, it would be odd to speak of having and yet

---

[15]Letty M. Russell, *The Future of Partnership* (Philadelphia: Westminster, 1979), 154.

[16]Jürgen Moltmann, "Theology as Eschatology," in *The Future of Hope*, ed. Frederick Herzog (New York: Herder & Herder, 1970), 33, quoted in Russell, *The Future of Partnership*, 165.

hoping to get the very same thing. Once arriving at work on time it would be strange to speak of hoping to get to work on time.[17]

Accordingly, when we hope we hope that some *possible* future state will obtain. "The person who hopes *believes* that the future is open, believes that something personally worthwhile is possible."[18] If we were timeless beings, hope would be an absurd notion. How could we speak of hoping for anything if there was no future and no possible? It is difficult to imagine simultaneously referencing notions of *hope* with an atemporal being. God, however, is quite likely a being who is not beyond or above temporality. Relational theists of every stripe affirm this statement.[19] God remembers the past, knows the present, and faces a significantly indeterminate future. God works to bring about a particular future both near and far. In working to bring about some desired future, God is affected by the past while currently working to affect the future in concert with other persons. As shown in chapter one, God cannot bring about the future God desires acting alone for the future reality God desires is only possible by cooperation. In fact, that is the future God desires—human and divine communion. However, for now, God still hopes—hopes that we will be cooperative partners in covenant with God.

As stated above, relational theists understand God to be a temporal being. But why? Should we not believe that God is somehow "above" or "outside" time and is thus able to see all past, present, and future in one glance? Should we profess that God only knows an eternal now and so

---

[17]It may be possible to hope for what you already have, provided you don't know you have it. A student can say, "I hope I get an A on my paper" or a person who checks the lotto results a few days after can rightly say, "I hope these are the winning numbers." In this way it might be possible for one who believes that every future state has already been worked out by God's sovereign will to still say, "I hope I have salvation," even though it has already been determined. And so, since the knowing of whether what is hoped for is still in the future, I will not push this point. But if one has full knowledge that they have won the lottery it is irrational to say, "I hope I won the lottery." As long as there is question about the veracity of the hoped-for state, hope is possible and logical.

[18]Joseph Godfrey, *A Philosophy of Human Hope*, Studies in Philosophy and Religion 9 (Dordrecht, The Netherlands: Martinus Nijhoff, 1987), 215.

[19]Open and relational theists are not the only ones who conceive of God as being situated in time. Molinists and some Simple Foreknowledge advocates hold that God experiences the passing of time. But as I will show in a moment, divine hope is not possible on their account since God exhaustively knows the future.

every instant of time is collapsed into a single moment for God? To answer this question thoroughly is beyond the scope and purpose of this book. My intent, rather, is to show why a God of unsurpassable love, as open and relational theists understand, should speak about God's hope, and God being temporal is one reason why there is divine hope. I will, however, make a few brief comments explaining why open and relational theists do believe God operates "in" time.

Discussing God's love in relation to time can feel a bit like the chicken or egg question. Does God's temporality necessitate how God loves, or does God's love necessitate the reality of time? While there might be very good reasons to begin with the nature of time and then argue why God is temporal, my preference, as I have tried to do throughout this book, is to begin with God's nature as personal, responsive love and see why this gives reason to believe God is temporal. Nicholas Wolterstorff asks the provocative question, "Does God have a history?" Asked another way, "Is there a story to be told about God's actions, about God's responses to what transpires in God's creation, and about the flow of knowledge which lies behind those?"[20] For Wolterstorff, and many others, the answer is a definite yes. The Bible depicts God as acting, responding, waiting, remembering, and anticipating. The Christ story is about God *becoming* human. Eschatology speaks to what God has promised to do. It may be the case that the whole of the biblical language about God acting at various times in this world is thoroughly metaphoric, but, given the overwhelming biblical language of God remembering the past and planning for the future, the burden of proof is on the classical theists and those who hold that God is timeless or eternal as opposed to temporal and everlasting.[21]

Out of love God made us beings who are free and able to respond to God's grace or to freely refuse it. This freedom means that if our choices are genuinely contingent, then much of the future must also be genuinely

---

[20]Nicholas Wolterstorff, "Unqualified Divine Temporality," in *God and Time: Four Views*, ed. Gregory E. Ganssle (Downers Grove, IL: InterVarsity Press, 2001), 203.
[21]Wolterstorff, "Unqualified Divine Temporality," 188.

contingent. If the future is at least in part contingent, then God can only know those aspects of the future contingently. If God knows them as future contingencies, then God is temporal.[22] The temporality of God means that God's love is responsive. God's love is not a single event, a "one and done" timeless act, but a continuous series of actions and responses. If God has acted in love and desires our love freely returned, then God acts in the hope for our good and loving responses. If God is not temporal and/or we are not genuinely free, then God cannot hope. But if we are free and our free contingent acts are known to God as contingencies, not actualities, then God as a loving being celebrates hope. Delights in hope.

Hope looks to overcome the arduous. If you could take one pill and your illness, whatever it might be, would be gone, guaranteed, would you likely speak of hoping for a cure? While such a pill or cure is currently our hope, once it is here and established we would no longer speak in terms of hoping. While people once hoped for a way of crossing America in less than a month, we no longer have that hope. If what you desire is immediately or easily at hand, it is unlikely you would think about that desire in terms of hoping. As I sit in this restaurant I have (at least) two clear desires: to make progress on this chapter and to drink my coffee. Plainly, only one of these two desires is arduous or demanding. It is quite easy for me to reach over, pick up the cup, and drink my coffee. When the cup is empty, I can simply walk over and refill. There was no feeling of "I hope I get some coffee," I just walked over and got it. Writing, however, is another story. It is difficult, consuming, and is often accompanied with the thought, "I hope I finish this book" and "I hope I am able to communicate my thoughts clearly." For this reason Aquinas "speaks of hoping only when the attainment of the good, future object involves some difficulty or an element of arduousness."[23]

---

[22]For a thorough discussion of this argument, see William Hasker, *God, Time, and Knowledge* (Ithaca, NY: Cornell University Press, 1989). For a brief summary of Hasker's argument, see Garrett J. DeWeese, *God and the Nature of Time* (Burlington, VT: Ashgate, 2004), 217-20.

[23]Cessario, "The Theological Virtue of Hope," 233.

I am not suggesting that one can only speak about hoping when the desired object or state is exceedingly difficult. If I were in a restaurant in which I had to wait on a server to refill my cup I could certainly say, "I hope she brings me coffee soon," and this would be a perfectly rational statement even though my waiting for a third cup is hardly arduous. Yet while statements about hope are not limited to the arduous, feelings of hope and its sustaining power are felt most in those demanding situations or trials of life. I will say more about this in a moment, but for now let's change the language a bit and say that while it is possible to feel a sense of hope when what one hopes for is not difficult, it is not a rational hope when what you desire is in hand, guaranteed, or a forgone certainty. Martin is correct that one cannot rationally speak about cases of hope that have a probability of either 0 or 1. "It is just crazy, clearly, to be hopeful . . . about an outcome one believes has literally no chance of occurring or that one believes is certain to occur."[24] One clear characteristic of hope then is that what is hoped for cannot be understood by the one hoping as certain, that is, it cannot have a probability of 1. That would hardly be arduous. It is simply irrational to hope for what you have (as shown above) or to hope for what is believed to be certain. If I were to think and feel at the very same moment, "I am certain I am in a coffee shop" and "I hope I am in a coffee shop," I would have to agree with Martin's assessment that this is "crazy" talk. While we may mistakenly hope for what is absolute and certain because of incomplete and fallible knowledge, what God knows to be true is in fact true. I could hope that I won last night's lottery since I do not know the numbers, but God could never hope I won last night's lottery since God currently knows I did not. God, therefore, never hopes for what is; God only rightly hopes for what could be.

Paul expresses an idea like the probability assessment that hope must be less than 1. He writes, "For in hope we were saved. Now hope that is

---

[24]Martin, *How We Hope*, 51. Martin speaks about believing a certain state is possible or impossible because our hope is less about the reality of a situation and more about our assessment of the situation. I can rationally feel hopeful about a future state that is either impossible or certain if I am unaware of conditions that make that state impossible or certain.

seen is not hope. For who hopes for what is seen? But if we hope for what we do not see, we wait for it with patience" (Rom 8:24-25). I think here Paul is equating "seen" with "attained."[25] Aquinas uses this passage to argue that there will be no hope for those in heaven. He writes that the object of (theological) hope is eternal happiness and once obtained hope is no longer future or arduous and so hope comes to its end or telos.[26] While there might be reason to challenge Aquinas's claim that hope ends once one enters the beatific vision, I think we can agree with him that hope ceases to be hope once that which has been hoped for is entirely gained.[27]

What if God is temporal but has exhaustive simple foreknowledge of the future? Can a God with complete and infallible foreknowledge genuinely hope? It seems to me that if the future is settled in such a way that God could have knowledge of how future contingent choices turn out, then there is no reason for God to hope since God is certain about every outcome. As already discussed, the open theist believes that God knows the truth of all actualities *as* actualities and the truth of all possibilities *as* possibilities. God cannot know with a probability of 1 that a person in the future will freely choose to keep a found wallet instead of returning it to its owner. Nevertheless, God can hope he returns the wallet. God does not know with certainty who in future generations will actually submit to God's will and love God and their neighbor, but God can hope that all do this. In fact, if the open and relational theists are right, then it is only good and moral that God hope for such things. This might be a good place to return to hope being arduous.

It seems to me that God's hope for Israel and the church, let alone the world, has been arduous at times. Israel is said to have been a "stiff-necked" people (Ex 32:9) and an unfaithful wife (Ezek 16). The church

---

[25]This is consistent with Paul's sense of "now and not yet." We have the first fruits of hope, but we do not have in full what we hope for. If we did it would be "seen" and thus no longer hoped for.
[26]Aquinas, *Summa Theologica*, 2-2.18.2.
[27]It may be the case that as long as there is temporal existence there will be hope. While I may have what I desire, I can have a sense of hope that I will not lose the good I have. This would not be a hope that overcomes fear but a general sense of hopefulness.

likewise has many times been on the wrong side of justice, opting for war, racism, bigotry, slavery, and misogamy. Yet God has not given up hope in the church. God's spirit still rests upon this failed and flawed amalgamation of people. Why? Because God still has hope that the church can be what God desires it to be, the embodiment of divine love and unmerited grace, the means of divine justice and mercy. Not because of the church's own abilities, but because of a God who continues to lavish the church with immeasurable faith.[28]

Hope is also born out of adversity. It is desire plus difficulty plus dubitability. What one hopes for must be desired, difficult to achieve, and its obtainment less than certain. Without trouble, there is no need for hope. Hope is arduous for God in that hope naturally brings with it doubts about the likelihood of the desired outcome.[29] God hopes that we return God's great love, but this is not a forgone conclusion. Divine hope is costly because there are real risks of God's hopes being dashed by our egoism. Other theologies do not have a God whose love is so vulnerable; by their understanding God risks nothing and so hopes for nothing. The God of meticulous providence cannot logically be disappointed since God is the cause of each and every moment. The future is utterly fixed and unchangeable in God's providence, and so God has no hope for anything since God has all that God desires. Some find this to be comforting, that God can neither hope nor be disappointed since everything God wants God gets. I, however, am not reassured by this depiction of God given the past and current state of the world.

Hope looks to the possible. A popular meme says, "Hope is a passion for the possible." We can wish the impossible were not impossible, but we cannot rightly hope for what is strictly impossible. As noted above, Aquinas argued, "Only something that is attainable elicits hope." This is as true for God as it is for us—hope is found only in the possible.[30]

---

[28]Thanks to Bryan Overbaugh for helping me articulate this.

[29]Sanders aptly puts it, "God freely enters into genuine give-and-take relations with us. This entails risk taking on his part because we are capable of letting God down." John Sanders, *The God Who Risks: A Theology of Providence*, 1st ed. (Downers Grove, IL: InterVarsity Press, 1998), 282.

[30]Most philosophers agree with Aquinas, noting the difficulty in saying God can do *all* things.

As shown above, Martin argues that it is illogical to be hopeful about an outcome that literally has no chance of happening. I cannot logically hope my great grandmother gets a baby sister. Even more definitive, I cannot hope that tomorrow it will be 1985. So, let's apply this to God. Most assuredly, God is not illogical and so God does not hope for what is logically impossible. God does not hope for things God infallibly knows can and will never be. For example, God does not hope anything about the past. God does not currently hope that the Holocaust did not happen. Notice that the language does not allow us to speak about hoping for the past. Even if I say, "I hope Matt got home safe last night," I am not so much hoping that the past can be other than what it was but that I currently hope that I will get good news about Matt's safe journey. We can wish that the past be other than it was, fantasize about "what if things had been different." To hold out hope that the past can be other than what it was, however, is thoroughly irrational.[31]

In the last section, I argued that God would not have hope if God is the sovereign cause of all events since it is illogical to hope for what you have. Still, what if God is not the cause of all but nonetheless has infallible knowledge of what is to come? If God is atemporal and knows each event as a single moment or if God is temporal but has exhaustive simple foreknowledge of every future event, then God again has no hope. If God knows that I will one day in the future accidently take a medication I am allergic to, and that results in grave consequences, and God's knowledge of the event cannot be mistaken, then I cannot do other than take that medication. God may desire that I not take the medication, but God cannot rightly hope I do not take it. At best, God can wish the future be other than what God knows it to be, but God cannot hope it be other. It is even questionable whether God can rightly desire what God infallibly

These philosophers suggest that God's omnipotence means God can do anything that is logically possible. For instance, God cannot cause an object to exist and not exist at the same time in the exact same manner (see *Summa Theologica*, 1.25.3). Relating this back to God's hope, just as God can only do what is logically possible, it seems only right that God would only hope for what is logically possible.

[31]For an interesting discussion of God's ability to change the past, see Kevin Tempe, "Prayer for the Past," in *Arguing About Religion*, ed. Kevin Tempe (New York: Routledge, 2009), 414-28.

knows is impossible unless we redefine desire in the weakest terms possible. God might think it would be nice if the future could be other than what God knows it will be, but God cannot be passionately desirous about an impossible alternative future.

This is where the *actual* and the *impossible* differ regarding hope and desire. It is possible and reasonable to have and desire something concurrently. God can rightly have and desire our love. To have and yet also hope for our love is problematic (unless we mean something like God has our love and hopes that we continue to love God into the future). It is also problematic, however, to say that God desire what God does not have and *can never have*. God as a perfectly logical being would not passionately desire the impossible. God does not desire two plus three equal seven for that would be irrational. God cannot rationally desire the past be other than what it is even if God might wish it were other. Again, I think it is reasonable to say that *if* God did have exhaustive simple foreknowledge of even all future contingents, then God could wish some were not so, but God could not rightly desire they be other than what they are. Said another way, God can be attracted to all sorts of states, but to rationally desire the impossible would be outside God's character as *omnisophic*.

If it is problematic to say God desires what is impossible, it is wildly foolish to say God hopes for the impossible. For God to know infallibly that I will have a reaction to a medication and yet hope I do not have this reaction is nonsense. Maybe God could hope that God's knowledge was somehow wrong, but this is equally nonsense. This would be God hoping to be something other than God. God cannot logically hope to change the future since this too would equate to God being wrong and thus, God being not God. If the future is fixed in God's knowledge, then God is unable to change the future. So, if God has not sovereignly caused all future states, but knows that at least some of the future will not be what God desires, then God can only face the future in one of two possible ways: stoic resignation or despair. God either sees undesirable but unchangeable aspects of the future and resigns God's self to the fact that this is simply the way it will be and chooses to cease being concerned about it, or God sees undesirable aspects of the future but despairs because there is nothing anyone can do about them, not even God. We are a long way from the Anselmian God who cannot be conceived to be any better. Certainly it is better that God have hope for the future than stoic resignation or outright despair!

This brings us back to the idea that the one who hopes must believe that what is desired is possible. Hope is more than fantasizing, wish fulfillment, and even more than desire. Hope believes that the desired is possible—even when highly improbable. God believes we are, by God's grace, capable of fellowship and communion. God believes that by means of unrelenting love there is hope in the divine project. God believes, and so acts on that hope, that God's love can bring us into divine fellowship. Since the future is open to contingent possibilities, God's hope, while at times disappointed, is nevertheless alive and well. If God is inexorable love, then God is inexorably hoping and ever hopeful.

Because hope is always an attraction and desire, hope is never idle. Hope is a future-oriented stance that drives present actions. We currently hope that the future state desired will come about, but we do not sit idle when our actions can help bring about what is hoped for. Hope requires we act when our efforts will increase the possibility of its obtainment. To hope without acting in such cases is mere fantasizing or waiting for the inevitable. Neither wish nor expectation will change a course of action. Hope, however, like belief, is active. It seeks and works to bring about that which is desired even if it is not completely within one's own power. God thus hopes as God works to bring about what God desires, all the while knowing that it is not wholly within God's control. God, as a dependent being, must hope from time to time if God is to be truly lovingly, relational, and good.

BIBLICAL EXAMPLES OF DIVINE HOPE

So far, we have seen that hope means being attracted to a favorable and good future state, not in absolute certainty nor in wish-laden fantasies.

The Bible does not speak univocally about God's hope—but it comes close. The following two examples speak to God's hope. The first example regards the translation of the word "perhaps," and the second concerns the implications of God being "patient."

"Perhaps." Conditional statements attributed to God reveal God's posture before an open future, but these statements at times also reveal God's hope. Exodus 4 reveals a dialogue between God and Moses that is replete with conditional language by both. God instructs Moses to go to the Israelite elders and reveal God's intentions for Moses to be God's delegate. Moses responds to God's instructions with, "But suppose they do not believe me or listen to me." God gives Moses a miraculous sign and replies, "so that they *may* believe that the LORD . . . has appeared to you" (Ex 4:1, 5 emphasis added).[32] In the event that this miracle is un-convincing, God gives further instructions followed by the statement, "*If* they will not believe you or heed the first sign, they *may* believe the second sign. *If* they will not believe even these two signs or heed you . . ." (Ex 4:8-9 emphasis added). Later in the narrative God's inner thoughts are said to contain deliberations and possible conditions concerning the path the Israelites should take in their exodus. "When Pharaoh let the people go, God did not lead them by way of the land of the Philistines, although that was nearer; for God thought, 'If the people face war, they may change their minds and return to Egypt'" (Ex 13:17). These state-ments of "if" and "may" not only reveal that God does not know the actual future outcome of the action but also seem to reveal that God is hopeful that such actions will produce their desired ends. God gives signs to Moses in the hope that the Egyptians may listen.

Along with the conditional statements "if" and "may," there are Old Testament passages in which God uses the word "perhaps" concerning future free actions of a person. The Hebrew word *'ûlay*, typically

---

[32]It could be suggested that the use of *may* would be better understood as *in order that*, eliminat-ing the conditionality of the statement. That God gives the sign "in order that they *will* believe." It is certainly the case that God intends for Pharaoh to believe, that God gives the sign "in order that they believe that the LORD . . . has appeared to you." But the context of God's continuing dialogue with Moses confirms the uncertainty of the outcome of God's intention.

translated as "perhaps" or "it may be," is primarily "used in human speech to indicate uncertainty regarding the future."[33] Of the forty-five occurrences of *'ûlay* in the Old Testament, in five passages the word is spoken by God (Is 47:12; Jer 26:3; 36:3, 7; 51:8; Ezek 12:3). Terence Fretheim suggests that the word *'ûlay* is "often tinged with a note of hope."[34] However, I believe there is more than a tinge of hope expressed in the usage of this word given the contexts. David Reimer, in his essay, "An Overlooked Term in Old Testament Theology: Perhaps," investigates *'ûlay* and how it is used in relation to both human and divine.[35] He first explores a few of the uses of *'ûlay* involving humans to get a clearer picture of divine uses.[36] First, in Genesis 16 we have Sarai planning to establish Abram's heir by having him conceive a child with Hagar. In verse two Sarai states, "Please go in to my maid; *perhaps* I will obtain children through her" (Gen 16:2 NASB).[37] Reimer suggests that we cannot precisely know what is meant by *'ûlay*, but it appears that "Sarai hopes by this plan to overcome her own barrenness."[38] Likewise, the story of Jacob's fearful meeting with his estranged brother Esau leads Jacob to pray for God's help and deliverance. Jacob also planned to give Esau many gifts desiring to win his brother's favor. This is all couched in contingent yet hopeful language. Jacob thought that after the gifts were delivered "perhaps he will accept me" (Gen 32:20). It could be said, "Jacob hopes for a favourable reception based not on his prayers, but on his presents."[39] Reimer deals with several other passages in which he argues that the human use of *'ûlay* clearly

[33]Fretheim, *The Suffering God*, 45.
[34]Fretheim, *The Suffering God*, 45.
[35]David J. Reimer, "An Overlooked Term in Old Testament Theology: Perhaps," in *Covenant as Context: Essays in Honour of E. W. Nicholson*, ed. A. D. H. Mayes and R. B. Salters (New York: Oxford University Press, 2003), 325-46.
[36]Reimer puts the uses of *'ûlay* into three categories: (1) *'ûlay* + hypothetical situation; (2) action/situation + *'ûlay* + possible past/future outcome [human]; (3) action/situation + *'ûlay* + possible past/future outcome [divine]. Reimer focuses upon examples of the second since these deal with possible future human outcomes and include three passages in which God utters *'ûlay* in relation to human action/situation (334).
[37]The NRSV reads, "Sarai said to Abram, 'You see that the Lord has prevented me from bearing children; go in to my slave-girl; it *may be* that I shall obtain children by her.' And Abram listened to the voice of Sarai." The connotation here still expresses Sarai's hope.
[38]Reimer, "An Overlooked Term in Old Testament Theology: Perhaps," 335.
[39]Reimer, "An Overlooked Term in Old Testament Theology: Perhaps," 335.

suggests that the person was hopeful.[40] It could be said then that 'ûlay expresses hope where knowledge is uncertain, even when God has made known divine commitments to a particular course of action. Amos, as well, holds out hope (Amos 5:15) that an Israelite "return to justice might possibly promote the chances of divine mercy" and also that God would "act for good in spite of his announced intention."[41] In each of these cases, the use of "perhaps" denotes more than an expression of the unknown; it expresses a hopefulness in a particular end.

The human use of this word is generally in situations where the user seems to be hoping that the outcome be other than what is likely. There is uncertainty about what will happen next, perhaps even a negative expectation, but there is hope that "perhaps" some other result will come. Can this be applied to the divine utterances and uses of 'ûlay? Reimer thinks so. "In the same way that human behaviour is the basis for a hoped-for response from God, so too God holds out such hopes for his people."[42] Of the five times 'ûlay is attributed to God, three can be said to convey the idea that God is hoping that the message will effect change in the hearers (Jer 26:3; 36:3; Ezek 12:3).[43]

Ezekiel 12:3 reads, "Perhaps they will understand, though they are a rebellious house." In context, God is hoping the stern words of the prophet might, perhaps, lead the Jerusalemites out of rebellion and coming exile. Likewise, both passages from Jeremiah reveal God's hopefulness: "Perhaps they will listen and everyone will turn from his evil way, that I may repent of the calamity which I am planning to do to them because of the evil of their deeds" (Jer 26:3 NASB) and "Perhaps the house of Judah will hear all the calamity which I plan to

---

[40]Caleb's hope of entering the promised land (Josh 14), Jonathan's hope and risk in attacking the Philistine garrison (1 Sam 14:6), David's hope for a good outcome after being cursed (2 Sam 16:12), and the story of Balaam (Num 22–24) contains five occurrences of 'ûlay in which a specific outcome is hoped for. For more information, see Reimer, "An Overlooked Term in Old Testament Theology: Perhaps," 335-39.

[41]Reimer, "An Overlooked Term in Old Testament Theology: Perhaps," 336-37.

[42]Reimer, "An Overlooked Term in Old Testament Theology: Perhaps," 339.

[43]The other two uses do not seem to convey a message of hope. Isaiah 47:12 is a hypothetical situation, and Jer 51:8, while it has a hopeful tone, is not directed to persons in order to change a situation.

bring on them, in order that every man will turn from his evil way; then I will forgive their iniquity and their sin" (Jer 36:3 NASB). Each statement delivered through the prophet reveals God's desired and hopeful outcome—a turning from evil. But the desire is not simply for a change in the audience but also in God's actions as well. Jeremiah 36:3 shows that God desires to forgive and thus hopes they will turn from their evil. Even more powerfully, Jeremiah 26:3 states that God desires to change God's mind concerning what is intended. In this passage, belief and hope are powerfully linked in the life of the divine. God believes disaster likely awaits Judah but nonetheless hopes they will listen and turn from evil. In this sense, God experiences what all humans have experienced: God's belief of an outcome at odds with God's hope. God knows Judah too well and believes it is unlikely they will heed the warning, but God still holds out hope.[44] "God in essence is hoping that an unpredictable event might in fact occur."[45] In the end, God's hope went unfulfilled—Judah did not listen. These passages support the case that God faces an open future since "perhaps" language is deceitful if God fully knows the outcome. More than revealing an open future, these examples reveal a God who hopes. As Reimer emphatically states, "In all three cases, the prophet, receiving a word from Yahweh, is instructed to convey a message which Yahweh hopes— it cannot be stated more strongly than that—will have an intended effect on his people."[46]

This hopeful expression of "perhaps" also appears in the New Testament, although only once. The Septuagint typically translates *'ûlay* into *isōs*,[47] a word found only in Luke 20:13, the parable of the vineyard

---

[44]It seems that God hopes that God's beliefs here will be changed.

[45]Fretheim, *The Suffering of God*, 46.

[46]Reimer, "An Overlooked Term in Old Testament Theology: Perhaps," 339. Steven C. Roy offers the suggestion that these passages reveal God speaking in anthropomorphic metaphor. God is speaking in terms of the uncertainty experienced by those hearing the message. In this view, God knows the future free choice of the audience but speaks to them from the human vantage point of Jeremiah. For more information, see Steven C. Roy, *How Much Does God Foreknow? A Comprehensive Biblical Study* (Downers Grove, IL: IVP Academic, 2006), 185-87.

[47]Ezekiel 12:3 is an exception, translating *'ûlay* as *hopōs*.

and tenants. The parable is clearly a lesson in Israelite history. God is
the vineyard owner, the servants are the prophets, and the "beloved
son" is Jesus.[48] Luke derived the parable from Mark 12:1-12 but with
some changes. Most important for this work is the addition of *isōs*.
After the tenants have rejected all of the vineyard owner's messengers,
the owner's son is introduced. Mark 12:6 says, "He had still one other,
a beloved son. Finally he sent him to them, saying, 'They will respect
my son.'" Luke, however, changes the story to include a soliloquy followed by a statement of hopefulness, yet unquestionably shy of certainty. Luke 20:13 reads, "Then the owner of the vineyard said, 'What
shall I do? I will send my beloved son; perhaps [*isōs*] they will respect
him.'" Luke's version has an added sense of hopefulness that Mark and
Matthew do not. The vineyard owner is hopeful that the workers, although they have beaten the messengers, will respect his son. There is
no sense of certainty in this passage. Luke's addition of "What shall I
do?" and the inclusion of *isōs* shifts and softens Mark's original definitive statement, "They will respect my son." The Lukan version
leaves Jesus' parable somewhat open-ended, with the readers wondering, along with the vineyard owner, "maybe so, maybe not."[49] Some
have suggested that Luke's redaction of Mark softens the reading and
"spare[s] God the error of not foreseeing the rejection of his son."[50]
Others, however, reject such ideas outright. Alfred Plummer writes,
"We must remember that it is the anthropos of ver. 9 who deliberates
as to what he shall do, says *isōs*, and expects that his son will be well
received. All this is the setting of the parable, and must not be pressed

---

[48]I. Howard Marshall, *The Gospel of Luke: A Commentary on the Greek Text*, The New International
Greek Testament Commentary 3 (Grand Rapids: Eerdmans, 1978), 726. Allusions to Israel's
history are made even stronger in Mark's and Matthew's renderings of the parable.

[49]Luke Timothy Johnson, *The Gospel of Luke*, Sacra Pagina 3 (Collegeville, MN: Liturgical Press,
1991), 305.

[50]Joseph A. Fitzmyer, *The Gospel According to Luke (X–XXIV): Introduction, Translation, and
Notes*, Anchor Bible 28a (New York: Paulist Press, 1982), 1284. Fitzmyer cites this approach as
found in Adolf Jèulicher, *Die Gleichnisreden Jesu*, 2 vols. (Tübingen: Mohr [Siebeck], 1910; repr.,
Darmstadt: Wissenschaftliche Buchgesellschaft, 1963), 2:391-92. Fitzmyer rejects this, stating,
"Luke was scarcely concerned with problems of God's foreknowledge. Luke has rather added
a dramatic touch!"

as referring to God. This man represents God, not by his perplexity, but by his long-suffering and mercy."[51] Likewise, Darrel Bock believes that the word *isōs* and the parable itself convey a message of "the master's hope for a respectful response," but that the soliloquy, and parable as a whole, "shows how a parable often does not correspond to reality, since God is never said to be hesitant or uncertain about the fate of his Son."[52]

It is possible these passages do not speak of God's hopefulness, but if that is the case, it leaves the reader a bit baffled, wondering just what the stories mean to convey. If God does not hope because the future is already fully known in the mind of God, then how can we be hopeful? While it is problematic to suggest that Mark ignored the fact that the vineyard owner was wrong, it is equally problematic to suggest that Luke adds *isōs* without any thought concerning its connotations of hope and uncertainty in relation to God. We have Luke redacting Mark and adding the element of hope amid uncertainty. Otherwise, the Lukan change makes no sense.[53]

In light of relational theology, Luke 20:13 supports the Old Testament passages in which God utters "perhaps" in a hopeful context. The Lukan version of the parable depicts God—not simply in error—but in hopefulness, sending the son in the hope that the tenants will ("perhaps") listen to him. In the end, the vineyard owner does not get what is hoped. This is true in both Mark and Luke, but I think that Luke is trying to make explicit what Mark's version leaves implicit. God is a God who hopes and waits in patient anticipation.

God is patient. It is interesting how often authors speak about God's patience but with seemingly little thought concerning what it would mean for God to be patient. Patience, like hope, assumes a God existing "in"

---

[51] Alfred Plummer, *A Critical and Exegetical Commentary on the Gospel According to St. Luke*, 5th ed. The International Critical Commentary on the Holy Scriptures of the Old and New Testaments 28 (New York: Scribner's Sons, 1902), 460. It should be asked why "long-suffering" is applicable to God but not hopefulness!

[52] Darrell L. Bock, *Luke*, vol. 2: *9:51–24:53*, Baker Exegetical Commentary on the New Testament (Grand Rapids: Baker Academic, 2007), 1599-1600.

[53] Could it be that both Plummer and Bock have their theological presuppositions driving their exegesis?

time with an unsettled future. If all things in the future were foreordained or foreknown there would be no need for patience. Patience makes no sense if God is timeless, for patience assumes waiting with a great sense of anticipation or in discomfort with the current process of events.

Patience is not identical with hope, but they are quite similar. Hope is an attitude and posture of positive anticipation. To hope is to believe that a good result is at least possible, even if not likely. Patience is the ability to wait without provocation. It is the capacity to take the time and care necessary to obtain the desired outcome. It is not being apathetic or indifferent but trusting over time and waiting for the best of all possibilities.[54] Stanley Hauerwas rightly notes the necessary relationship between the two, stating, "Without patience, those filled with hope threaten to destroy that for which they hope. Without hope, the patient threaten to leave the world as they find it."[55] If God is not patient in hope, the free expression of love by God's creation may not come to fruition. Without hope, God might simply abandon the relationship altogether. Thus, in the proper context, patience and hope are complementary if not at times synonymous. An example is 2 Peter 3:9, "The Lord is not slow about his promise, as some think of slowness, but is patient with you, not wanting any to perish, but all to come to repentance." This passage can easily be read as God patiently waiting in the hope that all will come to repentance. For what other reason could it be said that God is patient in this context?

The parables of Jesus quite often speak to the patient hope of God even if that is not the central focus. Luke 13:6-9, the parable of the barren tree, tells a story of mercy and warning but also of hope.[56] It speaks of a vineyard owner who has a barren tree. The tree has not produced fruit for three years, and as many might advise, the tree needs to come down. However, here is where the parable shocks the

---

[54]Abraham J. Heschel, *The Prophets*, 2 vols. (Peabody, MA: Prince Press, 1962), 2:65.
[55]Stanley Hauerwas, *Matthew*, Brazos Theological Commentary on the Bible (Grand Rapids: Brazos, 2006), 207.
[56]Joel B. Green, *The Gospel of Luke* (Grand Rapids: Eerdmans, 1997), 515.

sensibilities. The vinedresser asks the owner to give it one more year. The parable is a call for repentance. Jesus had just spoken of tragedies that had befallen some first-century Judeans, using this as an opportunity to a call for repentance, but then, strangely enough, this parable is given. "The parable is an encouragement. We live in the midst of God's absurd mercy, unbelievably patient and generous. Let us then respond to grace, grace stretched wide, and repent! God is waiting, waiting. . . . Quick! Take advantage of the divine ellipsis!"[57] The call for repentance is couched in the reality of God's hopefulness. The tree has been given enough time to produce fruit, but when by all accounts it should be removed, it is instead given one more year, a year of care and attention. The vinedresser will cultivate the soil around the tree and will supply it with the nourishment it needs. In the end, neither knows if the tree will bear fruit; the parable has no final act. In this sense, the parable is quite real, for no one knows if the tree will bear fruit. In fact, it *seems* hopeless. However, the pleading of the vinedresser and the openness of the ending is the basis for hope.[58] The parable is left to the hearers (readers) to complete, and thus it includes hopefulness (either cautious or radical hope, depending on your disposition) that the tree still has the ability to produce fruit. Otherwise why spend another year on a dead tree?

Luke 15 has three parables all pertaining to lost items and joyful returns. There is the lost sheep, coin, and son. Yet the focus and intent of the parables are somewhat missed when the focus is centered on the items lost and not on the activity of the persons seeking and the attitudes expressed in their finding. In the first parable, a person sets off to find a single lost sheep while leaving the other ninety-nine behind. What seems like a foolish and risky act pays off when the shepherd finds the lost sheep. That, however, is what faith does: it inspires

---

[57]David Buttrick, *Speaking Parables: A Homiletic Guide* (Louisville, KY: Westminster John Knox, 2000), 196.

[58]Bernard Brandon Scott, *Hear Then the Parable: A Commentary on the Parables of Jesus* (Minneapolis: Fortress, 1990), 337-38.

persons to do the risky in the hope of great reward. The second parable is of a woman who loses a coin, then lights a lamp and searches, either in desperation or in hope, until she finds the coin. While we are not told whether the woman is desperate or hopeful (perhaps some of each), I think the attitude presented is one of hopefulness when the found coin is compared to a repentant sinner and the angels rejoice. There is no shock or surprise over the sinner repenting but rejoicing seemingly born out of animated hope.

The parable of the prodigal son, as it is typically termed, has come to be renamed more appropriately "the parable of the waiting father."[59] This is a good shift for, even though the younger son seems to be the central character, the parable is actually about the character of God, not the nature of sinners. The parable is quite fascinating, and readers can discuss any number of aspects. Yet the image of the father would have been the most scandalous, and also the most revolutionary, to the original hearers. The story is a shock to first-century Hebrew sensibilities, primarily because it represents the father as quite undignified. The image of the father running was both unusual and unbecoming, but the father running to a child who had insulted and embarrassed him was unthinkable.[60] Yet this is how the parable depicts God, running in abandonment toward his returning son. The image of the father running to his son is first set up by the image of a father patiently waiting in hopeful anticipation of the son's return.

The story is not only of the son coming home and addressing the father, or even merely about the father seeing the son's return and then running to meet him. The parable also gives a beautiful picture of a father waiting, looking, and hoping. Unlike the parables of the lost sheep and coin, this parable speaks in terms that convey the reality of authentic relationships. The sheep and coin needed to be found and

[59]This title is typically credited to Helmut Thielicke, *The Waiting Father: Sermons on the Parables of Jesus*, trans. John W. Doberstein (New York: Harper, 1959). Joachim Jeremias titles the parable "The Father's Love," in *Rediscovering the Parables*, Scribner Lyceum library editions (New York: Scribner, 1966), 191.

[60]Robert H. Stein, *An Introduction to the Parables of Jesus* (Philadelphia: Westminster, 1981), 120.

put in their rightful place, but, as a free being, the son must return on his own. The father could not chase the son and drag him home because then the relationship between them would still be estranged. The father had to let the son return of his own volition for that is a condition of relationality. Because the son had to return to reestablish the relationship himself, a father of love and mercy could only wait and hope.

The point of a parable should not be stretched beyond recognition, but if the parable's emphasis is to teach us something about the character of God, is it too much to suggest that this parable depicts God not only as a waiting and running father but also as a patiently hoping father?[61] The idea of the father seeing the son while he was still far off, running to him, and falling on his neck with kisses only makes sense in light of a father whose hopes and desires were realized. If the father was not hoping for the son's return, then the actions of the father make no sense. The father loved the son and hoped to love him again.

This parable is certainly more about God's hope than God's belief, for there is little reason to suppose the son would return. The fact of requesting the inheritance for less than noble purposes leads the reader to believe that the son had disdain for the father. In that culture, this would be equivalent to wishing the father were dead.[62] Yet the father's waiting and looking for the son revealed a hope and enthusiasm amid hopelessness and despair. The father was not hopeless; he waited and looked for the son. The picture of the father running to his son shows he was surprised by the joy of a returning child and delighted in hope of a relationship restored. The parable's title has rightly shifted from the "prodigal son" to the "waiting father." I believe it may be time for another shift and that we address this as the parable of the "hopeful father."

---

[61]Stein, *An Introduction to the Parables of Jesus*, 122-23. Stein argues that the main point of the parable was not to teach that God is loving and gracious to sinners, something the parable teaches but only secondarily, but that the scribes and Pharisees' opposition to Jesus' ministry was wrong because of God's graciousness.

[62]Stein, *An Introduction to the Parables of Jesus*, 119. See also Scott, *Hear Then the Parable*, 111.

Patience is a natural consequence of hope when what is desired and hoped for is beyond the hoper's control. God desires and hopes that all repent, but humans have some say so in this end, God must be patient. The one hoping needs patience if what is hoped for is not near. God seems to be in this for the long haul and so divine hope requires divine patience.

CONCLUSION

Hope is what keeps one from despair. It is the power to continue to be in relation when there is evidence that the relationship is in want. Rosemarie Rizzo Parse summarizes hope most insightfully when she writes that hope is the "creative pull between now and the future, which persistently believes in the possibility of a thing becoming other than what it is."[63] This "thing" that God hopes for is the continuing but developing relationship the divine might have with creation. God continues in the hope that the relationship between God and creation will grow and mature in mutual love and a fellowship of communion.

Because the future is significantly open, and because God is in partnership with a free humanity, God will not always get what is planned or desired. Much of the future is in the hands of limited and fallible humanity. God has chosen to become dependent on others by entering into this partnership. There is no guarantee that the future will be shaped exactly as God desires, and thus when it seems that it is going wide of the mark and is out of God's control, hope is a natural and necessary element of any true relationship. God hopes that those entrusted with overseeing and fostering creativity, justice, and goodness will bring these to fruition. God hopes that the love shown is not given in vain but will be returned. God hopes the trusted will be true.

Since God has created a world with genuinely free agents who can and do sin, God's desires are not always realized. We have the

---

[63]Rosemarie Rizzo Parse, *Hope: An International Human Becoming Perspective* (Sudbury, MA: Jones and Bartlett, 1999), 15. Parse gives many definitions of hope from various sources, but her own is the most relationally oriented.

God-given ability and power to thwart many of God's plans and purposes. This is the risk that God has freely chosen, but because God has chosen this path, it must necessarily be a good and noble way. God, by creating the world that exists, chose to enter into a relationship of hope with humanity. God as a relational partner demonstrates the ironic power of restraint in order for the relationship to be authentic. In restraint, God truly hopes that we, as God's partner, will be faithful and trustworthy.

Hope is not divine hand-wringing, expecting disaster but acting, nonetheless, as if there is a chance. God's hope is rightly humanity's hope. Hope is what makes God's risky trust and binding faith a joyful experience. God anticipates and looks forward to reaping the fruit of God's patient but ever-present relationship with creation. In this sense, hope can never be separated from faith. They are inseparable companions.[64] Without hope God's faith in humanity, the commitment of a trusting partnership, would be a matter of obligation and not relationship. It is hope that makes God's commitment and faith a labor of love and joy. Hope reveals the power of restraint, a power too often neglected. Power is more than the ability to do; it can often be the power to wait and see what happens. As Brueggemann states, "We are dealing here with a peculiar kind of sovereignty. . . . It invites but does not compel. It hopes rather than requires."[65]

In the end, our hope rests on faithfulness and God's hope. Our hope is that God will never lose hope in us, that amid human failure and unfaithfulness God will not give up on us. God will continue to hope against hope in our continued process of maturing and reciprocal relationship. That God will continue to seek communion with us even though the situation at times seems dire. Our aim is to share in God's hope of a healed creation, something Moltmann sees in relational terms of sympathy. We

---

[64]Jürgen Moltmann, *Theology of Hope: On the Ground and the Implications of a Christian Eschatology*, trans. James W. Leitch (New York: HarperCollins, 1991; New York: Harper & Row, 1967), 20.

[65]Brueggemann, *Genesis*, 18. Brueggemann offers these words in the context of God's calling creation into being and the nature of that creation.

enter into union with God, a union of sympathy in which we share in the pathos of God. The one who does this is the one who is "with God," who "is angry with God's wrath. He suffers with God's suffering. He loves with God's love." Moltmann rightly concludes, "He hopes with God's hope."[66] Thankfully, God is a God of hope.

---

[66]Jürgen Moltmann, *The Crucified God: The Cross of Christ as the Foundation and Criticism of Christian Theology*, trans. R. A. Wilson and John Bowden (Minneapolis: Fortress, 1993; New York: HarperCollins, 1974), 272.

7

DIVINE FAITH AND
THE ADVENT OF CHRIST

*Jesus' trust in the Father becomes our trust. To believe
as Jesus believed is to be open, as he is open, in his
dependence. We depend on Jesus in his dependence
on the Father. Our faith in Jesus is to have his faith.*

Arthur Anton Vogel, *Christ in His Time and Ours*

Up to this point my focus has been the faith of God, but in this chapter, I will expand upon that and explore Jesus' faith in God the Father as well as God's faith in the Son. The faith of Jesus is unique in that it is both a revelation of what God's faith is, as well as what human faith should be. Any discussion of Jesus' faith as revelation of God the Father's faith requires a brief discussion of incarnational theology.

FAITH AND THE INCARNATION

I see no reason not to suppose that if love has eternally existed within God's triunity then so too has faith. The triunity of God provides interesting avenues for discussions of precreational divine love. God's love was not first made manifest with the creation of physical substance, living creatures, or even sentient beings. God's love was living and active within the Godhead. I argued above that love needs trust to be complete, that love longs to trust and be trusted. Therefore, faith, a perfect faith to be sure, may be as eternal as God. But just as the divine love that existed prior to creation differs from the love that God has poured out on creation, it would certainly be right to suggest that any sort of precreational faith that has existed within the Godhead is distinct from the faith that God now has in creation. The love within the Godhead would have had no need for grace, mercy, or forgiveness, whereas the love God has for creation is most manifested in these manners and expressions. Likewise, any faith within the Godhead would seemingly have minimal place for risk or doubt, while these make perfect sense in God's faith and partnership with a fallible humanity.

Just as God's love evolved into something more dynamic with the act of creation, we can say that God's faith transformed as well to accommodate the situation. Perhaps it is enough to say this—God's love surely did not originate with the creation but found new opportunities and new modes of expression. Those new opportunities and modes of expression such as patience, forgiveness, and healing would also include faith. So too, God's faith may not have originated with creation but was tested by the introduction of free humans who are other and can act for or against God. Whether God's love *and* faith were unleashed and grew with the advent of creation or whether God's love took on new and dynamic forms that necessarily included faith, what is sure and good is that God's relationship to this creation is one of both love and faith.

Open theists are not single-minded in their trinitarian theories. Clark Pinnock, for example, defends a robust social trinitarianism, that "God is constituted by three subjects, each of whom is distinct from the other and is the subject of its own experiences in the unity of one divine life."[1] Keith Ward, on the other hand, is critical of such approaches and worries that "this 'social Trinity' idea is more misleading than helpful." Ward takes a "unitive" view, the idea that the Trinity consists of "three 'forms of existing' of one divine subject."[2] While I believe there is reason to

---

[1]Clark H. Pinnock, *Flame of Love: A Theology of the Holy Spirit* (Downers Grove, IL: InterVarsity Press, 1996), 35.
[2]Keith Ward, *Christ and the Cosmos: A Reformation of the Trinitarian Doctrine* (New York: Cambridge University Press, 2015), 145.

ponder intratrinitarian faith, such discussions would require a fully expressed doctrine of the Trinity—something outside the scope of this work. Whether God is a society of divine subjects with independent wills and experiences or whether God is a single subject with unique forms of expression does not immediately affect the claim of this chapter, that God and Jesus had faith in one another. Thus, my discussion is limited to the trust expressed between the heavenly Father and the earthly Son.

The incarnation of the Son, like the creation of the universe, provided God new opportunities for love and faith within the Godhead. In the incarnation and on the cross, God experienced not only pain and suffering but also faith as both the Father and the Son. The Father and Son's latent trust was made explicit in the incarnation. Said another way, the ready attitude of faith became realized acts of faith. Each needed to trust that the other would be true to their mission, love, and promises.

I must make it clear that I am working with an "incarnational Christology." That is, I am affirming that the second person of the Trinity, the preexistent Logos, became fully human in the person of Jesus of Nazareth. My affirmation is in line with the Chalcedon creedal statement: "Jesus Christ . . . truly God and truly man." This creed naturally leads to questions such as, what does it mean to say the Logos became human? Likewise, what does it mean that Jesus was truly God? These are important questions too enormous for this study. I will simply say I believe a theology of divine faith may help foster responses to these questions.

While there may be many formulations of the incarnation that could be receptive to a theology of divine faith, a kenotic Christology is what makes most sense to me. In short, kenotic Christologies seek to resolve some of the paradoxes that exist in affirming that Jesus was truly God and truly man. Philippians 2:6-7 states that Christ "emptied" himself and took on the form and likeness of a human. I understand this to mean that the Logos gave up such divine traits as omniscience, omnipotence, and omnipresence. These could be set aside and the Logos still be divine as long as the fullness of love remained.[3]

I certainly believe that a "Christology that goes beyond yet is faithful to Chalcedon may legitimately speak of a 'kenotic unity' of God and humanity in Jesus Christ."[4] There is room to rethink and even disagree with the creeds and councils, but the first order is to seek ways to interpret these traditional teachings by means faithful to Scripture, experience, and reason. The approach I take in the remainder of this chapter seeks to be faithful to the councils while going beyond what the architects of this creed may have had in mind.[5]

Is the kenosis of the Logos in the person of Jesus Christ an act of both love and faith? While the literature is abundant concerning the kenosis being an expression of divine love, I have found no authors who suggest the kenosis was also an act of faith. However, I find it utterly incomprehensible that the self-emptying of God into a first-century Jewish man for the purposes of a relational salvation can be understood as anything less than an act of faith. The thought of God becoming a powerless and dependent child, a human who suffers physically, emotionally, and spiritually, a servant who eventually dies that others might live suggests Jesus lived more than a life of love. The life of Jesus is made even more beautiful when we recognize images of monumental and historic faith. It is a faith that perhaps only God could have. In the act of becoming fully human, the Son became utterly dependent on the Father in ways never before experienced. Jesus, as a human being, had no guarantee of

---

[3]For more concerning kenotic Christology, see C. Stephen Evans, ed., *Exploring Kenotic Christology: The Self-Emptying of God* (New York: Oxford University Press, 2006); Donald G. Dawe, *The Form of a Servant: A Historical Analysis of the Kenotic Motif* (Philadelphia: Westminster, 1963); John Polkinghorne, ed., *The Work of Love: Creation as Kenosis* (Grand Rapids: Eerdmans, 2001); David Brown, *Divine Humanity: Kenosis and the Construction of a Christian Theology* (Waco, TX: Baylor University Press, 2011). Brown explores the compelling analogy of "method acting" in order to better frame the incarnation (246-59).

[4]Daniel L. Migliore, *Faith Seeking Understanding: An Introduction to Christian Theology*. 2nd ed. (Grand Rapids: Eerdmans, 2004), 181.

[5]I agree with C. Stephen Evans when he states, "I do not conceive of kenotic Christology as an alternative to Chalcedonian orthodoxy, but rather as one particular way of trying to make sense of the Incarnation and remain within the boundaries of orthodox Christian belief." C. Stephen Evans, "Kenotic Christology and the Nature of God," in C. S. Evans, *Exploring Kenotic Christology*, 195.

health, safety, or security. The mission was to become a ransom and to give up what little Jesus did have—his life—in the hope of saving humanity. The kenosis is typically spoken of as an act of love and it is. But it is a love that is most completely demonstrated in faithful submission. God's faith is demonstrated in the Logos becoming something other than divine—emptied in order to become a human. But the emptying did not stop at being human, for Jesus was a slave who was obedient unto death. Not the death of a grey-haired man at the end of a long righteous life (Prov 16:31), but the death of a young man cursed and forsaken by God (Mt 27:46). In the end, one's acceptance of a theology of divine faith may depend on the degree to which one embraces a kenotic Christology.

If Jesus was God while at the same time in the fullness of humanity, then God had to trust those who were the caretakers of the child Jesus. What kind of faith did it take for God to entrust Jesus to the care of a young Palestinian Jewish girl?[6] What kind of faith did God display in having Jesus grow and develop in such an unstable time in Israel's history? What kind of faith did God have in facing the unknown, not as God in power but as human in the person of Jesus? What kind of faith did God have to become that which would suffer a cruel death? What monumental faith God must have had in order to die in the hope that humanity would respond to such a sacrificial death on its behalf. Perhaps this is the kind of faith that God wants to see in us. Perhaps this is the kind of faith Jesus called for in his disciples when he said that if they had the "faith of God" they could move a mountain into the sea.[7]

---

[6]This statement makes most sense from either a Lukan or Matthean reading of the birth narratives. The idea of God entrusting Jesus to Mary is somewhat unsettling in the Markan depictions of Jesus' family as "outsiders" (Mk 3:31) who believe Jesus is "out of his mind" (Mk 3:21).

[7]Mark 11:22 has the curious statement *echete pistin theou*, which is most often translated as "have faith in God." The issue is whether this should be read with God as the objective genitive ("have faith *in* God") or the subjective genitive, which allows the translation to read ("have the faith *of* God") even though no translations do so. Eugene LaVerdiere is one of the few who reads *echete pistin theou* to mean "have the faith of God." He argues that Mark's gospel uses the subjective genitive in other places when speaking of faith and we would not read these as meaning persons had faith in themselves (Mk 2:5; 5:34; 10:52). "I suggest the same may be true in this case, and that the genitive is subjective. Jesus would be telling Peter and others that this faith must equal

By offering a theology of divine faith we can approach the kenosis, not without mystery or paradox, a condition necessary with any incarnation theory, but relationally.[8] Faith, as a kind of relationship, a mutual fellowship or communion, offers a way to understand the divinity of Jesus without diminishing either his divinity or humanity. Jesus, as the incarnate Son of God, is divine, not merely because of a preincarnate history but because of a love and faith in and with the Father. Jesus' sacrificial love for humanity and radically obedient faith makes Jesus one with the Father—and the Father one with Jesus. I see no reason why this should be understood as a diminished sense of divinity. The argument that Jesus' divinity is found in a faith and love that makes him one with the Father is not meant to suggest that Jesus was not truly or ontologically God. If love and faith constituted the relationship between the Father and Son before the incarnation, then they surely typified the relationship in the incarnation as well.

In the following two sections, I intend to show that the incarnation created a way for God to experience two kinds of divine faith. First, the man Jesus had faith in the Father. The Father was the object of Jesus' faith. While this is not often emphasized, Jesus' life and death should be understood as an example of radical faith in action. Second, God the Father had faith in the Son. Jesus was the object of God the Father's faith. Jesus, as human, had his own will and freedom. This free will on Jesus' part must have included the ability to not only succeed but possibly to fail in this sacrificial mission. The Father, while empowering the Son,

---

the faith that God himself has." LaVerdiere does not read this to mean that God is dependent upon others but that this is an expression of divine confidence. This form of faith would enable the disciples to do what only God can do. Eugene LaVerdiere, *The Beginning of the Gospel: Introducing the Gospel According to Mark*, vol. 2: *Mark 8:22–16:20* (Collegeville, MN: Liturgical Press, 1999), 160-61. For more on the translation of this passage, see Craig A. Evans, *Mark 8:27–16:20*, Word Biblical Commentary 34B (Nashville: Thomas Nelson, 2001), 186-87; R. T. France, *The Gospel of Mark: A Commentary on the Greek Text* (Grand Rapids: Eerdmans, 2002), 448-49. For an argument against this text meaning "faith of God," see Moisés Silva, *God, Language, and Scripture: Reading the Bible in the Light of General Linguistics*, Foundations of Contemporary Interpretation 4 (Grand Rapids: Zondervan, 1990), 106-8. Silva also references several others who argue against such a reading.

[8]Stephen T. Davis, "Is Kenosis Orthodox?" in C. S. Evans, *Exploring Kenotic Christology*, 120.

had to trust that the Son would do what the Father could not, die for the world.

THE SON'S FAITH IN THE FATHER: FAITH IN THE LIFE OF JESUS

Theologically it is important to affirm the incarnation. Jesus is the *true* revelation of God even if he is not the *whole* revelation of God. When Jesus' love led him to die the sacrificial death for the world, is this not also a demonstration of God's love? I believe all Christians would affirm it is. Jesus' sacrificial love is not merely a representation of his humanity but also of his divinity. The power that Jesus demonstrated over oppression, illness, and death displayed God's power. Yet if these are revelations of divine love and power, might we then also suggest that the faith that led Jesus to live and eventually die is also a revelation of divine faith? Is the faith of Jesus that empowered him to heal and do mighty works the very faith of God? I believe we can and should conclude that the faith of Jesus, like the love and power of Jesus, is a revelation of God's faith. I begin this section affirming these conclusions. Given the arguments made in previous chapters, I see no reason to parse out the life of Jesus and suggest that love and power are divine revelations while faith is simply a human trait. Jesus' faith describes divine faith and prescribes human faith. Thus, I understand these accounts of Jesus' faith to be revelations of the God-man. The faith of Jesus is the faith of a man who is the true revelation of God. It is the faith of the kenotic God in the person of Jesus Christ.

The faith of Jesus, as the subject of theological and biblical study, has been relatively unexplored compared to other faith studies. John Haughey notes, "Christians have expended so much energy on what is entailed in having faith in Jesus that they have failed to ask whether Jesus himself had faith."[9] This may be due to a long history proclaiming that Jesus had

---

[9]John C. Haughey, *Housing Heaven's Fire: The Challenge of Holiness* (Chicago: Jesuit Way, 2002), 67. Haughey believes that the reason for the paucity of these sorts of studies is that people believe that the demonstration of Jesus as a person of faith would produce a sense of disenchantment in Jesus.

complete and utter knowledge of God the Father—"beatific vision."
Thomas Aquinas, for example, is rather forthright in denying Jesus had
faith; "from the first moment of his conception Christ had the full vision
of God in his essence . . . therefore he could not have had faith."[10] For
others, Jesus' full and complete understanding of God meant that he
"lived by sight, not by faith."[11] Even so, there have been some helpful
studies on the faith of Jesus. The subject of Jesus' faith has been explored
in narrative,[12] historical,[13] and theological studies.[14]

"Here is a call for the endurance of the saints, those who keep the com-
mandment of God and the faith of Jesus" (Rev 14:12). This is the only
time the phrase "faith of Jesus" is used in Scripture. While the "Faith of
Jesus Christ," and similar expressions are found eight times in Pauline
literature (Rom 3:22, 26; Gal 2:16a, 16b, 20; 3:22; Eph 3:12; Phil 3:9), they
are typically understood as objective genitives.[15] That is, faith *in* Jesus
Christ. However, there are those who believe that these Pauline passages
"must contain *some* reference to the faith of Christ himself."[16] Ian Wallis,
after an extensive study of Pauline uses of *pistis Christou*, concludes that
"in each case Paul had Christ's own faith in mind." Furthermore, "faith is
a characteristic of Christ's inclusive humanity through which the power
of sin is broken on the cross and all people are given a way of responding
to God's grace."[17]

[10]Aquinas, *Summa Theologica*, 3.7.3, quoted in Haughey, *Housing Heaven's Fire*, 67.
[11]Gerald O'Collins and Daniel Kendall, "The Faith of Jesus," *Theological Studies* 53, no. 3 (1992): 407.
[12]Richard B. Hays, *The Faith of Jesus Christ: The Narrative Substructure of Galatians 3:1–4:11*, 2nd ed.
(Grand Rapids: Eerdmans, 2002). Hays's study focuses on Paul's thought and more specifically
how to translate *pistis Christou*. Hays argues this should be read as a subjective genitive, "faith
of Jesus" or "faithfulness of Jesus."
[13]James P. Mackey, "The Faith of the Historical Jesus," *Horizons* 3, no. 2 (1976): 155-74; Ian G. Wallis, *The Faith of Jesus Christ in Early Christian Traditions*, Society for New Testament Studies
Monograph Series 84 (New York: Cambridge University Press, 2005).
[14]O'Collins and Kendall, "The Faith of Jesus"; Gerald O'Collins, *Christology: A Biblical, Historical,
and Systematic Study of Jesus* (New York: Oxford University Press, 1995), 250-68; Christian D.
Kettler, *The God Who Believes: Faith, Doubt, and the Vicarious Humanity of Christ* (Eugene, OR:
Cascade, 2005).
[15]O'Collins and Kendall, "The Faith of Jesus," 411.
[16]Morna D. Hooker, "ΠΙΣΤΙΣ ΧΡΙΣΤΟΥ," *New Testament Studies* 35 (1989): 341, quoted in
O'Collins and Kendall, "The Faith of Jesus," 412.
[17]Wallis, *The Faith of Jesus Christ in Early Christian Traditions*, 124-25.

The epistle to the Hebrews is also a source of fruitful discussion concerning the faith of Jesus.[18] Two passages are especially enlightening: "Although he was a Son, he learned obedience through what he suffered; and having been made perfect, he became the source of eternal salvation for all who obey him" (Heb 5:8-9). Add to that, "Jesus the pioneer and perfecter of our faith" (Heb 12:2). The first passage can be understood to mean that Jesus, through the experiences of his life, especially those times of testing and suffering, learned to be faithful, that is obedient, to God. This text is saying that just as human beings "*learn* faith or obedience through what we suffer," so too did Jesus. Moreover, Jesus' "faith was perfected, and he was freed from the fear of death which makes us slaves, and he thus became the pioneer and perfecter of faith, the one we follow when we have faith like this."[19] Hebrews 12:2 places Jesus at the end of a long list of Old Testament faith heroes. By placing him at this point, Jesus is revealed as the perfect example of faith. "Jesus exhibited faith in the highest form. As the head of a great army of heroes and heroines of faith, he carried faith" and brought it to perfection and triumph.[20] According to the author of Hebrews, Jesus is more than our source of faith. He is also the pioneer, model, and exemplar of faith.[21] In Hebrews, Jesus is the archetype of the faithful. His "life of faith, evident in learning obedience, suffering and death, incarnates faith and constitutes a focus for inspiration and emulation."[22]

This discussion of Hebrews leads me to three events found in the Gospel of Mark that I believe resolutely point to Jesus as a person of faith. I believe these three events are key in Mark's narrative, for they not only

---

[18]Wallis suggests this letter provides the "most explicit reference to Jesus' faith in the New Testament." Wallis, *The Faith of Jesus Christ in Early Christian Traditions*, 145.

[19]James Mackey, *Jesus, the Man and the Myth: A Contemporary Christology* (New York: Paulist Press, 1979), 169, quoted in O'Collins and Kendall, "The Faith of Jesus," 413.

[20]O'Collins and Kendall, "The Faith of Jesus," 413.

[21]O'Collins and Kendall, "The Faith of Jesus," 414. This point is made even more forcefully when one notes that the Greek does not have the word "our" as a qualifier of the following word "faith." Therefore, the passage could (should?) read, "Jesus the pioneer and perfecter of faith." Without the "our" it is no longer a passage directed only at Christ's followers but to all who wish and seek to be in relationship with God the Father.

[22]Wallis, *The Faith of Jesus Christ in Early Christian Traditions*, 159.

highlight Mark's theme of faith, but they also demonstrate that Jesus' earthly ministry is bookended by faith acts. The three events are Jesus' wilderness testing (Mk 1:12-13), exorcism of the demon-possessed boy (Mk 9:14-29), and the agony at Gethsemane (Mk 14:32-42). It is important to remember that these stories are not isolated events but are principal examples of the fuller life of Jesus. As Gordon Fee emphatically states, "Jesus is portrayed not as acting out of a position of divine power, but as a truly human figure who is totally dependent on God his Father."[23] Jesus' whole life, and not a few dotted moments here and there, reveal that Jesus relied on the Father at all times—that Jesus lived a life of faith.

The ministry of Jesus, in the Gospel of Mark, is bookended by two testing stories: testing in the wilderness and testing at Gethsemane. These two testing stories are also bookended by "baptism" stories, the first being Jesus' baptism by John and the second Jesus' "baptism" by crucifixion.[24] Immediately after Jesus is baptized by John, the heavenly voice declares Jesus is the Son and he is driven into the wilderness by the Spirit to face forty days of testing by Satan. The testing of Jesus in the wilderness is reminiscent of the forty years of testing that the Israelites faced after the Exodus (Deut 8:2, 16). Even though neither Mark nor Deuteronomy uses the word "faith," the context clearly points to that conclusion.[25] Deuteronomy 8:2 states that God led the Israelites for the forty years to humble them, "testing you to know what was in your heart, whether or not you would keep his commandments." It was not only a test of obedience, an Old Testament concept closely associated with trust, but a test of faith. Just as the wilderness served as the backdrop of the testing of the Israelites' faith, the wilderness is used by Mark to demonstrate that Jesus' ministry begins with a similar testing of faith and obedience. The notation of this event is very quick and without fanfare, but it was very

---

[23]Gordon D. Fee, "The New Testament and Kenosis Christology," in C. S. Evans, *Exploring Kenotic Christology*, 38.

[24]Jesus refers to his crucifixion as a baptism in Mark 10:38-39.

[25]The psalmist links the wilderness event to the testing of Israel's faith and trust when he writes "Therefore, when the LORD heard, he was full of rage; a fire was kindled against Jacob, his anger mounted against Israel, because they had no faith in God, and did not trust his saving power" (Ps 78:21-22).

important for Mark, for whom faith is a central theme.[26] It was thematically important for Mark to begin Jesus' ministry in a manner representative of Israel and the testing of obedience and faith.[27]

While other passages of Mark also speak of Jesus' faith, the story of the demon-possessed boy is most vivid. The story begins with Jesus coming down from the mountain after the transfiguration and finding that his disciples could not cast out a demon and heal the boy. Jesus chastises them for being a "faithless generation" (Mk 9:19) and calls the boy and his father over. The father asks, "If you are able to do anything, have pity on us and help us" (Mk 9:22). Jesus replies, "If you are able!—All things can be done for the one who believes" (Mk 9:23). After the father cries out, "I believe; help my unbelief!" Jesus heals the boy, and the story ends with Jesus' statement, "This kind can come out only through prayer" (Mk 9:29). The question is by whose faith was it that the boy was healed? The disciples were the "faithless generation," the father believed but still had unbelief, and the boy's possible faith is never addressed. It is unlikely, then, to have been the faith of any of these persons. Since it was Jesus who healed the boy after exclaiming that "all things can be done for the one who believes," it makes most sense to attribute the healing faith to Jesus. Christopher Marshall suggests the story has several foci, one of which is "the faith of Jesus himself."[28] Marshall argues that in Mark, it can be understood that it is both the faith of the one who performs the miracle and the faith of the ones for whom the miracle is performed in which healing comes.[29] This story "discloses by implication the secret of Jesus' great power, his complete confidence in God. The father is being implicitly called to emulate the faith of Jesus, and it is the faith of both parties that permits the

---

[26]Christopher D. Marshall, *Faith as a Theme in Mark's Narrative*, Society for New Testament Studies Monograph Series 64 (New York: Cambridge University Press, 1989). Even though Marshall unpacks faith as a theme in Mark's gospel, including the faith of Jesus, he does not begin his treatment until after Jesus' baptism and testing. I believe this is an unfortunate omission in an otherwise excellent work.

[27]Kettler writes, "The story of the faith of Jesus in the Father is never portrayed apart from his obedience to the will of the Father in contrast to the rest of humanity." See *The God Who Believes*, 29.

[28]Marshall, *Faith as a Theme in Mark's Narrative*, 111.

[29]Marshall, *Faith as a Theme in Mark's Narrative*, 119-20.

success."[30] Ronald Kernaghan also believes Jesus' faith is key to this story: "The child was raised not because his father's faith was perfect, but because Jesus believed all things were possible. Jesus helped the father's unbelief by raising the boy."[31] Jesus is portrayed as one who believes (trusts) all things can be done. He is the exemplar of faith that has the power to heal and even move mountains (Mk 11:22-24). Jesus is not one who works in faith alone, however. Rather, he calls others to faith and praises them for their faith. Jesus seeks to have faith *with* others and not merely *for* others.

The testing of Jesus' faith in the wilderness following his baptism by John is an allusion to his testing in Gethsemane, which precedes his baptism of passion. The agony at Gethsemane, unlike the wilderness passage, is a more detailed account of Jesus' grief, doubt, and ultimate triumph of faith. In Mark 14:34 Jesus reveals to the disciples that he is "deeply grieved, even to death" a state that hardly depicts one who is above the need for faith.[32] While we are not told what it is that grieves Jesus, it certainly involves the painful death he is about to experience and quite possibly a sense of distance he is experiencing as God the Father begins to forsake him. The event not only reveals Jesus' faith but also his doubt when he "prayed that, if it were possible, the hour might pass from him" (Mk 14:35). Earlier, Jesus responded to the father of the possessed boy who asked, "If it is possible," saying, "All things can be done for the one who believes" (Mk 9:23). Again, during the prophetic demonstration against the temple Jesus says, "Whatever you ask for in prayer, believe that you have received it, and it will be yours" (Mk 11:24). But this is not what Jesus does. He prays like the father of the possessed boy, "*If* it were possible." However, in contradiction to what Jesus proclaims in chapters 9 and 11, Jesus does not get what he prays for! It is for this reason that Jesus' faith is so monumental. Jesus' Gethsemane prayer is not "a simple petition: 'Give me strength to drink

---

[30]Marshall, *Faith as a Theme in Mark's Narrative*, 120.

[31]Ronald J. Kernaghan, *Mark* (Downers Grove, IL: InterVarsity Press, 2007), 177. For arguments that it was the faith of the father that brought about the healing of the boy, see Eugene LaVerdiere, *The Beginning of the Gospel*, 50-53; France, *The Gospel of Mark*, 369.

[32]John's gospel, with its high Christology, has no agony in the garden. Jesus, seemingly, has no reservations about going to the cross. For more on John's Christology, see Frank J. Matera, *New Testament Christology* (Louisville, KY: Westminster John Knox, 1999), chap. 6.

this cup.' Rather, he prayed: 'Remove this cup from me.'"[33] Jesus is asking for the impossible to be made possible! Does this mean Jesus did not have faith? Was Jesus' doubt so great that his prayer was ineffective?

I don't believe Mark's intent was to reveal Jesus' doubt but, in fact, to show the faith of Jesus. Just as the testing in the wilderness proved Jesus to be obedient at the outset of his ministry, he was just as obedient in the painful and doubting close of his ministry. And yet, Jesus' struggle between faith and doubt speaks loudly. Jesus intimately prays again, but this time with, "Abba, Father, for you all things are possible . . . yet, not what I want, but what you want" (Mk 14:36).[34] In Jesus' words I can hear the cry of the father, "I believe; help my unbelief!" "I have faith, help me through the doubt." Jesus is said to have prayed this not once but three times (Mk 14:39-41). The point is that Jesus truly desired this cup removed, but it was not to be. Jesus thus had to come to terms with a faith whose power is not in the healing of illnesses or the casting of mountains but rather in accepting the will of God when it is not your own will. Jesus' faith was most dramatically shown not in getting what he asked for but in accepting he would not. This is what makes Jesus a pioneer of faith.

Just as the incarnation itself is a revelation of both genuine divinity and genuine humanity, the faith of Jesus reveals not merely a human faith but also a divine faith. The faith of Jesus in the Father is paradigmatic for it shows us what it means to be truly faithful and full of faith. "Christians don't just believe in Jesus as Lord and Savior. We believe in trusting and obeying God the way Jesus trusted and obeyed God."[35] This is not a demonstration of merely human faith any more than the cross is a demonstration of merely human love. The love of Jesus should not be parsed out and deemed human

---

[33]E. Frank Tupper, *A Scandalous Providence: The Jesus Story of the Compassion of God* (Macon, GA: Mercer University Press, 1995), 324, quoted in John Sanders, *The God Who Risks: A Theology of Providence*, rev ed. (Downers Grove, IL: InterVarsity Press, 2007), 101.

[34]Prayer itself is also a sign or demonstration of faith. Prayer reveals a "deep sense of dependence and trust—in other words, a strong relationship of faith in God." O'Collins and Kendall, "The Faith of Jesus," 417. While the NRSV uses the words "able" (9:23) and "possible" (14:35-36), they are the same Greek word *dynatos*.

[35]Art Ross and Martha M. Stevenson, *Romans*, Interpretation Bible Studies (Louisville, KY: Geneva Press, 1999), 31.

at some points and divine at others. A robust Christology seeks to understand the love and truth of Christ as reflecting both humanity and divinity. The faith of Jesus should be understood no differently. Jesus' faith, while unique in the way that it was lived out in relation to the Father, was nonetheless the faith of God. In his book *The God Who Believes*, Christian Kettler works out a Christology of vicarious faith. Jesus' faith is more than an exemplar, it is a faith on our behalf, a faith that we may never experience. "The trust of Jesus . . . is not just an example of how to believe. No, the faith of Jesus is vicarious, on our behalf and in our place."[36] For Kettler, the faith of Jesus is a faith for us, a faith when we cannot overcome our own doubts and fears. Jesus then is the incarnation of the "God who believes." Kettler understands that by affirming the incarnation and the faith of Jesus we must at the same time affirm the faith of God. "The God of the Bible is a God who can *believe*, dare we say it, just as much as he can create and sustain. This is what we find in the vicarious humanity of Christ."[37] Furthermore, "God provides the belief, the faith, the trust, as well as the revelation. This is the message of the incarnation, of a truly Chalcedonian Christology that takes seriously the full humanity as well as the full deity of Christ."[38] Jesus is the kenotic God incarnate, and therefore the faith of Jesus is the faith of God. "The faith of Jesus reveals great truths about God. . . . God loves the world so much, God is willing to become incarnate to suffer and die so that the world might know the greatness of God's love."[39] It is the incarnational faith of Jesus that brings about God's faith in the power of the cross.

THE FATHER'S FAITH IN THE SON:
THE CROSS AND THE MISSION OF CHRIST

We understand Jesus to be the self-emptied Son of God, the divine Logos, who was tested and tempted, who entirely submitted his own will to the

---

[36]Kettler, *The God Who Believes*, 140.

[37]Kettler, *The God Who Believes*, 140.

[38]Kettler, *The God Who Believes*, 139.

[39]Ross and Stevenson, *Romans*, 31. Ross and Stevenson actually suggest the faith of Jesus reveals two great truths. The second truth is that "because of the revelation that occurs through Jesus, Christians believe that God's love and God's power are victorious over every power that seeks to defeat us, including the self-centeredness of betrayal, denial, and death."

will of the Father. If Jesus was fully human and God has entered into relationships of faith with humanity, then we must also speak about the Father's faith in the Son. The faith of Jesus, displayed in his obedience, reveals a God who trusted Jesus to be faithful and obedient. It may seem like a difficult idea, maybe even more challenging than the faith of God in humanity, but if Jesus was "one who in every respect has been tested as we are" (Heb 4:15), then we have to take seriously the Father's faith in the Son. And this faith was vindicated since Jesus was tested "yet without sin." While the New Testament affirms that Jesus was sinless (Jn 8:46; Heb 7:26) and fully obedient (Phil 2:8; Heb 5:8), this does not address whether Jesus *could* sin or be disobedient.

Thomas Oden affirms that Jesus' temptations and testing were authentic and reminiscent of the testings of Moses, Elijah, and all Israel.[40] Jesus, like the rest of humanity, had the freedom to sin. "His temptations were real appeals to his real freedom. His resistance was a real act of freedom in saying no on behalf of a larger yes to his vocation. . . . His temptation was real and required choice and effort to overcome. A faith that remained forever unchallenged would be a faith untested and inadequately experienced, hence unprepared for mediatorial work."[41] Oden further argues that Jesus' sinlessness was "inevitable but not necessary," meaning that "His sinlessness *is not necessitated because it is an act of freedom, but inevitable because it is the freedom of the eternal Son.*"[42] Yet Oden still argues that the potential for sin had to be real. "Arguably, there could have been no genuine temptation of Jesus had he not been subject to some possibility of spiritual pride, fatigue of spirit, or inordinate desire. If he were in his human nature absolutely immune to any potential pride or sensuality, then what could the temptation have meant, and how could he then have been truly like us, sharing our infirmities?"[43]

---

[40]Thomas C. Oden, *The Word of Life*, vol. 2 of *Systematic Theology* (New York: Harper & Row, 1989), 243.
[41]Oden, *The Word of Life*, 244-45.
[42]Oden, *The Word of Life*, 246. Italics Oden's.
[43]Oden, *The Word of Life*, 245.

If Jesus was fully human with the ability to freely enter into sin and disobedience, then seemingly God had to trust that Jesus, in the fullness of his freedom and humanity, would not sin or be disobedient.[44] However Jesus was able to remain sinless, either by his own free will or by the strength of the Spirit, it seems that if he could sin, then God, to some extent, was dependent upon Jesus. This does not mean God the Father was pacing the floor wondering if Jesus would at any moment sin, but that does not mean faith was somehow missing. God's faith was most likely a confident trust given all that God knew of the Son. Nonetheless, divine faith was there, and so discussions of Jesus being faithful should include God having faith in Jesus because Jesus was faithful, trustworthy, to the Father.

The cross of Christ presents us with a paradox no less than that found in the incarnation. In the cross we have both the faith of the Son and the faith of the Father. The Father's faith is demonstrated in empowering Jesus with the freedom to choose, giving Jesus the capacity to say, "Not your will but my will." There was nothing outside of Jesus that compelled him to accept the way of the cross. This was a sacrifice freely chosen, a life generously given. If Jesus was compelled by the Father to die, then there was no *giving* of his life as a ransom, nor was there anything necessarily loving or affirming about his death. In fact, if Jesus was compelled then his death is far more a tragedy than a living sacrifice. The death of Jesus is only a sacrifice in love, only a sacrifice if it is freely given. Love cannot be compelled. Jesus' act of sacrifice was a life given out of love for the Father and for humanity.

God the Father knew that as the time of the cross grew nearer greater trust in Jesus would become even more necessary. Jesus seemed to feel increasingly distant from the Father as the cross and his death approached. The agony at Gethsemane makes this distancing quite evident. Moltmann writes, "On other occasions he had withdrawn from them, in order to be joined with God in the prayer of his heart. Here for the first

---

[44]For reasons Jesus could not sin, see O'Collins, *Christology*, 270.

time he does not want to be alone with his God, and seeks the protection of his friends."[45] Jesus prays three times that the cup might pass from him, but God does not affirm his prayer. Jesus is not only experiencing an unprecedented distance from the Father but is also being betrayed and abandoned by his friends. While he grieves, they sleep. The situation is ripe for Jesus to abandon his mission, to give up and flee. The testing of Jesus did not end in the wilderness; that is where it began. Jesus' real testing is not in confrontation with Satan but in his utter isolation. The garden is not a testing followed by angels ministering to him but with soldiers coming to arrest him. Gethsemane was also not the end of his testing, for Jesus could have cursed the Father at any point. Perhaps, like Job, Jesus knew that if he would only curse God his torment would be over. Yet during what may be the most intense moment of pain and agony, when Jesus cries out, "Eloi, Eloi, lema sabachthani?" (Mk 15:34), he does not abandon God—even while God abandons him. There is a distance between Jesus and the Father as Jesus does not cry out to his Abba but to Eloi. The cries of Jesus to God and not to his Father reveal that his faith is being tested, perhaps in ways we may never fathom. In this event God surely must have known how difficult this would be for Jesus. It does not take an omniscient being to know the agony felt as one experiences abandonment and alienation.

God's faith in Jesus is demonstrated, ironically, by his willingness to abandon and forsake Jesus. The unwillingness to remove Jesus' cup of suffering is a sign of, among other things, God's faith in Jesus. To remove the cross would have been a sign, not of Jesus' triumph, but of failure. The fact that Jesus experienced agony, suffering, and God-forsakenness and not a supernatural sense of power and vision reveals God trusted Jesus to drink the cup given. A supernatural power or vision would have eliminated both risk and faith—trust and trustworthiness. God recognizes Jesus' continued faith even among his doubts and meets Jesus' faith with divine faith. Jesus never stops praying even in his isolation. When

---

[45]Jürgen Moltmann, *The Way of Jesus Christ: Christology in Messianic Dimensions*, trans. Margaret Kohl (Minneapolis: Fortress, 1993), 166.

he cries out from the cross he shows he has not given up on God even as he struggles with feeling that God has given up on him. "Jesus, like his Old Testament predecessors, exhibits an element of faith as he cries out to his Abba, the God of the covenant community, and expects to be heard and answered. Jesus is still speaking to God, and he has not lost his faith."[46]

The faith between Father and Son at the cross event is monumental. It is a faith shown and a faith shared. God's love, again ironically, is shown in the abandonment and forsakenness of Jesus for this was a love that could trust. God's love of Jesus led to a monumental act of divine faith— leaving Jesus on his own. Likewise, Jesus loved the Father enough to trust the Spirit, which not only led him to the wilderness for his pre-ministry testing but also to Gethsemane and the cross—the ultimate of tests. The faith of God in the cross does not end with Jesus' death. No, this is where God's faith in the cross only begins.

GOD'S FAITH IN THE EFFICACY OF THE CROSS

In the death and resurrection of Jesus something absolute and objective happens. "Jesus Christ, Savior" is the affirmation of all Christians, and this affirmation is directly tied to what God accomplished in Jesus by the cross and resurrection. Understanding what it means to say that Jesus Christ is Savior and how salvation is imparted has generated many theories of atonement. Generally, these views have fallen under the titles of "Christus victor," "satisfaction," and "moral exemplar."[47] There can be great agreement and diversity among these various models of atonement, and to some extent each includes elements of objectivity and subjectivity. Objective salvation emphasizes that "in the cross event something is actually achieved on behalf of humanity by God in Christ."[48] Subjective salvation means that "the cross makes possible or enables a necessary

---

[46]Sanders, *The God Who Risks*, 106.

[47]Gustaf Aulén, *Christus Victor: An Historical Study of the Three Main Types of the Idea of Atonement*, trans. A. G. Herbert (New York: Macmillan, 1969).

[48]Roger Olson, *The Mosaic of Christian Belief: Twenty Centuries of Unity and Diversity* (Downers Grove, IL: IVP Academic, 2002), 256.

response within the human person needing salvation and that the actual benefit of Christ's death is in that response."[49] Add to this several biblical motifs regarding salvation, which include justification, sacrifice, redemption, and reconciliation.

In this section, I am not arguing for any one model or motif of atonement, nor am I championing subjective salvation over the objective. While some motifs make more sense given the acceptance of other metaphors and models, I do not believe any one should be given final approval to the negation of all others. All of these ideas and concepts have a place and should be discussed as part of the great theological conversation. With this said, there is a realistic qualification. As one approaching theology through the framework of relational theism, it will be relationship that I use as a guiding metaphor. In a relational model, the primary, though hardly only, problem dealt with on the cross is not a legal problem but a relational one. The cross and resurrection are the means and hope of healing a broken relationship.[50]

Sin is the denial of an authentic and mutually loving relationship with God. It is an act of mistrust that gives birth to rebellion and pride and leads to the harm and destruction of other relationships. From a relational approach, the cross and resurrection are about the healing of the relationship and reestablishment of the broken trust. If sin is primarily damage to the divine-human relationship and the heart of salvation is the restoration of broken relationships, the first and foremost being the relationship between God and humanity, then the cross is a means of repairing or healing the relational damage done.

Because salvation is primarily about the restoration of a broken relationship, there is a deeply subjective aspect to salvation. Salvation, that is, the healing of a broken relationship, cannot be accomplished by God

---

[49]Olson, *The Mosaic of Christian Belief*, 256. Olson puts atonement in this category, suggesting that "atonement itself happens outside of the individual human subject even if it remains to be realized and appropriated by him or her." I believe it is better to suggest that atonement be placed equally within the objective and subjective categories.

[50]Clark H. Pinnock and Robert C. Brow, *Unbounded Love: A Good News Theology for the 21st Century* (Downers Grove, IL: InterVarsity Press, 1994), 99.

alone but requires a response and willingness from the other in the relationship. This is why salvation is both objective and subjective. Objectively Christ becomes sacrifice and God justifies the sinner. But even
with the objective effects of Christ's sacrifice, a subjective element is still
necessary.[51] We must desire and enter into a healed relationship. There
must be a willingness respond to the death and resurrection positively,
affirming God's love and submitting to God's will. The sinner is called to
return to relationship with the Father, affirming the objective work of the
cross. Restoration is possible only by the objective aspect of salvation via
the cross and resurrection. Subjectivity—giving individuals the power to
decide their own future concerning being in relationship with God—is
risky. There is the possibility of disappointment in that there are those
who might ultimately reject God's love and the divine sacrifice. Yet, if
God is truly to restore relationship, God must trust humanity because
God cannot establish relationships of mutual fellowship unilaterally. Salvation began with love (the cross) and was manifested in power (the
resurrection), but now God must demonstrate the third component of
salvation—faith.

If salvation is to be understood as atonement and reconciliation, then
it is necessary to briefly discuss the relational nature of these ideas as well
as the necessity of divine faith. I will suggest that both atonement and
reconciliation make little sense without the notion of relationship, and
relationships, by nature, are about faith. Also, if the cross is to be understood as an act of divine risk, then the cross was also an act of divine faith.

ATONEMENT

At the heart of atonement is the idea of bringing together alienated parties,
the reconciliation and restoration of a damaged relationship.[52] While

---

[51]I agree with Macquarrie that there can be neither a purely objective nor purely subjective salvation. Macquarrie suggests that salvation and atonement ideas transcend the subjective-objective
distinction and that thus "there could be no satisfactory view of the atonement that was purely
objective, any more than there could be an acceptable subjective view." See John Macquarrie,
Principles of Christian Theology, 2nd ed. (New York: Charles Scribner's Sons, 1977), 316-17.

[52]It is often stated that the development of the English word "atonement" began as "at-one-ment,"
but this may be "entirely fanciful." See *Vine's Complete Expository Dictionary of the Old and New*

there is certainly more to atonement than reconciliation, it is nonetheless a prominent concept in the word and may be, according to some, "the best way of understanding the atonement."[53] Reconciliation coveys the idea that a friendship has been restored or that two (or more) persons have reunited after a quarrel.[54] While reconciliation need not always be couched in personal relational terms, that is most often the idea being conveyed.[55] John Stott asserts that reconciliation, unlike other images, is about experiences of home and family.[56] Stott, as one of those scholars who believe that reconciliation is the meaning of atonement, seems to suggest that reconciliation may be the prime image of salvation. Other images such as justification and redemption are not ends in themselves but are meant to transpire in hope of reconciliation.[57] Pinnock and Brow also develop salvation and atonement under the idea of relational reconciliation. They argue that salvation, and theology as a whole, should move out of the imagery of "courtroom" and into the "family room." "God primarily seeks a restored relationship with sinners not a legal settlement."[58] The issue of reconciliation is not settled when the "debt is paid" for there is no restored relationship at that moment. While the cross makes possible the restoration of relationship, it does not guarantee it.

Reconciliation: A two-party affair. Appeasement, satisfaction, and justification may all take place in the life of God, but without a human

---

Testament Words and Topical Index, ed. W. E. Vine, Merrill F. Unger, and William White Jr. (Nashville: Thomas Nelson, 1996), 44.

[53]Leon Morris, *The Atonement: Its Meaning and Significance* (Downers Grove, IL: InterVarsity Press, 1983), 132.

[54]Morris, *The Atonement*, 132.

[55]For example, Macquarrie defines reconciliation in nonrelational terms, suggesting that it means "the activity whereby the disorders of existence are healed, its imbalances redressed, its alienations bridged over." See Macquarrie, *Principles of Christian Theology*, 268.

[56]John R. W. Stott, *The Cross of Christ* (Downers Grove, IL: InterVarsity Press, 1986), 168. Stott suggests there are three additional images of salvation along with reconciliation: "propitiation," which is linked to rituals at the shrine; "redemption," which brings to mind images of the marketplace; and "justification," which is linked to law-court imagery. For more information on how Stott understands these images, see pages 168-203.

[57]Stott, *The Cross of Christ*, 193. Stott also believes that other images not generally associated with atonement also speak of reconciliation, including "adoption" and "access." Stott develops this on pages 192-94.

[58]Pinnock and Brow, *Unbounded Love*, 9.

response there is no reconciliation. God has been impacted by the cross, no doubt, for at the cross God experienced the agony and alienation of death as well as the experience of being the Father of an abused and murdered child. These are two objective effects of the cross on the life of God. Yet even in God's pain and loss there is no reconciliation until the children return to the Father. The relationship cannot be healed and restored until humans freely return to God with cries for mercy and prayers of repentance. Reconciliation therefore requires a response. For "just as it takes two to quarrel it takes two to make a reconciliation."[59] God has done all the work, there is nothing that a person must do to gain God's love and forgiveness other than receive it. We are not wholly sure how or why God chose to act in the person of Christ and die on the cross. Somehow death and sin are dealt with by God through Christ on our behalf. In one sense it is not our worry how God brought about the demise of sin, guilt, and death. There is something deeply mysterious in the objective aspects of the cross. We should simply rejoice that they have been dealt with. Our concern is that by the love of God reconciliation and healing await, if we are willing to submit and receive it.

Atonement requires that humans freely respond to God's love. While God has been wronged and is owed a great debt, God has, instead, chosen to forgive and justify. God acts to reconcile us to God by demonstrating that God believes that the evil of a broken fellowship is greater than the injury and wrong inflicted on the divine. God, in choosing to forgive, has adopted our interests as God's own.[60] Forgiveness is costly, however, for "the one who forgives suffers."[61] This is why forgiveness is different from condoning. One is not harmed when one condones a behavior since nothing is risked. Condoning says no harm was done and no further action is required. Forgiveness, however, does not excuse but puts aside the harm done for the sake of the relationship.

---

[59]Morris, *The Atonement*, 144.
[60]Vincent Brümmer, *Atonement, Christology and the Trinity: Making Sense of Christian Doctrine* (Burlington, VT: Ashgate, 2005), 41.
[61]J. Edwin Orr, *Full Surrender* (Edinburgh, 1951), 22, quoted in Brümmer, *Atonement, Christology and the Trinity*, 41.

Forgiveness is also risky because it requires the one who committed the harm to be penitent and contrite. The relationship is not reconciled if only one is willing. "Loving fellowship is a two-way affair that cannot be one-sidedly established, maintained or restored."[62] Reconciliation requires forgiveness and also a penitent change of heart. Authentic forgiveness on God's part does not come after repentance but is made available beforehand. God extends forgiveness and grace, risking greater vulnerability, and then waits for the forgiven to respond, to enter into a new fellowship. Forgiveness is thus freely given, unconditionally, and not on order of a right response. God risks that the costly forgiveness extended might be refused and rejected. But on faith God still extends the forgiveness, believing and hoping it will not return empty. And while forgiveness is freely and unconditionally given, it is only finally effective in restoring fellowship when a repentant partner is willing to return. "It takes two to repair personal fellowship just as it takes two to establish it in the first place."[63]

Restored fellowship and love cannot be forced. God gives love and forgiveness in the hope and faith that humanity will respond. God cannot demand, but only invite, persons to freely repent and offer contrite hearts. Any understanding of salvation that is one-sided, that does not require the will of both parties, is not a salvation involving faith—divine or human. Such an understanding, known as "irresistible grace," is an act of "loving" an individual even if he has no desire for that love. A forced love cannot restore an estranged relationship. Forced love, no matter how beneficial, cannot establish mutual fellowship. Forced love cannot build trust between the parties. God can only give grace, offer love, and extend forgiveness, but then must wait.

It should also be noted that the problem of reconciliation does not lie with God but with humanity. Willingness to extend faith and enter into relationship is not something God refuses until satisfaction has been met. That is not forgiveness. Humans are the ones in need of reconciliation

---

[62]Brümmer, *Atonement, Christology and the Trinity*, 41.
[63]Brümmer, *Atonement, Christology and the Trinity*, 42.

and are the ones who need to respond in faith to faith and love given. Unfortunately, it is typical to read that it is God who needs reconciliation, that the cross reconciles God to God's self.[64]

It is difficult to harmonize the concept of God needing to be reconciled to humanity with God's love being the catalyst of the cross. If God requires sacrifice and appeasement before being willing to love, then love is a byproduct of the cross and not its motive. Pinnock and Brow, however, argue that God in fact needs no reconciliation, no appeasement.

> When it comes to salvation, we must not see God as the problem. God is committed to saving us and does not need to be coaxed—even by Jesus—into loving sinners. The only problem is how to repair the broken relationship with humanity. Obviously, if God was in Christ reconciling the world to himself, God does not need to be reconciled to us—it is we who need to be reconciled to him. The problem is how to get sinners to repent and turn from sin, to come back home and follow the new path of love.[65]

They go on to argue that a God who requires payment prior to reconciliation creates problems for the concept of costly forgiveness. "What place is there for forgiveness if Christ paid the price?"[66]

> We must realize that Jesus did not die in order to change God's attitude toward us but to change our attitude to God. God, who took the initiative of reconciling the world, does not need reconciling. It is in us that the decisive change is needed. The cross was not a sacrifice without which God could not love or forgive us; it was a sacrifice without which we would not have been able to accept forgiveness. The problem lies with us, not with God. He requires no sacrifice except a broken and contrite heart (Psalm 51:16-17).[67]

This is what makes the cross so risky and faith affirming. If God was the only one in need of reconciliation, then there is pain and suffering on the cross, but no peril. There is no question whether God will be "satisfied" in

---

[64]For example, see Stott, *The Cross of Christ*, 198; Emil Brunner, *The Mediator: A Study of the Central Doctrine of the Christian Faith* (London: Lutterworth, 1934), 519; Carl F. H. Henry, *God, Revelation, and Authority*, vol. 6: *God Who Stands and Stays*, part 2 (Waco, TX: Word, 1976), 358.
[65]Pinnock and Brow, *Unbounded Love*, 101.
[66]Pinnock and Brow, *Unbounded Love*, 102.
[67]Pinnock and Brow, *Unbounded Love*, 103.

the death of Christ. There is peril, however, in the fact that as free persons we may not respond to the sacrifice of Christ. The risk of the cross comes from the fact that God does not know whether the cross and divine grace will be effective in winning the hearts of a capricious humankind.

In a very odd bit of wisdom, God takes the way of the cross to win humanity. This was a very risky plan given that the cross was a sign of curse and God forsakenness. And yet God uses ungodliness to demonstrate love and forgiveness. John Macquarrie realizes that "man needs some concrete manifestation of God's activity, some manifestation that can seize him and bring him to an attitude of faith."[68] Is this what the cross is? We, after two thousand years of sermons, hymns, and artistry, have lost sight of what foolishness the cross was. In 1 Corinthians 1:18-31, Paul speaks about the foolishness of the cross for he knew that the cross was not a symbol of love and forgiveness, not a means of justification, but of rejection and wrath. Indeed, God chose the cross as a symbol of love and mercy. The wisdom of God is not found by analyzing the cross but by receiving its power of reconciliation. Its wisdom is found in God's love. The cross, because it is a stumbling block and foolishness, is God's great act of faith. God trusted, not in the wisdom that appeals to humanity, not in the power that seduces, but in the cross, an image of suffering and humiliation. Only by the faith of God could one trust in something so foolish.

God's faith in humanity's response. If the cross is to be understood as a risk, then it is also an act of faith. God's agony, suffering, and loss on the cross were not a risk if there was no doubt in the mind of God that all whom God desired to be saved would be saved. That is, if God either foreknew or foreordained all who would respond and seek reconciliation, then the cross was painful, perhaps even loving, but not risky. If God foreknew all those who would respond to this outpouring of love, then God took no chance with the cross. It was merely a difficult step in the process of reconciling those whom God knew would respond.[69] If God

---

[68]Macquarrie, *Principles of Christian Theology*, 270.
[69]It might be argued that if God infallibly knew, from the beginning of time, who would positively respond to the cross and be reconciled to God, then the entire process of creation and redemption

foreordained those who would be reconciled, the cross was a pointless, even cruel, event since those God has not chosen have no chance of reconciliation. The cross only for the foreordained is cruel both for Jesus, whose death affected nothing that was not already decided, and for a world of people who only have a false hope of salvation. These are the ways of a cross without risk, a cross without faith.

The cross was not an act of desperation, but neither was it a cold, calculated act. The cross was a deliberate undertaking of love. "Will this strategy of being resourceful, receptive and responsive succeed? Will the disciples come to trust God's way? Will their lives be turned around? Will other people come to trust God through Jesus? Will reconciliation come about? Is God crazy to take this path?"[70] The cross is a risk that God has faith will work—otherwise God would not have engaged in such an undertaking. The fact that Christ died to reconcile a sinful world means that God hoped, and certainly believed, the cross would be effective. God trusts that humans will respond to this act. God hopes that all will participate in Christ's resurrection. And yet, we still see God may have doubts about the final and complete victory. Biblical teachings that speak of death, perishing, and destruction in hell mean that God may be far less than sure if all will ultimately seek reconciliation and mutual loving fellowship. Biblical teachings on hell give testimony to the fact that God trusts that persons will freely respond to God's faith with faith of their own, but that God will compel no one.[71]

---

was superfluous. If God knew the entirety of all free acts, then the cross was unnecessary for God could (should?) have simply created the final state. The entire history of the world is pointless for God is merely "going through the motions" to get to what is and always has been inevitable. For more on this, see Sanders, "The Uselessness of Simple Foreknowledge for Providence," in *The God Who Risks*, 200-207.

[70]Sanders, *The God Who Risks*, 106.

[71]Hell need not be conceived as eternal conscious torment. Many have conceived of hell as a place of ultimate and final destruction for those who finally do not wish to participate in God's faith and love. For explorations into hell as annihilation or conditional immortality, see Edward William Fudge, *The Fire That Consumes: A Biblical and Historical Study of Final Punishment* (Fallbrook, CA: Verdict Publications, 1982); Edward William Fudge and Robert A. Peterson, *Two Views of Hell: A Biblical and Theological Dialogue* (Downers Grove, IL: InterVarsity Press, 2000); Clark Pinnock, "The Conditional View," in *Four Views on Hell*, ed. William v. Crockett (Grand Rapids: Zondervan, 1992), 135-66; Christopher M. Date, Gregory G. Stump, and Joshua W. Anderson, eds., *Rethinking Hell: Readings in Evangelical Conditionalism* (Eugene, OR: Cascade, 2014).

Some believe that God's act of love and grace might actually be universally successful. Keith Ward proposes that we can hold out hope that in the end God's act of love will be effective in winning the whole world, that the message of God's love will have the power to effect universal reconciliation. Ward, when speaking of God's "hope of turning perpetrators of evil to penitence" writes, "Even though God will not compel free creatures to love, it might seem unnatural for anyone truly to experience the destructive effects of self-regard and then to encounter such self-giving, empowering, fulfilling love and reject it."[72] I believe Ward is right to hold out such hope as I see God hoping for nothing less. Yet even with Ward's belief in a universal salvation, he acknowledges there are no guarantees when it comes to resistible grace.

> If God is omnipotent love, therefore, the divine purpose can be frustrated in many particulars, since divine love will not compel. But it cannot be frustrated in its final outcome, since God's power in its ultimately irresistible attraction, will not suffer love to be defeated. One cannot positively guarantee that this will happen. Yet it is an outcome one can rightly hope for and pray for, if God's universal love indeed wills the salvation of all created beings.[73]

Even with God's power and universal love, salvation is still a hope on many levels. This is a hope we must share with God, a hope that none will perish but all will come to repentance (2 Pet 3:9).

The resurrection of Jesus is God's victory over the powers of sin, alienation, and death. The resurrection means that the cross was not merely a sad ending to a noble attempt. It is the sign that God's love is not powerless but has the authority to make all things new, including relationships. However, because God raised Jesus from the grave to glory does not mean that the final victory has fully come or that the risk of the cross is over. The resurrection, like the cross, has an objective and a subjective side. Objectively, the resurrection reveals that Jesus conquered the power of death and alienating forces of sin. Yet subjectively the resurrection is a beacon of God's effective love—a sign of God's sacrificial love. The resurrection

---

[72]Keith Ward, *Religion and Creation* (New York: Oxford University Press, 1996), 264.
[73]Ward, *Religion and Creation*, 265.

shows what God has planned for those who hope and trust in God. The resurrection awaits those who wish to deny themselves and enter into mutual fellowship of love and faith with God. But this is still the free choice of human beings. God's life in Jesus cannot compel us to relationship any more than God's death in Jesus can. The reconciliation of the breached relationship requires that we respond to the love of God (the cross) and the power of God (the resurrection). God has acted in faith for faith and hopes and trusts that we will respond in kind. William Vanstone writes that the triumph or tragedy of God's love is dependent upon the response it receives. "The vulnerability of God means that the issue of His love as triumph or tragedy depends upon His creation. There is given to the creation the power to determine the love of God as either triumphant or tragic love. This power may be called 'power of response': upon the response of the creation the love of God depends for its triumph or tragedy."[74] Can a love that allows creation to play a role in whether it is triumphant or tragic be understood as anything other than a love given in faith? Even though we are weak, our hope is that God's love never fails (1 Cor 13:8).

God's faith in the church. Given all that has been put forward, that God's relationship with the world is one of faith, hope, and love, a few words concerning God's special faith in the church are due. Here I will touch on the fact that God has entrusted the church with the ministry of reconciliation. God's faith in particular church leaders of the first century extends out to the broader church and today to all Christians. God, through the Holy Spirit, has emboldened and entrusted the body of Christ to participate and partner with God in bringing reconciling love and healing.

God's mission of salvation did not begin on the cross nor end with the resurrection. "From the beginning, God was reaching out to humankind to be in relationship."[75] The story of Scripture reveals that God has been working toward the reconciliation and restoration of the whole world

---

[74]W. H. Vanstone, *The Risk of Love* (New York: Oxford University Press, 1978), 67.
[75]Kevin Lines, *Who Do the Ngimurok Say That They Are? A Phenomenological Study of Turkana Traditional Religious Specialists in Turkana, Kenya*, American Society of Missiology Monograph Series 35 (Eugene, OR: Pickwick, 2018), 29.

since its creation. Since God is a God who adores and seeks relationship, a God who "refuses to be alone,"[76] God has not endeavored to complete this mission alone. The mission of God is found in the call of Abraham, the liberation of Israel, the life, death, and resurrection of Jesus, the coming of the Spirit, and many points in between. God's sharing of the mission with the church may be a unique partnership, but it's not unique for God to be in partnership. God's covenant with Israel was made new through Christ, extending to the whole world. It is to this new covenant that the church serves as ministers.

Paul says, "In Christ God was reconciling the world to himself, not counting their trespasses against them, and entrusting the message of reconciliation to us. So we are ambassadors for Christ, since God is making his appeal through us; we entreat you on behalf of Christ, be reconciled to God" (2 Cor 5:19-20).[77] Contextually, Paul most likely meant that he and his companions were those entrusted, the ambassadors of the ministry. However, I do not think Paul believed the ministry of reconciliation altogether excluded other Christians—either those in Corinth or those of today. Paul seems to think that his teachings should be extended to the wider body of believers. He writes to Timothy, "And what you have heard from me through many witnesses entrust to faithful people who will be able to teach others as well" (2 Tim 2:2). Therefore, just as Paul has been entrusted and has entrusted Timothy, Timothy should in turn entrust it to other teachers. Paul then tells Timothy (and his coworkers), "Do your best to present yourself to God as one approved by him, a worker who has no need to be ashamed, rightly explaining the word of truth" (2 Tim 2:15). "Approved" in the context is synonymous with "trusted." Show yourselves to be persons that demonstrate God's trust was not in vain. These words, most would affirm, should be extended to all Christians.[78]

---

[76]William H. Willimon, *Who Will Be Saved?* (Nashville: Abingdon, 2008), 1.

[77]Craig S. Keener, *The IVP Bible Background Commentary: New Testament*, 2nd ed. (Downers Grove, IL: IVP Academic, 2014), 1:508.

[78]Second Timothy is one of the disputed letters of Paul which means scholars do not agree whether this letter was actually written by Paul or possibly a disciple of his. If the letter is pseudonymous

Christians have been called to participate in the ministry of reconciliation. This two-dimensional ministry involves the vertical: God's reconciling the world to God's self (Rom 5:1-11); and the horizontal: the reconciliation of human to human (Eph 2:12-20); and even the healing of all of creation (Col 1:19-20). The model of missions being exclusively about evangelistic conversion (Mt 28:19-20) has given way to a much more robust idea of mission that involves the church being an instrumental partner in God's work to make all things new.[79] The reconciling ministry of the church has broadened then to include, along with proclamation, efforts toward dialogue, liberation, justice, healing, and building.

Robert Schreiter rightly recognizes that "true reconciliation does not come about because of what we do. Our effectiveness as messengers and ministers of reconciliation arises out of our co-operation with God."[80] Yes, *true*, that is, complete and thorough, reconciliation is beyond our ability and efforts, but this does not mean that the church plays no part. Quite the contrary, Schreiter notes that this mission's effectiveness rests in part on us—*our* cooperation with God. This suggests that if the effectiveness of missions, in part, rests on us, then God's cooperation with the church involves divine faith. God has entrusted the church to work and cooperate with God's Spirit. Schreiter further argues that the ministry of reconciliation is "more a spirituality than a strategy," and that it is "rooted in a deep and ongoing communion with God."[81] This means that the ministry of the church is centered on relationship with God—not simply cooperation or partnership, but intimate communion.

---

that does not hurt my argument and may actually bolster it. This would mean that by the end of the first century a tradition had developed that workers had been entrusted with the gospel and this entrusting serves as motivation. The church then has a tradition of each generation entrusting the next with the message and ministry of the gospel.

[79]This broader perspective is often called *missio Dei*. Kevin Lines, quoting missiologist David Bosch, offers a very nice summary of *missio Dei*: "A missiological metanarrative recognizing that missions are the particular activities of the church and missionaries, while *mission* 'is not primarily an activity of the church, but an attribute of God.'" Lines, *Who Do the Ngimurok Say That They Are?* 28-29.

[80]Robert Schreiter, "The Emergence of Reconciliation as a Paradigm of Mission: Dimensions, Levels, and Characteristics," in *Mission as Ministry of Reconciliation*, ed. Robert Schreiter and Knud Jørgensen (Oxford: Regnum, 2013), 15.

[81]Schreiter, "The Emergence of Reconciliation as a Paradigm of Mission," 15.

God's trust in the church should not be understood to mean God *uses* the church in the sense of a mechanic using a wrench. God can and has used all sorts of persons to affect God's plans, but these have not been people God has partnered with nor necessarily trusted even if God relied on them.[82] God makes use of the church by working with this community in the ministry of reconciliation. I, like many others, am bewildered as to why God remains hidden, relying on the church to be the principal means of delivering the gospel.[83] While I am perplexed as to why God has chosen to engage in missions the ways God has, I am undaunted that God has faith in each Christian individually and trusts the church collectively to impact the world and work with God in its healing.

It must be made clear that divine faith does not mean God has handed over the mission, left it to the church to do *for* God. This is God's mission because *"reconciliation is first and foremost the work of God*, who makes it a gift to us in which we in turn are called to co-operate."[84] But it is nonetheless a mission the church has procured and been entrusted to advance as it works *with* God. The church has been entrusted with the ministry of reconciliation, but not left on its own to sink or swim. Furthermore, the church does not take Christ into the world but is led into the world by the Spirit. God's trust is not a replacement for grace, nor does God's employment and partnership with the church imply that God's grace does not go out to all. God's prevenient grace has gone throughout the world preparing the way for Christian workers. I am not suggesting that God's ability to save the lost is wholly dependent on the efforts of the church. God is completely capable of saving the unevangelized.[85] But this does not mean mission efforts are pointless any

---

[82]Some examples might include the Babylonians, Herod, and Pilate.
[83]The problem of divine hiddenness, which some see as a branch of the greater problem of evil, poses the question of why God remains hidden, silent, if some are willing to believe if God would only manifest God's self to them. For more on the issue, see Daniel Howard-Snyder and Paul K. Moser, eds., *Divine Hiddenness: New Essays* (Cambridge: Cambridge University Press, 2002).
[84]Schreiter, "The Emergence of Reconciliation as a Paradigm of Mission," 15.
[85]This statement should not be read as an endorsement of any particular theory regarding the scope and means of God's salvation even though prominent open theists such as Clark Pinnock and John Sanders have affirmed inclusivism. For Clark H. Pinnock, see *A Wideness in God's Mercy: The Finality of Jesus Christ in a World of Religions* (Grand Rapids: Zondervan, 1992);

more than is seeking medical aid for a nonlife-threatening disorder. I affirm that it is God who saves, and my hope is that in the end God will make right what we neglected.

This brief discussion of God's faith in the church raises a new set of questions. Is there a difference between trusting a pastor and trusting the church? Can the church itself be understood as faithful and trustworthy or is trustworthiness a category limited to individuals? Trusting the church or any institution, system, or nation poses challenges that trusting an individual does not.[86] An institution can seem untrustworthy if its spokesperson or leaders are suspicious, even if most of its members are reliable. Can the church as a whole be trustworthy even if some of its branches, movements, and denominations have strayed into heresy, injustice, and/or immorality? Institutions like the church, however, may be greater than the sum of its parts and so even though the church is made up of sinful persons and wayward periods and parts, it can, as a whole, be deemed trustworthy. Or, at the very least, worth investing in and working with while it matures into a faithful institution. I do not always understand God's historic trust in this institution of the church any more than I understand God's trust in the many unsavory characters we see God trusting throughout Scripture or even God's apparent trust in me. God has chosen the church to make known God's wisdom (Eph 3:9-10), and while the church itself may not always understand that wisdom, we need to believe that God is not foolish in trusting the church.

Pinnock, "An Inclusivist View," in *More Than One Way? Four Views on Salvation in a Pluralistic World*, ed. Dennis L. Okholm and Timothy R. Phillips (Grand Rapids: Zondervan, 1995), 254-55; Pinnock, *Flame of Love*. For John Sanders, see *No Other Name? An Investigation into the Destiny of the Unevangelized* (Grand Rapids: Eerdmans, 1992); Sanders, "Inclusivism," in *What About Those Who Have Never Heard? Three Views on the Destiny of the Unevangelized*, ed. John Sanders (Downers Grove, IL: InterVarsity Press, 1995), 21-55.

   While I believe it is most reasonable that inclusivists affirm open theism given that it would be odd for God to genuinely desire and work to save all persons while infallibly knowing that would not be the case, there is not a logical disconnect in an open theist rejecting inclusivism and affirming particularism or universalism.

[86]Katherine Hawley has written on institutional trustworthiness; see *Trust: A Very Short Introduction* (Oxford: Oxford University Press, 2012), chap. 8; and "Trustworthy Groups and Organizations," in *The Philosophy of Trust*, ed. Paul Faulkner and Thomas Simpson (Oxford: Oxford University Press, 2017), 230-50.

Finally, some might suggest I am being inconsistent by affirming that God trusts the church in particular and humanity in general, if God is ultimately the one who brings reconciliation and, furthermore, that our hope is in God, not the church. I do not see it this way. As a former professional house painter I can still hire and trust a crew to paint my house, knowing that if there are flaws I can touch them up myself. Likewise, my wife and I can trust our daughter to do her chores and help keep the house clean even if I have to do some things she either cannot (because she is too short) and did not (because she was distracted by friends). Simply because I can complete and perfect what I have entrusted others to do does not negate the reliance I have and the trust I gave. Likewise, God has chosen to work with the church, and this work is important, but this does not mean God cannot to a large degree clean up our mistakes. How deep and wide God's reconciliation will finally be is beyond my abilities. Even if I do not quite understand how God will do it, my faith remains that God will keep the promise of making all things new (2 Cor 5:17; Rev 21:5).

CONCLUSION

God's faith in the efficacy of the cross is not idle. Just as God's strength and love are at work reconciling the world to God's self, God's faith is at work as well. "It is God's faith in us and God's love for us that creates the gift Paul describes as *justification*. The conviction that we are justified by God's faith in us and God's love for us creates peace with God."[87] God's faith in us, whether we recognize it as faith or not, is calling us to love and trust in God. We know God's love and faith are efficacious in bringing about justification, reconciliation, and mutual fellowship for we know God. Just as God's love sparks a love within us, God's faith is the means of our own faith. Mike Mason says it well:

> True faith depends not at all upon itself, nor upon its own system of piety, but rather upon the Lord alone and his faithfulness. It knows that our faith in God

---

[87]Ross and Stevenson, *Romans*, 37.

is only a reflection of God's faith in us. For our Father does believe in us; He *faithed* us into existence in the first place, and he continues day by day "sustaining all things by his powerful word" (Heb. 1:3). To have faith is to have trust in the faithfulness of our God, knowing that faithfulness is first and foremost not a human but a divine attribute. All we human beings can do is to become empty, in order that God's character of perfect faithfulness may flow into us. Genuine faith is not the faith to *do* anything at all, except to fall to the ground and die.[88]

The risk God took in the incarnation and the cross demonstrates that God does not love from a distance but has the faith to become that which God hopes to save. God had the faith to become godforsaken for us. Salvation is the restoring of broken fellowship and the healing of human sin, but it is also the healing of divine hurt. If God is truly wounded by human sin and if salvation is the restoring of broken fellowship, can we speak about God being healed, somehow "saved," by faith? Is Jesus more than our Christ but also God's Christ?

Human salvation as healing is one of the many metaphors for salvation. Sanctification, justification, liberation, and forgiveness are deep metaphors in the language of salvation and are extremely important, with a richness and depth of meaning for all who taste salvation. However, these are often individualized concepts that do not necessarily have to speak in terms of relationality. Healing, in many instances, may also have the sense of personal and individual healing. Biblically, the idea of salvation as healing, quite common with the Greek term *sōzō*, is used to speak of both physical healing and eschatological healing.[89] Paul even connects the concepts of reconciliation and healing when he writes, "For if while we were enemies, we were reconciled to God through the death of his Son, much more surely, having been reconciled, we will be saved by his life" (Rom 5:10). Here the idea of reconciliation, that is, the restoring of broken fellowship, is tied to the idea of healing. We are saved, that is, the relationship has been restored.

---

[88]Mike Mason, *The Gospel According to Job* (Wheaton, IL: Crossway, 1994), 69-70.

[89]Perhaps the most interesting example is found in Acts 4:9 and 4:12, in which the same word is used to speak of both physical and eschatological healing.

In theological terms, Bruce Reichenbach argues that salvation should be understood in terms primarily, although not exclusively, of healing. For him salvation is about restoration of the person, a perfecting and maturing. Sin is a form of spiritual sickness; God is the healer, Jesus the physician.[90]

The healing is *curative* in that it deals with our fundamental human predicament of sin, removing our sin from us. It is *restorative* because it returns us to wholeness—to the wholeness of our relation to God from whom we have been cut off because of sin in rejecting his covenant and his forgiving attempts to reconcile us, to the wholeness of our person from which sickness have been removed, and to the wholeness of God's community from which we were ostracized.[91]

According to Reichenbach, the healing is not simply a removal of sin or a curing of the individual but a restoration of the whole person, which includes reconciling and restoring the person to God. Salvation heals the relationship and the damages caused by sin. But as we know, humans are not the only ones hurt by sin nor are humans the only ones affected by the estrangement. God, too, is hurt and estranged from humans by sin and rebellion. One of the most significant tenets of relational theology is the rejection of the classical doctrine of impassability, the idea that God can never suffer. Significant in open and relational theology is the affirmation that God does suffer, both willingly and unwillingly. God not only suffers in and with Jesus on the cross, but God suffers the ill effects of sin before the cross. It is the suffering of humanity and divinity that leads to the cross. God suffers the effects of a love rejected. This is one reason why God must act in faith and love in the hope of restoring the relationship. God acts in faith in order to reconcile humanity to God's self, heal the breach in the relationship, and experience peace with creation. God's faith, the willingness to suffer in order to end suffering, is also healing for God. God's hope is that by reaching out in faith and love, God, as well as humanity, will be saved, that is, healed.

---

[90]Bruce R. Reichenbach, "Healing View," in *The Nature of Atonement: Four Views*, ed. James Beilby and Paul R. Eddy (Downers Grove, IL: IVP Academic, 2006), 117-42.
[91]Reichenbach, "Healing View," 133.

The faith of God in the advent of Christ is the most dramatic act of faith ever displayed. Our faith is in the one who is faithful. God's faith is unsafe because it is often faith in a faithless humanity. Jesus' faith in the Father, while having to face the threat of God forsakenness, was a faith that was rewarded by his glorification. The Father's faith in the Son was a faith in the true human, a human with a perfected yet autonomous will. The Father's faith was rewarded when Jesus effected the atonement with his death and resurrection. The final effects of God's faith in humanity's subjection to the cross are yet to be seen. Certainly, there have been many men and women who have come to God with repentant hearts seeking God's will for their lives. But there are others who we cannot be sure about. For those we are not sure of, we can only follow Ward's advice to hope and pray that God's willful salvation for the entire world will not fail. This is not merely a human hope but a divine hope as well. Fortunately, God is as wise as God is faithful, and we have reason to hope that God will be successful in these plans for all to live in Christ.

CONCLUSION

As that faith grows, it becomes a God's faith, strong
in its roots, lofty in its branches, overshadowing the
whole soul in its influence, it can do mightier things.

GEORGE HENRY DAVIS,
THE FAITH NECESSARY TO PREVAILING PRAYER

THROUGHOUT THIS WORK I have endeavored to demonstrate that
God has faith. In ways we may never fully comprehend, God believes in
us, trusts us, and has hope for us—all because God deeply loves us. In
faith God reaches out to humanity in the hope that humanity will respond in kind. By faith God sends grace to all persons, empowering
them to freely respond to the divine lure of love (Jn 12:32). We can ask,
why is it that without faith it is impossible to please God (Heb 11:6)? The
answer says that relationship, at its most intimate, is impossible without
mutual faith. Only by faith can one be in relationship with God. Only
faith pleases God because it is our positive response to God's own love,
trust, and hope. Feeble as it may be, our faith, even when less than that
of a mustard seed, derives from our being in the likeness of God.

The Scriptures speak to us about being imitators of God and Christ.
"You shall be holy, for I the LORD your God am holy" (Lev 19:2). "Be
perfect, therefore, as your heavily Father is perfect" (Mt 5:48). "Be merciful, just as your Father is merciful" (Lk 6:36). "Therefore be imitators
of God, as beloved children" (Eph 5:1). "Whoever says, 'I abide in him

[Christ],' ought to walk just as he walked" (1 Jn 2:6). Christ, "suffered for you, leaving you an example, so that you should follow in his steps" (1 Pet 2:21). While theologies known as *imitatio Dei* and *imitatio Christi* are typically applied to moral theology, it has in fact application with the faith of God.[1] Moral exemplars are a key element to moral development and maturity. But Christ is not only our moral but also our faith exemplar. Hebrews 11 discusses the heroes of faith: Abraham, Moses, Rahab, and others, but these exemplars are penultimate. The ultimate exemplar is "Jesus the pioneer and perfecter of our faith" (Heb 12:2). Jesus, as the Word of God made flesh, shows us perfect faith—faith not only in God the Father but in his disciples as well.

We know that God is love (1 Jn 4:8), and 1 Corinthians 13 highlights what love is and is not so that we too might walk in the ways of love. As I suggested earlier, if it is true that God is love, then God is patient (2 Pet 3:9); God is kind (Eph 2:7); God is not envious or boastful, arrogant or rude (Ps 113:5-6[2]). God does not insist on God's own way (Ex 33:1-3, 14); God is not irritable or resentful (Ps 103:8). God does not rejoice in wrongdoing (1 Jn 1:9) but rejoices in the truth (1 Jn 5:6). If God is our exemplar in all these ways, then God too is our example in faith! There is no limit to what God can bear, no limit to God's trust, hope, or endurance (1 Cor 13:7)! What better model of faith could we have than the God who is love?

The Bible is often referred to as the "story of God," and while it may be more than that, it is not less. It is a story that begins with God's acts

---

[1]For more concerning *imitatio Dei*, see Roberto Sirvent, *Embracing Vulnerability: Human and Divine* (Eugene, OR: Pickwick, 2014), esp. chap. 3; John Sanders, *Theology in the Flesh: How Embodiment and Culture Shape the Way We Think About Truth, Morality, and God* (Minneapolis: Fortress, 2016), chap. 6; Howard Kreisel, "*Imitatio Dei* in Maimonides' *Guide of the Perplexed*," *Association for Jewish Studies* 19, no. 2 (1994): 169-212; John Barton, "Imitation of God in the Old Testament," in *The God of Israel*, ed. R. P. Gordon (Cambridge: Cambridge University Press, 2007), 35-46. Concerning *imitatio Christi*, see Jason B. Hood, *Imitating God in Christ: Recapturing a Biblical Pattern* (Downers Grove, IL: InterVarsity Press, 2013); Richard A. Burridge, *Imitating Jesus: An Inclusive Approach to New Testament Ethics* (Grand Rapids: Eerdmans, 2007).

[2]"Who is like the LORD our God, / Who is enthroned on high, / Who humbles Himself to behold / The things that are in heaven and on earth?" (NASB). We should also look to Philippians 2:5-8 when speaking of the humility of God.

of creation and ends with the vision and promise of a new creation. Between these creative acts we see God call Abraham, lead Israel, live and die as the man Jesus, raise to new life, and establish the church. The story of God is not only a love story, but also a faith story. Psalm 115 reminds us that we become what we worship, what we trust. If it is faith that pleases God, then we should worship, trust, and imitate the God of faith—the God who trusts.

FINAL REMARKS

Faith, when complete, has the attribute of belief, the intellectual activity of affirming the truth of an idea that is outside the range of possible knowledge.[3] A second quality of faith is trust. Trust, unlike belief, is primarily an action or disposition to act. Trust is living out and acting upon the hope that one has. Hope is that future-facing quality of anticipating and longing for some good. Finally, love is that quality of faith that draws us near to the other or object of faith. To have faith is not merely to believe, trust, and hope—it is to long for the one we have faith in. Love moves us beyond belief *that* to faith *in*. Faith is lived out in the cognitive, affective, and conative plans and works toward a desired future. Faith seeks and yearns for values and goods—beauty and creativity—beyond the assuredness of security.

The idea of faith cannot be reduced to a single conception. It is multifaceted in that it includes the qualities of belief, trust, hope, and love. Faith functions as noun and verb, theoretical and experiential, complex and simple, of the mind and the body. Faith has a value all its own and is also a means to its own end, that is, the purpose of faith is to generate faith. Faith, like love, is not something that will one day run its course and cease to be useful or necessary. For as long as there are free beings there will be faith. As long as there are relationships of mutual fellowship and communion between the divine and the human there will be faith. Over time faith becomes stronger and the relationship galvanized by

---

[3] As noted in chap. 4, God only believes what is true, so this aspect of faith is thoroughly human.

the mutual trust, but faith never runs its course. Faith is perfected, but never completed.

As stated above, faith is ultimately for the fostering of relationships. In fact, faith should be understood as a particular kind of relationship, a relationship that love or trust alone could never produce. Faith is a kind of relationship that connects love and trust so there can be an intimacy, friendship, and devotion. Love and trust produce a relationship of faith where there is guidance without control, care without overpowering, and freedom without apathy. As any parent knows, it is difficult to work out a healthy balance of love that seeks to protect and trust and that allows for freedom and maturity. But in many ways, this is the kind of faith a parent has in a child, a faith that can be typified as a careful infusion of love with trust. I am not suggesting that faith should supersede the ideas of love or trust. I am merely approaching the idea of faith from a relational perspective, seeking ways in which the concepts of love and trust might be enriched and expanded.

Open and relational theology has produced theological innovations while inviting theologians and laity, believers and seekers, to engage the Scriptures and traditions in light of this approach. The focus of open and relational theology is that God is essentially loving and relational, which means God refuses absolute control over all facets of creation. God is responsive to the real and free choices of creatures. The relational conceptualization of God has generally included the notions that God is self-limited for the purposes of relationship.[4] And God loves relationship, so God loves self-limitation. Or said better, God loves when we are free, and God is active in securing our freedom in the fullest. The relationships that God desires are relationships of genuine love, which produce goods and values, many of which God alone could never achieve. For the sake of love and immeasurable values, God becomes limited in

---

[4]It is here that a major disagreement among relational theists can be found. Some theologians will argue that God is necessarily limited by a metaphysical truth independent of God or by God's own nature as a being defined by love, while other relational theologians will argue that God is only limited by God's free choice—or perhaps some combination of the three.

giving humans the ability to freely enter into relationship with God and likewise the ability to ignore relationship with God. For the sake of authentic love—genuine relationship—God created a universe with potential and the novelty that God could not and wanted not, to control at each step of its unfolding. It is a universe in which God cannot and wants not to foreknow all that will transpire as creatures have real freedom. God, for the sake of freedom and the purposes of love, has chosen to enter into relationship with humanity—a relationship of faith.

Given that faith is relationship-centered and that open and relational theists seek to understand and explain God in terms of loving relationship, is there any reason not to celebrate faith as a divine attribute? This work suggests that given the nature of faith and the relational conception of God, it makes the most sense to speak of God as a being, a perfect being, of perfect faith. Thus, faith should be included among God's great-making qualities. Like love, faith is not a weakness but a strength. Faith does not restrain God; rather, it empowers God to work with other free beings. In faith God is most creative. Faith allows God to bring about goods otherwise impossible. It enables God to love in the fullest. Faith is a necessary quality of genuine relationship. If God has authentically partnered with humanity to produce values and beauties that God cannot produce alone, then faith is not only an attribute of God, it is an essential attribute.

God is rightly spoken of as being first and foremost love. God acts out of and for the purposes of love. Yet to make sense of God's love we also speak of divine power, for love without power is helpless sentimentality. God's love is also just because it works to right all wrongs. God is all-wise, and so God's love is never foolish or wrongheaded. God is faithful, for God's love has empowered humans to make their own choices. While God's sharing of power can rightly be seen as an act of love, it is no less an act of faith, for the sharing of power shows that God does not love from afar but is vulnerable and risky. God shares God's very nature and being with a limited and fallible creature. Can this be anything less than an act of faith?

The faith demonstrated in the advent of Christ was not merely Jesus' faith in the Father, but equally the Father's faith in Jesus. The Father had to trust that Jesus would take the cross and fulfill his messianic mission. God trusted that Jesus would remain faithful and trustworthy, even when forsaken. Even though God had to give up Jesus, God never gave up on Jesus. God's faith is most clear in Jesus' prayer that his suffering be removed. God trusted Jesus with that hour even when Jesus himself had doubts. In the advent of Christ, we see not only the Father's faith in Christ but also the Father's faith through Christ. Thank God for the Father's faith in the Son and the Son's faith in the Father, for without either we would be lost in our sins!

Jesus' faith was not only in the Father but in his disciples as well. Jesus taught the disciples to follow his way. He empowered them to do great works and entrusted his church with the Spirit of God to be a light of God's love and truth. These acts are not to be taken lightly since the empowering of the church is risky, and many times the church has failed. But God has not lost faith. God continues to entrust the church with the gospel and as the body of Christ.

The Scriptures have been called a love story, but they are no less a faith story. God has acted by faith for faith (Rom 1:17). God hopes that we respond to faith with faith. God loves and desires love, but without also longing for fellowship and communion, faith is unnecessary. This is what open and relational theism seeks to bring to the forefront of theology—a God who loves, desires, and values fellowship—a God who loves mutual faith.

The history of a theology of divine faith is sparse, yet the faith of God is not a wholly foreign idea. Authors have alluded to God's faith, as noted throughout this work, and have even used statements such as "God's faith." Authors have spoken about God's risking, trusting, and hoping. In 1919, Frederick Shannon produced the collection *God's Faith in Man: And Other Sermons*, in which he proclaims the creation of humans is an act of divine faith.[5] Shannon mentions biblical heroes such as Moses and

---

[5]Frederick F. Shannon, *God's Faith in Man: And Other Sermons* (New York: Fleming H. Revell, 1919), 9-25. The sermon is interesting given that its date of publication is 1919, just after World

David as being the object of God's faith, but states that the twelve apostles are its "supreme illustration."

> The Will that can bind or loose the bands of Orion chose twelve frail human wills to inaugurate the kingdom of God among men. Unlettered, without social prestige, devoid of political power, lacking the emoluments of wealth, yet these twelve men—bigoted, selfish, sinful—are sent forth to conquer the world. Many times they were without faith in themselves, in man, or God. While apparently doing everything in their power to make it impossible for even God to trust them, yet the Lord Christ goes on believing in them, inspiring them, strengthening them, loving them unto the end, and on across the beckoning frontiers of "the Land of Beginning Again."[6]

Shannon ends his sermon with a call to those who have lost faith to remember God's faith in them.[7] The sermon, while not a deeply developed theological argument, nonetheless calls us to ponder God's trust and faith in a weak yet hopeful humanity.

Some insist that religious trust in God is a "degenerate form of absolute and unreciprocated trust."[8] While it may be true that our trust in God should be absolute, I have shown there is ample reason to challenge the notion that it is unreciprocated. Jürgen Moltmann, too, understands that trust between God and human is reciprocal. "Trust is always a mutual affair, and this is true of trust in God too: We trust in God because God trusts in us. That is the heart of the biblical stories and message: God trusts in us, God believes in us, God hopes in us and awaits us. People who understand this become God's trusted and familiar friends."[9] Perhaps if we reimagine our relationship with God, we will see that faith creates a particular reality. We will see that the future is fashioned and formed by who we trust and how we trust—and this is no different for God. Trust brings about a positive expectation and hopeful

---

War I, yet the sermon reads as if it were written in the heyday of Idealism. If the sermon is post–World War I, it is a remarkable statement of hopefulness.

[6]Shannon, *God's Faith in Man*, 23-24.

[7]Shannon, *God's Faith in Man*, 24.

[8]Annette Baier, "Trust and Antitrust," *Ethics* 96, no. 2 (1986): 252.

[9]Jürgen Moltmann, "Control Is Good—Trust Is Better: Freedom and Security in a 'Free World,'" *Theology Today* 62, no. 4 (2006): 473.

relationship, while distrust and suspicion stations persons in anxiety or fear.[10] God's relationship with humanity is, in effect, created by God's willingness to have faith. God creates a reality of intimate relationship by trusting humans to be genuine partners of the divine.

God's faith in the church certainly fosters a theology of divine faith. God's faith is not simply a theoretical notion but has real and practical implications. First John 4:19 says, "We love because he first loved us." We know love and can give love because of the example and revelation of God's love. The same could be said for faith. Just as we learn love by Christ's example, we also should turn to Christ to learn faith. We risk because God risked. We will for the things God has willed. We hope for what God hopes. We trust as God trusts. We doubt what God doubts. We hate what God hates. We are angered by what angers God. And we should have faith as God has faith. This is the prayer, this is the purpose, and this is maturity. This is the story of Scripture. "The stories of scripture are not only a story of our faith in God. They are also magnificent, tear-inducing stories of God's faith in us. We learn to trust as we realize we are being trusted. We become responsible as we understand we are being handed responsibility as a gift."[11] We love because God first loved us—we have faith because God first had faith in us.

---

[10]Trudy Govier, *Social Trust and Human Communities* (Montreal: McGill-Queen's University Press, 1997), 35.

[11]John W. Wimberly Jr., "God's Faith in Us," *Living Pulpit* 6, no. 1 (1997): 19.

BIBLIOGRAPHY

Adams, Robert Merrihew. *Finite and Infinite Goods: A Framework for Ethics.* New York: Oxford University Press, 1999.

———. *A Theory of Virtue: Excellence in Being* for *the Good.* Oxford: Oxford University Press, 2006.

Alfaro, Juan. "The Dual Aspect of Faith: Entrusting Oneself to God and Acceptance of the Christian Message." In *Man as Man and Believer*, edited by Edward Schillebeeckx and Boniface Willems, Concilium 21. New York: Paulist Press, 1967.

Alston, William P. "Belief, Acceptance, and Religious Faith." In *Faith, Freedom, and Rationality*, edited by Jeff Jordan and Daniel Howard-Snyder. Lanham, MD: Rowman & Littlefield, 1996.

———. *Divine Nature and Human Language: Essays in Philosophical Theology.* Ithaca, NY: Cornell University Press, 1996.

Aristotle. *Nicomachean Ethics.* Translated by Terence Irwin. 2nd ed. Indianapolis: Hackett, 1999.

Audi, Robert. "Belief, Faith, and Acceptance." In *Ethics of Belief: Essays in Tribute to D. Z. Phillips*, edited by Eugene Thomas Long and Patrick Horn. Dordrecht: Springer, 2008.

———. "Faith, Belief, and Rationality." *Philosophical Perspectives 5, Philosophy of Religion* (1991): 213-39.

Augustine. *The Enchiridion on Faith, Hope and Love.* Edited by Henry Paolucci and J. J. Shaw. Chicago: Henry Regnery, 1961/1996.

Aulén, Gustaf. *Christus Victor: An Historical Study of the Three Main Types of the Idea of Atonement.* Translated by A. G. Herbert. New York: Macmillan, 1969.

Baier, Annette C. *Moral Prejudices: Essays on Ethics.* Cambridge, MA: Harvard University Press, 1994.

———. *Trust: The Tanner Lectures on Human Values.* https://tannerlectures.utah.edu/_documents/a-to-z/b/baier92.pdf (accessed February 28, 2018).

———. "Trust and Antitrust." *Ethics* 96, no. 2 (1986): 231-60.

Barth, Karl. *Church Dogmatics*. Edited by Geoffrey W. Bromiley and T. F. Torrance. Vol. 2. Edinburgh: T&T Clark, 1957.

———. *Evangelical Theology: An Introduction*. Translated by Grover Foley. Grand Rapids: Eerdmans, 1963.

Barton, John. "Imitation of God in the Old Testament." In *The God of Israel*, edited by R. P. Gordon. Cambridge: Cambridge University Press, 2007.

Basinger, David. *The Case for Freewill Theism: A Philosophical Assessment*. Downers Grove, IL: InterVarsity Press, 1996.

Bedford, Nancy Elizabeth. *Galatians*. Louisville, KY: Westminster John Knox, 2016.

Beilby, James K., and Paul R. Eddy, eds. *Divine Foreknowledge: Four Views*. Downers Grove, IL: InterVarsity Press, 2001.

Berkhof, Louis. *Systematic Theology*. Grand Rapids: Eerdmans, 1962.

Bishop, John. "Trusting Others, Trusting in God, Trusting the World." In *Religious Faith and Intellectual* Virtue, edited by Laura Frances Callahan and Timothy O'Connor. Oxford: Oxford University Press, 2014.

Bloeser, Claudia, and Titus Stahl. "Hope." In *The Stanford Encyclopedia of Philosophy*, edited by Edward N. Zalta. Spring 2017 ed. https://plato.stanford.edu/archives/spr2017/entries/hope/.

Blomberg, Craig. *1 Corinthians*. The NIV Application Commentary. Grand Rapids: Zondervan, 1994.

Bock, Darrell L. *Luke*. Vol. 2: *9:51–24:53*. Baker Exegetical Commentary on the New Testament. Grand Rapids: Baker Academic, 2007.

Bohler, Carolyn Jane. *God the What? What Our Metaphors for God Reveal About Our Beliefs in God*. Woodstock, VT: SkyLight Paths, 2008.

Bonhoeffer, Dietrich. *Letters and Papers from Prison*. Translated by Reginald H. Fuller et al. New York: Macmillan, 1972.

Borg, Marcus J. *The God We Never Knew: Beyond Dogmatic Religion to a More Authentic Contemporary Faith*. San Francisco: HarperSanFrancisco, 1997.

Borgman, Paul. *Genesis: The Story We Haven't Heard*. Downers Grove, IL: InterVarsity Press, 2001.

Boring, M. Eugene, and Fred B. Craddock. *The People's New Testament Commentary*. Louisville, KY: Westminster John Knox, 2004.

Boyd, Gregory A. "God Limits His Control." In *Four Views on Divine Providence*, edited by Dennis W. Jowers. Grand Rapids: Zondervan, 2011.

———. *God of the Possible: A Biblical Introduction to the Open View of God*. Grand Rapids: Baker Books, 2000.

———. "The Open-Theism View." In *Divine Knowledge: Four Views*, edited by James K. Beilby and Paul R. Eddy. Downers Grove, IL: InterVarsity Press, 2001.

Brown, David. *Divine Humanity: Kenosis and the Construction of a Christian Theology*. Waco, TX: Baylor University Press, 2011.

Brown, Raymond Edward. *The Epistles of John*. New Haven, CT: Yale University Press, 2008.

Brown, Robert McAfee. *Is Faith Obsolete?* Philadelphia: Westminster, 1974.

Brueggemann, Walter. "Covenant as a Subversive Paradigm." *Christian Century*, November 12, 1980, 1094-98.

———. *Genesis*. Interpretation: A Bible Commentary for Teaching and Preaching. Atlanta: John Knox, 1982.

Brümmer, Vincent. *Atonement, Christology and the Trinity: Making Sense of Christian Doctrine*. Burlington, VT: Ashgate, 2005.

———. *Brümmer on Meaning and the Christian Faith: Collected Writings of Vincent Brümmer*. Edited by John R. Hinnells. Burlington, VT: Ashgate, 2006.

———. *The Model of Love: A Study in Philosophical Theology*. Cambridge: Cambridge University Press, 1993.

Brunner, Emil. *The Christian Doctrine of Creation and Redemption*. Vol. 2 of *Dogmatics*. Translated by Olive Wyon. Philadelphia: Westminster, 1952.

———. *The Mediator: A Study of the Central Doctrine of the Christian Faith*. London: Lutterworth, 1934.

Buber, Martin. *Two Types of Faith*. Translated by Norman Goldhawk. New York: Harper, 1961.

Buchak, Lara. "Can It Be Rational to Have Faith?" In *Philosophy of Religion: An Anthology*, edited by Louis P. Pojman and Michael Rea, 7th ed. Boston: Cengage Learning, 2014.

Buckley, James J. "The End." In *The Blackwell Companion to Catholicism*, edited by James Buckley, Frederick Christian Bauerschmidt, and Trent Pomplun. Oxford: Wiley Blackwell, 2011.

Burridge, Richard A. *Imitating Jesus: An Inclusive Approach to New Testament Ethics*. Grand Rapids: Eerdmans, 2007.

Buttrick, David. *Speaking Parables: A Homiletic Guide*. Louisville, KY: Westminster John Knox, 2000.

Calvin, John. *The Gospel According to St. John: 1–10*. Edited by David W. Torrance and Thomas F. Torrance. Translated by T. H. L. Parker. Grand Rapids: Eerdmans, 1995.

—————. *Institutes of the Christian Religion*. Edited by John McNeil. Translated by Ford Lewis Battles. 2 Vols. Library of Christian Classics. Philadelphia: Westminster, 1960.

Campbell, Alexander, and W. A. Morris. *The Writings of Alexander Campbell: Selections Chiefly from the Millennial Harbinger*. Austin, TX: Eugene Von Boeckmann, 1896.

Caputo, John D. *The Weakness of God: A Theology of the Event*. Indiana Series in the Philosophy of Religion. Bloomington: Indiana University Press, 2006.

Case-Winters, Anna. *God's Power: Traditional Understandings and Contemporary Challenges*. Louisville, KY: Westminster John Knox, 1990.

Cessario, Romanus, OP. "The Theological Virtue of Hope." In *The Ethics of Aquinas*, edited by Stephen Pope. Washington, DC: Georgetown University Press, 2002.

Chambers, Oswald. *My Utmost for His Highest*. Grand Rapids: Discovery House, 2003.

Clines, David J. A. *Job 1–20*. Word Biblical Commentary 17. Dallas: Word, 1989.

Cobb, John, Jr., and David Ray Griffin. *Process Theology: An Introductory Exposition*. Philadelphia: Westminster, 1976.

Coleman, James Samuel. *Foundations of Social Theory*. Cambridge, MA: Belknap Press of Harvard University Press, 1990.

Coppedge, Allan. *Portraits of God: A Biblical Theology of Holiness*. Downers Grove, IL: IVP Academic, 2008.

Creel, Richard. *Divine Impassibility: An Essay in Philosophical Theology*. Cambridge: Cambridge University Press, 1986.

Date, Christopher M., Gregory G. Stump, and Joshua W. Anderson, eds. *Rethinking Hell: Readings in Evangelical Conditionalism*. Eugene, OR: Cascade, 2014.

Davis, George Henry. *The Faith Necessary to Prevailing Prayer: A Sermon . . . with an Introductory Address to the Congregation at Old King Street*. Bristol, 1854.

Davis, Stephen T. "Is Kenosis Orthodox?" In *Exploring Kenotic Christology: The Self-Emptying of God*, edited by C. Stephen Evans. New York: Oxford University Press, 2006.

Dawe, Donald G. *The Form of a Servant: A Historical Analysis of the Kenotic Motif*. Philadelphia: Westminster, 1963.

Day, J. P. "Hope." *American Philosophical Quarterly* 6, no. 2 (1969): 89-102.

Descartes, Rene. *Passions of the Soul*. Translated by Stephen Voss. Indianapolis: Hackett, 1989.

DeWeese, Garrett J. *God and the Nature of Time*. Burlington, VT: Ashgate, 2004.

pography* 239

Dulles, Avery. *The Assurance of Things Hoped For: A Theology of Christian Faith*. New York: Oxford University Press, 1994.

Dyrness, William. *Themes in Old Testament Theology*. Downers Grove, IL: InterVarsity Press, 1983.

Eichrodt, Walter. *Theology of the Old Testament*. Vol. 1. Translated by J. A. Baker. Philadelphia: Westminster, 1961.

Erickson, Millard J. *Introducing Christian Doctrine*. Edited by L. Arnold Hustad. Grand Rapids: Baker, 1992.

Evans, C. Stephen, ed. *Exploring Kenotic Christology: The Self-Emptying of God*. New York: Oxford University Press, 2006.

Evans, Craig A. *Mark 8:27–16:20*. Word Biblical Commentary 34B. Nashville: Thomas Nelson, 2001.

Fedler, Kyle D. *Exploring Christian Ethics: Biblical Foundations for Morality*. Louisville, KY: Westminster John Knox, 2006.

Fee, Gordon D. "The New Testament and Kenosis Christology." In *Exploring Kenotic Christology: The Self-Emptying of God*, edited by C. Stephen Evans. New York: Oxford University Press, 2006.

Feinberg, John. "God Ordains All Things." In *Predestination and Free Will: Four Views of Divine Sovereignty and Human Freedom*, edited by David Basinger and Randall Basinger. Downers Grove, IL: InterVarsity Press, 1986.

Ferré, Nels F. S. *The Christian Understanding of God*. New York: Harper & Brothers, 1951.

Fiddes, Paul. "Creation Out of Love." In *The Work of Love: Creation as Kenosis*, edited by John Polkinghorne. Grand Rapids: Eerdmans, 2001.

———. *The Creative Suffering of God*. Oxford: Oxford University Press, 1988.

Fischer, John Martin. Introduction to *God, Foreknowledge, and Freedom*. Stanford Series in Philosophy. Stanford, CA: Stanford University Press, 1989.

Fischer, John Martin, Patrick Todd, and Neal Tognazzini. "Engaging with Pike: God, Freedom, and Time." *Philosophical Papers* 38, no. 2 (2009): 247-70.

Fitzmyer, Joseph A. *The Gospel According to Luke (X–XXIV): Introduction, Translation, and Notes*. Anchor Bible 28a. New York: Paulist Press, 1982.

Fowler, James W. *Stages of Faith: The Psychology of Human Development and the Quest for Meaning*. Rev. ed. New York: HarperOne, 1995.

France, R. T. *The Gospel of Mark: A Commentary on the Greek Text*. Grand Rapids: Eerdmans, 2002.

Fretheim, Terence E. *Exodus*. Interpretation: A Bible Commentary for Teaching and Preaching. Louisville, KY: John Knox, 1991.

———. "God, Abraham, and the Abuse of Isaac." *Word & World* 15, no. 1 (1995): 49-57.

———. *God and World in the Old Testament: A Relational Theology of Creation.* Nashville: Abingdon, 2005.

———. "Is Genesis 3 a Fall Story?" *Word & World* 14, no. 2 (1994): 144-53.

———. *The Suffering of God: An Old Testament Perspective.* Philadelphia: Fortress, 1984.

Fudge, Edward William. *The Fire That Consumes: A Biblical and Historical Study of Final Punishment.* Fallbrook, CA: Verdict Publications, 1982.

Fudge, Edward William, and Robert A. Peterson. *Two Views of Hell: A Biblical and Theological Dialogue.* Downers Grove, IL: InterVarsity Press, 2000.

Garrett, Leroy. *The Stone-Campbell Movement: The Story of the American Restoration Movement.* Rev. ed. Joplin, MO: College Press, 2002.

Geach, P. T. "The Future." *New Blackfriars* 54, no. 636 (1973): 208-18.

Geisler, Norman L. *Chosen but Free: A Balanced View of God's Sovereignty and Free Will.* Bloomington, MN: Bethany House, 2010.

Gellman, Jerome. "The God of the Jews and the Jewish God." In *The Routledge Companion to Theism*, edited by Charles Taliaferro, Victoria S. Harrison, and Stewart Goetz. New York: Routledge, 2013.

Godfrey, Joseph J. *A Philosophy of Human Hope.* Studies in Philosophy and Religion 9. Dordrecht, The Netherlands: Martinus Nijhoff, 1987.

———. *Trust of People, Words, and God: A Route for Philosophy of Religion.* Notre Dame, IN: University of Notre Dame Press, 2012.

González, Justo L. *Essential Theological Terms.* Louisville, KY: Westminster John Knox, 2005.

Govier, Trudy. *Dilemmas of Trust.* Montreal: McGill-Queen's University Press, 1998.

———. *Social Trust and Human Communities.* Montreal: McGill-Queen's University Press, 1997.

Green, Joel B. *The Gospel of Luke.* Grand Rapids: Eerdmans, 1997.

Grenz, Stanley J., and Roger E. Olson. *20th-Century Theology: God and the World in a Transitional Age.* Downers Grove, IL: InterVarsity Press, 1992.

Guleserian, Ted. "Can God Be Trusted?" *Philosophical Studies: An International Journal for Philosophy in the Analytic Tradition* 106, no. 3 (2001): 293-303.

Habel, Norman C. *The Book of Job.* Cambridge Bible Commentary: New English Bible. New York: Cambridge University Press, 1975.

Hagner, Donald A. *Matthew 14–28.* Word Biblical Commentary 33b. Dallas: Word, 1995.

Hamilton, Victor P. *The Book of Genesis: Chapters 1–17*. The New International Commentary on the Old Testament. Grand Rapids: Eerdmans, 1990.

Hardin, Russell. *Trust*. Malden, MA: Polity Press, 2006.

Harrington, Daniel J. *The Gospel of Matthew*. Sacra Pagina 1. Collegeville, MN: Liturgical Press, 1991.

Hartley, John E. *The Book of Job*. The New International Commentary on the Old Testament. Grand Rapids: Eerdmans, 1988.

Hasker, William. *God, Time, and Knowledge*. Ithaca, NY: Cornell University Press, 1989.

———. "Yes, God Has Beliefs!" *Religious Studies* 24, no. 3 (1988): 385-94.

Hauerwas, Stanley. *Matthew*. Brazos Theological Commentary on the Bible. Grand Rapids: Brazos, 2006.

Haughey, John C. *Housing Heaven's Fire: The Challenge of Holiness*. Chicago: Jesuit Way, 2002.

Hawley, Katherine. *Trust: A Very Short Introduction*. Oxford: Oxford University Press, 2012.

———. "Trustworthy Groups and Organizations." In *The Philosophy of Trust*, edited by Paul Faulkner and Thomas Simpson. Oxford: Oxford University Press, 2017.

Hays, Richard B. *The Faith of Jesus Christ: The Narrative Substructure of Galatians 3:1–4:11*. 2nd ed. Grand Rapids: Eerdmans, 2002.

Helm, Paul. "Classical Calvinist Doctrine of God." In *Perspectives on the Doctrine of God: Four Views*, edited by Bruce A. Ware. Nashville: B&H Academic, 2008.

———. *Faith with Reason*. New York: Oxford University Press, 2000.

———. "The Impossibility of Divine Passibility." In *The Power and Weakness of God*, edited by Nigel M. de S. Cameron. Edinburgh: Rutherford House, 1990.

Helseth, Paul Kjoss. "God Causes All Things." In *Four Views on Divine Providence*, edited by Dennis W. Jowers. Grand Rapids: Zondervan, 2011.

Henry, Carl F. H. *God, Revelation, and Authority*. Vol. 6: *God Who Stands and Stays*, Part 2. Waco, TX: Word, 1976.

Heschel, Abraham J. *God's Search for Man: A Philosophy of Judaism*. Northvale, NJ: Jason Aronson, 1987.

———. *The Prophets*. 2 vols. Peabody, MA: Prince Press, 1962.

Highfield, Ron. *Great Is the Lord: Theology for the Praise of God*. Grand Rapids: Eerdmans, 2008.

Hillers, Delbert R. *Covenant: The History of a Biblical Idea*. Baltimore, MD: Johns Hopkins Press, 1969.

Holton, Richard. "Deciding to Trust, Coming to Believe." *Australian Journal of Philosophy* 72 (1994): 63-76.

Holtzen, Wm. Curtis. "Believe It or Not, God Has Faith in You." In *Uncontrolling Love: Essays Exploring the Love of God*, edited by Chris Baker et al. San Diego, CA: SacraSage, 2017.

———. "Faith in Relations." In *Relational Theology: A Contemporary Introduction*, edited by Brint Montgomery, Thomas J. Oord, and Karen Winslow. Eugene, OR: Wipf and Stock, 2012.

Hood, Jason B. *Imitating God in Christ: Recapturing a Biblical Pattern*. Downers Grove, IL: InterVarsity Press, 2013.

Horsburgh, H. J. N. "The Ethics of Trust." *The Philosophical Quarterly* 10, no. 41 (1960): 343-54.

Horton, Michael. *For Calvinism*. Grand Rapids: Zondervan, 2011.

Howard-Snyder, Daniel. "Does Faith Entail Belief?" *Faith and Philosophy* 33, no. 2 (2016): 142-62.

———. "Propositional Faith: What It Is and What It Is Not." *American Philosophical Quarterly* 50, no. 4 (2013): 357-72.

Howard-Snyder, Daniel, and Paul K. Moser. *Divine Hiddenness: New Essays*. Cambridge: Cambridge University Press, 2002.

Hume, David. *A Treatise of Human Nature*. Edited by David Fate Norton and Mary J. Norton. Oxford: Oxford University Press, 2007.

Immink, F. Gerrit. *Faith: A Practical Theological Reconstruction*. Studies in Practical Theology. Grand Rapids: Eerdmans, 2005.

Janzen, J. Gerald. *Job*. Interpretation: A Bible Commentary for Teaching and Preaching. Atlanta: John Knox, 1985.

Jeremias, Joachim. *Rediscovering the Parables*. Scribner Lyceum Library Editions. New York: Scribner, 1966.

Johnson, Luke Timothy. *The Gospel of Luke*. Sacra Pagina 3. Collegeville, MN: Liturgical Press, 1991.

Kane, Robert, ed. *The Oxford Handbook of Free Will*. Oxford: Oxford University Press, 2011.

Keener, Craig S. *A Commentary on the Gospel of Matthew*. Grand Rapids: Eerdmans, 1999.

———. *Galatians*. New Cambridge Bible Commentary. Cambridge: Cambridge University Press, 2018.

———. *The IVP Bible Background Commentary: New Testament*. 2nd ed. Downers Grove, IL: IVP Academic, 2014.

———. *Matthew*. The IVP New Testament Commentary Series. Downers Grove, IL: InterVarsity Press, 1997.

Kellenberger, J. "Three Models of Faith." *International Journal for Philosophy of Religion* 12, no. 4 (1981): 217-33.

Kenny, Anthony. *Action, Emotion, and Will*. London: Routledge & Kegan Paul, 1963.

———. *What Is Faith?* Oxford: Oxford University Press, 1992.

Kernaghan, Ronald J. *Mark*. The IVP New Testament Commentary Series. Downers Grove, IL: InterVarsity Press, 2007.

Kettler, Christian D. *The God Who Believes: Faith, Doubt, and the Vicarious Humanity of Christ*. Eugene, OR: Cascade, 2005.

Kierkegaard, Søren. *Christian Discourses*. Edited and translated by Howard V. Hong and Edna H. Hong. Princeton, NJ: Princeton University Press, 1997.

———. *Fear and Trembling*. Translated by Alastair Hannay. London: Penguin, 1985.

———. *Samlede Vaerker*. Edited by A. B. Drachmann, J. L. Heiberg, and H. O. Lang. Translated by Paul Sponheim. 15 vols. Copenhagen: Guldendals, 1901–1936.

Koehn, Daryl. *Rethinking Feminist Ethics: Care, Trust and Empathy*. New York: Routledge, 1998.

König, Adrio. *Here Am I: A Believer's Reflection on God*. Grand Rapids: Eerdmans, 1982.

Kreisel, Howard. "*Imitatio Dei* in Maimonides' *Guide of the Perplexed*." *Association for Jewish Studies* 19, no. 2 (1994): 169-212.

Lamm, Norman. *Faith and Doubt: Studies in Traditional Jewish Thought*. New York: KTAV, 1971.

LaVerdiere, Eugene. *The Beginning of the Gospel: Introducing the Gospel According to Mark*. Vol. 2: *Mark 8:22–16:20*. Collegeville, MN: Liturgical Press, 1999.

Lewis, C. S. *The Four Loves*. New York: Houghton Mifflin Harcourt, 1960.

———. *Mere Christianity*. New York: Macmillan, 1952.

Lines, Kevin. *Who Do the Ngimurok Say That They Are? A Phenomenological Study of Turkana Traditional Religious Specialists in Turkana, Kenya*. American Society of Missiology Monograph Series 35. Eugene, OR: Pickwick, 2018.

MacIntosh, J. J. "Belief-In." *Mind*, New Series, 79, no. 315 (1970): 395-407.

Mackey, James P. "The Faith of the Historical Jesus." *Horizons* 3, no. 2 (1976): 155-74.

———. *Jesus, the Man and the Myth: A Contemporary Christology.* New York: Paulist Press, 1979.

Macquarrie, John. *Principles of Christian Theology.* 2nd ed. New York: Charles Scribner's Sons, 1977.

Marshall, Christopher D. *Faith as a Theme in Mark's Narrative.* Society for New Testament Studies Monograph Series 64. New York: Cambridge University Press, 1989.

Marshall, I. Howard. *The Gospel of Luke: A Commentary on the Greek Text.* The New International Greek Testament Commentary 3. Grand Rapids: Eerdmans, 1978.

Martin, Adrienne M. *How We Hope: A Moral Psychology.* Princeton, NJ: Princeton University Press, 2014.

Martin, Ralph P., and Carl N. Toney. *New Testament Foundations: An Introduction for Students.* Eugene, OR: Cascade, 2018.

Mason, Mike. *The Gospel According to Job.* Wheaton, IL: Crossway, 1994.

Matera, Frank J. *New Testament Christology.* Louisville, KY: Westminster John Knox, 1999.

McFague, Sallie. *Metaphorical Theology: Models of God in Religious Language.* Philadelphia: Fortress, 1982.

———. *Models of God: Theology for an Ecological, Nuclear Age.* Philadelphia: Fortress, 1987.

McGeer, Victoria. "Trust, Hope, and Empowerment." *Australasian Journal of Philosophy* 86, no. 2 (2008): 237-54.

McGeer, Victoria, and Philip Pettit. "The Empowering Theory of Trust." In *New Philosophical Perspectives on Trust*, edited by Paul Faulkner and Thomas Simpson. Oxford: Oxford University Press, 2017.

McGrath, Alister E. *Reformation Thought: An Introduction.* 3rd ed. Malden, MA: Blackwell, 1999.

McKenzie, Steven L. *Covenant.* St. Louis, MO: Chalice, 2000.

McMyler, Benjamin "Deciding to Trust." In *The Philosophy of Trust*, edited by Paul Faulkner and Thomas Simpson. Oxford: Oxford University Press, 2017.

McReynolds, Paul R. *Word Study Greek-English New Testament.* Carol Stream, IL: Tyndale House, 1999.

Migliore, Daniel L. *Faith Seeking Understanding: An Introduction to Christian Theology.* 2nd ed. Grand Rapids: Eerdmans, 2004.

Miller, Patrick D. *The Ten Commandments.* Louisville, KY: Westminster John Knox, 2009.

Moltmann, Jürgen. *The Church in the Power of the Spirit: A Contribution to Messianic Ecclesiology.* London: SCM, 1977.

———. "Control Is Good—Trust Is Better: Freedom and Security in a 'Free World.'" *Theology Today* 62, no. 4 (2006): 465-83.

———. *The Crucified God: The Cross of Christ as the Foundation and Criticism of Christian Theology.* Translated by R. A. Wilson and John Bowden. Minneapolis: Fortress, 1993.

———. *God in Creation: A New Theology of Creation and the Spirit of God.* Minneapolis: Fortress, 1993.

———. "Theology as Eschatology." In *The Future of Hope*, edited by Frederick Herzog. New York: Herder & Herder, 1970.

———. *Theology of Hope: On the Ground and the Implications of a Christian Eschatology.* Translated by James W. Leitch. New York: HarperCollins, 1991; New York: Harper & Row, 1967.

———. *Trinity and the Kingdom of God.* Translated by Margaret Kohl. Minneapolis: Fortress, 1981.

———. *The Way of Jesus Christ: Christology in Messianic Dimensions.* Translated by Margaret Kohl. Minneapolis: Fortress, 1993.

Moltz, Howard. "God and Abraham in the Binding of Isaac." *Journal for the Study of the Old Testament* 96 (December 2001): 59-69.

Morris, Leon. *The Atonement: Its Meaning and Significance.* Downers Grove, IL: InterVarsity Press, 1983.

Moser, Paul K. "The Virtue of Friendship with God." In *Religious Faith and Intellectual Virtue*, edited by Laura Frances Callahan and Timothy O'Connor. Oxford: Oxford University Press, 2014.

Myers, Allen C., ed. *The Eerdmans Bible Dictionary.* Grand Rapids: Eerdmans, 1987.

Nagel, Thomas. *The Last Word.* New York: Oxford University Press, 1997.

Nash, Henry S. *Ethics and Revelation.* New York: Macmillan, 1899.

Neusner, Jacob. *Theological Dictionary of Rabbinic Judaism: Principal Theological Categories.* Lanham, MD: University Press of America, 2005.

Niebuhr, Reinhold. "Reflections on Faith, Hope, and Love." *The Journal of Religious Ethics* 2, no. 1 (1974): 151-56.

Nygren, Anders. *Agape and Eros.* Translated by Philip S. Watson. New York: Harper & Row, 1953.

O'Callaghan, Paul. *Christ Our Hope: An Introduction to Eschatology.* Washington, DC: Catholic University of America Press, 2011.

O'Collins, Gerald. *Christology: A Biblical, Historical, and Systematic Study of Jesus.* New York: Oxford University Press, 1995.

O'Collins, Gerald, and Daniel Kendall. "The Faith of Jesus." *Theological Studies* 53, no. 3 (1992): 403-23.

Oden, Thomas C. *The Living God.* Vol. 1 of *Systematic Theology.* San Francisco: HarperSanFrancisco, 1992 [1987].

―――. *The Word of Life.* Vol. 2 of *Systematic Theology.* New York: Harper & Row, 1989.

Oh God! DVD. Directed by Carl Reiner. 1977. Burbank, CA: Warner Home Video, 2003.

Olson, Roger E. *Arminian Theology: Myth and Realities.* Downers Grove, IL: IVP Academic, 2006.

―――. "The Classical Free Will Theist Model of God." In *Perspectives on the Doctrine of God: Four Views,* edited by Bruce A. Ware. Nashville: B&H Academic, 2008.

―――. *The Mosaic of Christian Belief: Twenty Centuries of Unity and Diversity.* Downers Grove, IL: IVP Academic, 2002.

Oord, Thomas Jay. *Defining Love: A Philosophical, Scientific, and Theological Engagement.* Grand Rapids: Brazos, 2010.

―――. *The Nature of Love: A Theology.* St. Louis, MO: Chalice, 2010.

―――. *The Uncontrolling Love of God: An Open and Relational Account of Providence.* Downers Grove, IL: InterVarsity Press, 2015.

Parse, Rosemarie Rizzo. *Hope: An International Human Becoming Perspective.* Sudbury, MA: Jones and Bartlett, 1999.

Peckham, John C. *Canonical Theology: The Biblical Canon, Sola Scriptura, and Theological Method.* Grand Rapids: Eerdmans, 2016.

―――. *The Love of God: A Canonical Model.* Downers Grove, IL: IVP Academic, 2015.

Penelhum, Terence. *Reason and Religious Faith.* Boulder, CO: Westview, 1995.

Peperzak, Adriaan P. *Trust: Who or What Might Support Us?* New York: Fordham University Press, 2013.

Peters, Ted. *Sin Boldly! Justifying Faith for Fragile and Broken Souls.* Minneapolis: Augsburg, 2015.

Peterson, Michael, William Hasker, Bruce Reichenbach, and David Basinger. *Reason and Religious Belief: An Introduction to the Philosophy of Religion.* 5th ed. Oxford: Oxford University Press, 2013.

Pettit, Philip. "The Cunning of Trust." *Philosophy and Public Affairs* 24, no. 3 (1995): 202-25.

Pike, Nelson. "Divine Omniscience and Voluntary Action." In *God, Foreknowledge, and Freedom*, edited by John Martin Fischer, Stanford Series in Philosophy. Stanford, CA: Stanford University Press, 1989.

Pinches, Charles. "On Hope." In *Virtues and Their Vices*, edited by Kevin Tempe and Craig A. Boyd. Oxford: Oxford University Press, 2014.

Pink, Thomas. *Free Will: A Very Short Introduction*. Oxford: Oxford University Press, 2004.

Pinnock, Clark H. "The Conditional View." In *Four Views on Hell*, edited by William V. Crockett. Grand Rapids: Zondervan, 1992.

———. *Flame of Love: A Theology of the Holy Spirit*. Downers Grove, IL: InterVarsity Press, 1996.

———. "An Inclusivist View." In *More Than One Way? Four Views on Salvation in a Pluralistic World*, edited by Dennis L. Okholm and Timothy R. Phillips. Grand Rapids: Zondervan, 1995.

———. *Most Moved Mover: A Theology of God's Openness*. Grand Rapids: Baker Academic, 2001.

———. *A Wideness in God's Mercy: The Finality of Jesus Christ in a World of Religions*. Grand Rapids: Zondervan, 1992.

Pinnock, Clark H., and Robert C. Brow. *Unbounded Love: A Good News Theology for the 21st Century*. Downers Grove, IL: InterVarsity Press, 1994.

Pinnock, Clark, et al. *The Openness of God: A Biblical Challenge to the Traditional Understanding of God*. Downers Grove, IL: InterVarsity Press, 1994.

Placher, William C. *Narratives of a Vulnerable God: Christ, Theology, and Scripture*. Louisville, KY: Westminster John Knox, 1994.

Plantinga, Alvin. *Knowledge and Christian Belief*. Grand Rapids: Eerdmans, 2015.

Plummer, Alfred. *A Critical and Exegetical Commentary on the Gospel According to St. Luke*. 5th ed. The International Critical Commentary on the Holy Scriptures of the Old and New Testaments 28. New York: Scribner's Sons, 1902.

Pojman, Louis P. "Faith, Hope, and Doubt." In *Philosophy of Religion: An Anthology*, edited by Louis P. Pojman and Michael Rea, 7th ed. Boston: Cengage Learning, 2014.

———. "Faith Without Belief?" *Faith and Philosophy* 3, no 2 (1986): 157-76.

Polkinghorne, John ed. *The Work of Love: Creation as Kenosis*. Grand Rapids: Eerdmans, 2001.

Pool, Jeff B. *God's Wounds: Hermeneutic of the Christian Symbol of Divine Suffering*. Vol. 1: *Divine Vulnerability and Creation*. Cambridge: James Clarke, 2009.

Post, Stephen G. "The Inadequacy of Selflessness: God's Suffering and the Theory of Love." *Journal of the American Academy of Religion* 56, no 2 (1988): 213-28.

Price, H. H. "Belief 'In' and Belief 'That.'" *Religious Studies* 1, no. 1 (1965): 5-27.

Reading, Anthony. *Hope and Despair: How Perceptions of the Future Shape Human Behavior*. Baltimore, MD: Johns Hopkins University Press, 2004.

Regan, Jane E. *Where Two or Three Are Gathered: Transforming the Parish Through Communities of Practice*. New York: Paulist Press, 2016.

Reichenbach, Bruce R. "Healing View." In *The Nature of Atonement: Four Views*, edited by James Beilby and Paul R. Eddy. Downers Grove, IL: IVP Academic, 2006.

Reimer, David J. "An Overlooked Term in Old Testament Theology: Perhaps." In *Covenant as Context: Essays in Honour of E. W. Nicholson*, edited by A. D. H. Mayes and R. B. Salters. New York: Oxford University Press, 2003.

Rhoda, Alan R. "Generic Open Theism and Some Varieties Thereof." *Religious Studies* 44, no. 2 (2008): 225-34.

Rhoda, Alan R., Gregory A. Boyd, and Thomas G. Belt. "Open Theism, Omniscience, and the Nature of the Future." *Faith and Philosophy* 23 (2006): 432-59.

Rice, Richard. *God's Foreknowledge and Man's Free Will*. Minneapolis: Bethany House, 1985.

———. *Reason and the Contours of Faith*. Riverside, CA: La Sierra University Press, 1991.

Rogers, L. Edna. "The Meaning of Relationship in Relational Communication." In *The Meaning of "Relationship" in Interpersonal Communication*, edited by Richard L. Conville and Lilian Edna Rogers. Westport, CT: Praeger, 1998.

Ross, Art, and Martha M. Stevenson. *Romans*. Interpretation Bible Studies. Louisville, KY: Geneva Press, 1999.

Roy, Steven C. *How Much Does God Foreknow? A Comprehensive Biblical Study*. Downers Grove, IL: IVP Academic, 2006.

Russell, Letty M. *The Future of Partnership*. Philadelphia: Westminster, 1979.

Ryken, Leland, James C. Wilhoit, and Tremper Longman III, eds. *Dictionary of Biblical Imagery*. Downers Grove, IL: IVP Academic, 1998.

Sanders, John. "Divine Providence and the Openness of God." In *Perspectives on the Doctrine of God: Four Views*, edited by Bruce Ware. Nashville: B&H Academic, 2008.

———. "Divine Suffering in an Openness of God Perspective." In *The Sovereignty of God Debate*, edited by D. Stephen Long and George Kalantzis. Eugene, OR: Wipf and Stock, 2009.

———. *The God Who Risks: A Theology of Providence*. Downers Grove, IL: InterVarsity Press, 1998; Rev. ed. 2007.

———. "Inclusivism." In *What About Those Who Have Never Heard? Three Views on the Destiny of the Unevangelized*, edited by John Sanders. Downers Grove, IL: InterVarsity Press, 1995.

———. *No Other Name? An Investigation into the Destiny of the Unevangelized*. Grand Rapids: Eerdmans, 1992.

———. *Theology in the Flesh: How Embodiment and Culture Shape the Way We Think About Truth, Morality, and God*. Minneapolis: Fortress, 2016.

Schreiter, Robert. "The Emergence of Reconciliation as a Paradigm of Mission: Dimensions, Levels, and Characteristics." In *Mission as Ministry of Reconciliation*, edited by Robert Schreiter and Knud Jørgensen. Oxford: Regnum, 2013.

Scott, Bernard Brandon. *Hear Then the Parable: A Commentary on the Parables of Jesus*. Minneapolis: Fortress, 1990.

Sessions, William Lad. *The Concept of Faith: A Philosophical Investigation*. Ithaca, NY: Cornell University Press, 1994.

Shannon, Frederick F. *God's Faith in Man: And Other Sermons*. New York: Fleming H. Revell, 1919.

Shapiro, Gerald. *Bad Jews and Other Stories*. Cambridge: Zoland Books, 1999.

The Shawshank Redemption. DVD. Directed by Frank Darabont. 1994. Burbank, CA: Warner Home Video, 1999.

Silva, Moisés. *God, Language, and Scripture: Reading the Bible in the Light of General Linguistics*. Foundations of Contemporary Interpretation 4. Grand Rapids: Zondervan, 1990.

Sirvent, Roberto. *Embracing Vulnerability: Human and Divine*. Eugene, OR: Pickwick, 2014.

Smedes, Lewis B. *Mere Morality: What God Expects from Ordinary People*. Grand Rapids: Eerdmans, 1995.

Smick, Elmer B. "Job." In *The Expositor's Bible Commentary*, edited by Frank E. Gaebelein, vol. 4. Grand Rapids: Zondervan, 1992.

Smith, James B. *Embracing the Love of God: The Path and Promise of Christian Life*. New York: HarperCollins, 2010.

Smith, Mont W. *What the Bible Says About Covenant*. Joplin, MO: College Press, 1981.

Soelle, Dorothee. *Of War and Love*. Maryknoll, NY: Orbis, 1983.

———. *The Silent Cry: Mysticism and Resistance*. Minneapolis: Fortress, 2001.

———. *Theology for Skeptics: Reflections on God*. Minneapolis: Fortress, 1995.

Speak, Daniel. *The Problem of Evil*. Malden, MA: Polity Press, 2015.

———. "Salvation Without Belief." *Religious Studies* 43, no. 2 (2007): 229-36.

Sponheim, Paul R. *Speaking of God: Relational Theology*. Philadelphia: Fortress, 1988.

Stein, Robert H. *An Introduction to the Parables of Jesus*. Philadelphia: Westminster, 1981.

Stott, John R. W. *The Cross of Christ*. Downers Grove, IL: InterVarsity Press, 1986.

Swinburne, Richard. *The Coherence of Theism*. Rev. ed. Oxford: Clarendon, 1993.

———. *Faith and Reason*. Oxford: Clarendon, 1981.

Taylor, Daniel. *The Myth of Certainty: The Reflective Christian and the Risk of Commitment*. Downers Grove, IL: InterVarsity Press, 1992.

Tempe, Kevin. "Prayer for the Past." In *Arguing About Religion*, edited by Kevin Tempe. New York: Routledge, 2009.

Tempe, Kevin, and Craig A. Boyd, eds. *Virtues and Their Vices*. Oxford: Oxford University Press, 2014.

Tempe, Kevin, and Daniel Speak, eds. *Free Will and Theism: Connections, Contingencies, and Concerns*. Oxford: Oxford University Press, 2016.

Thielicke, Helmut. *The Waiting Father: Sermons on the Parables of Jesus*. Translated by John W. Doberstein. New York: Harper, 1959.

Thiselton, Anthony C., ed. *A Concise Encyclopedia of Philosophy of Religion*. Grand Rapids: Baker Academic, 2002.

———. *The First Epistle to the Corinthians: A Commentary on the Greek Text*. New International Greek Testament Commentary. Grand Rapids: Eerdmans, 2000.

Tillich, Paul. *Dynamics of Faith*. New York: Harper & Row, 1957.

———. *Systematic Theology*. 3 vols. Chicago: University of Chicago Press, 1951–1963.

Todd, Patrick. "Geachianism." *Oxford Studies in Philosophy of Religion* 3 (May 2011): 222-51.

Tupper, E. Frank. *A Scandalous Providence: The Jesus Story of the Compassion of God*. Macon, GA: Mercer University Press, 1995.

Utley, Fiona. "Trust and the Experience of Love." In *Thinking About Love: Essays in Contemporary Continental Philosophy*, edited by Dianne Enns and Antonio Calcagno. University Park: Pennsylvania State University Press, 2015.

Vacek, Edward Collins, SJ. *Love, Human and Divine: The Heart of Christian Ethics*. Washington, DC: Georgetown University Press, 1994.

Vanhoozer, Kevin J. *Remythologizing Theology: Divine Action, Passion, and Authorship*. New York: Cambridge University Press, 2010.

Vanstone, W. H. *The Risk of Love*. New York: Oxford University Press, 1978.

Väyrynen, Pekka. "Thick Ethical Concepts." In *The Stanford Encyclopedia of Philosophy*, edited by Edward N. Zalta. Winter 2016 ed. https://plato.stanford.edu/archives/win2016/entries/thick-ethical-concepts/.

Vine's Complete Expository Dictionary of Old and New Testament Words with Topical Index. Edited by W. E. Vine, Merrill F. Unger, and William White Jr. Nashville: Thomas Nelson, 1996.

Vitz, Rico. "Doxastic Voluntarism." *The Internet Encyclopedia of Philosophy*. http://www.iep.utm.edu/ (accessed May 22, 2017).

Vogel, Arthur Anton. *Christ in His Time and Ours*. Kansas City, MO: Sheed & Ward, 1992.

Wallis, Ian G. *The Faith of Jesus Christ in Early Christian Traditions*. Society for New Testament Studies Monograph Series 84. New York: Cambridge University Press, 2005.

Ward, Keith. *Christ and the Cosmos: A Reformation of the Trinitarian Doctrine*. New York: Cambridge University Press, 2015.

———. *Divine Action: Examining God's Role in an Open and Emergent Universe*. West Conshohocken, PA: Templeton Foundation Press, 2007.

———. *God, Chance and Necessity*. Oxford: Oneworld, 1996.

———. *God, Faith and the New Millennium: Christian Belief in an Age of Science*. Oxford: Oneworld, 1998.

———. *Rational Theology and the Creativity of God*. New York: Pilgrim Press, 1982.

———. *Religion and Creation*. New York: Oxford University Press, 1996.

Ware, Bruce A. "A Modified Calvinist Doctrine of God." In *Perspectives on the Doctrine of God: Four Views*, edited by Bruce A. Ware. Nashville: B&H Academic, 2008.

Watson, Gary, ed. *Free Will*. Oxford: Oxford University Press, 1982.

Weinandy, Thomas G. *Does God Suffer?* Notre Dame, IN: University of Notre Dame Press, 2000.

Wenham, Gordon J. *Genesis 1–15*. Word Biblical Commentary 1. Waco, TX: Word, 1987.

Wierenga, Edward. "Omniscience." In *The Oxford Handbook of Philosophical Theology*, edited by Thomas P. Flint and Michael C. Rea. Oxford: Oxford University Press, 2009.

Wilkens, Steve, ed. *Faith and Reason: Three Views*. Downers Grove, IL: IVP Academic, 2014.

Willimon, William H. *Who Will Be Saved?* Nashville: Abingdon, 2008.

Wimberly, John W., Jr. "God's Faith in Us." *Living Pulpit* 6, no. 1 (1997): 18-19.

Wolterstorff, Nicholas. "Unqualified Divine Temporality." In *God and Time: Four Views*, edited by Gregory E. Ganssle. Downers Grove, IL: InterVarsity Press, 2001.

Yancey, Philip. *Disappointment with God: Three Questions No One Asks Aloud.* Grand Rapids: Zondervan, 1988.

―――. *Reaching for the Invisible God: What Can We Expect to Find?* Grand Rapids: Zondervan, 2000.

AUTHOR INDEX

SUBJECT INDEX

SCRIPTURE INDEX

Finding the Textbook You Need

The IVP Academic Textbook Selector
is an online tool for instantly finding the IVP books
suitable for over 250 courses across 24 disciplines.

---

ivpacademic.com
